WITHDRAWN

HARVARD LIBRARY

WITHDRAWN

ERASMUS GRANDESCENS

BIBLIOTHECA
HUMANISTICA & REFORMATORICA

VOLUME XLIII

R. J. SCHOECK

ERASMUS GRANDESCENS

The Growth of a Humanist's Mind
and Spirituality

NIEUWKOOP
DE GRAAF PUBLISHERS
1988

CIP-GEGEVENS KONINKLIJKE BIBLIOTHEEK, DEN HAAG

Schoeck, R.J.

Erasmus grandescens: the growth of a humanist's mind and spirituality / R.J. Schoeck. – Nieuwkoop: De Graaf. – (Bibliotheca humanistica & reformatorica; vol. 43)
Met index, lit. opg.
ISBN 90-6004-398-7 geb.
SISO 155.2 UDC 929 Erasmus, Desiderius + 165.74-051(492)"14/15"
Trefw.: Erasmus, Desiderius.

© R.J. SCHOECK, 1988

As with most intellectuals, the development of Erasmus' mind is far more interesting than mere biography.

LEWIS W. SPITZ,
The Religious Renaissance of the German Humanists (1963)

... haec est uberior fecundiorque felicitas non ventre gravescere sed mente grandescere, non lactescere pectore sed corde candescere ...

AUGUSTINE, *Epist.* 150/17-9

TABLE OF CONTENTS

Preface		7
List of Abbreviations		13
I	The Place of Erasmus Today	17
II	The Early Erasmus	31
	A. The *Devotio moderna* and the Brethren of the Common Life	31
	B. Agricola and Erasmus	40
III	The Monastery Years	49
	A. Augustinian Erasmus (1487-1492)	49
	B. The Early Letters of Erasmus: Problems of Interpretation	79
IV	Liminality – Into Another World	89
	A. A Bishop's Secretary	90
	B. Erasmus' Theological Studies at Paris	101
V	*Translatio studii* and the *studia humanitatis*	111
VI	The Mastering of Craft: *The Praise of Folly*	127
VII	The Afterlife of Erasmus and His Works	137
	A. That Influential Clerk Erasmus	137
	B. Erasme et Postel: les traditions de la civilité et de la tolérance	144
VIII	Conclusion	157
A Selective Bibliography		161
Index Nominorum		171

PREFACE

Erasmus has been a part of my life for several decades, and a reproduction of the famous Holbein portrait of him has hung for more than 30 years in my office in Toronto, my study in Washington, and my office in Boulder. Erasmus' studies and writing as well as his teaching in universities took him around Europe; and, like his, my own career and working on this biography of him have been linked with a number of places. An academic traveller myself, I think that I understand Erasmus as a wandering scholar, yet one with a keen love of place: still, *peregrinus ubique*, everywhere a wanderer (as Petrarca called himself).

From 1961 on, and for the next decade, I was at the University of Toronto as a professor of English but also as a professor ordinarius in the Pontifical Institute of Mediaeval Studies, where I was able to understand the matrix from which Erasmus emerged at the end of the fifteenth century: not so much the waning as in the true sense of Huizinga's title the harvest of the middle ages. At Toronto I was also privileged to be the first coordinating editor of the Collected Works of Erasmus – that splendid edition of Erasmus' correspondence and other writings for our times; and I have continued to be a member of the Executive Committee of the Collected Works of Erasmus since its inception. My debt to the University of Toronto Press and to colleagues of CWE has been and continues to be a large and living debt.

In 1970 I went to the Folger Shakespeare Library as its first Director of Research Activities, and as well as all that I experienced by being at one of the great world-centers of Renaissance scholarship (truly a scholar's Café de la Paix), I was fortunate also to be able to offer a seminar in the Folger Institute for Renaissance and 18th-century Studies on Erasmus: a semester seminar for doctoral and post-doctoral students that dealt with all aspects of Erasmus' work; and for this seminar a number of Erasmians were brought weekly to the Folger, including Craig R. Thompson, the *doyen* of Erasmian scholars in the United States, and others. Learning, I am sure, at least as much as other members of the seminar, I have not looked back upon pre-Erasmian days nor slackened in my zeal to read and understand Erasmus more fully.

Since 1971, IANLS (the International Association for Neo-Latin Studies), which was born at Louvain under the inspiration of Jozef IJsewijn and took shape at Amsterdam two years later under the hospitality and good offices of

C. S. Rademaker and Pierre Tuynman, with the help of Professors Walther Ludwig, Leonard Forster, and others, has for me revolved in large part around Erasmus and Erasmian scholarship, and I acknowledge with gratitude the collegiality and friendship of Jozef IJsewijn, Pierre Tuynman, Gerdien Kuiper, Eckhard Kessler, J.-C. Margolin, Leonard Forster, L. V. Ryan, and others in this nobly Erasmian enterprise. For IANLS, with its stress on Latin as the medium of scholarship and civility during the Renaissance period (and beyond), and extolling the achievement of Latin letters, might well have Erasmus as a patron saint of good humanistic scholarship and of the Republic of Letters: he would have approved heartily of the enterprise. And through IANLS, which I have served as a member of its Executive Committee and which honored me in electing me President for 1976-1979, I have been able to visit many of the Erasmian places and, even more, in a warm and genuine Erasmian spirit to come to know many European scholars as friends. Specific acknowledgements are scattered in the footnotes; this preface must serve as a communal acknowledgment for much support, advice, and friendship.

Six months at Wolfenbüttel in the Herzog August Bibliothek during the summer and autumn of 1986 were invaluable both for access to its incomparable resources and for the manifold opportunities to exchange views with Renaissance and Reformation scholars. A discussion of problems of interpretation of Erasmus' early letters and poems was offered as a colloquium in September 1986 and I wish to thank the Director of the Library Prof. Dr. Paul Raabe, and the Leiterin for Research, Frau Dr. Sabine Solf, for their good offices, hospitality, and kindness.

A word needs to be said about the biographical focus of these essays and studies, and about the concept of growth by stages. The epigraph taken from Lewis W. Spitz's volume on *The Religious Renaissance of the German Humanists* (1963) rather admirably stresses the interest in the development of Erasmus' mind; and that, together with a concern for the development of his spirituality, provides the focus of this volume of essays and studies. Our line of investigation must keep steadily in view the development of Erasmus from school to monastery to bishop's court to Paris, and so onward through his life. Erasmus was an intellectual, and from his earliest writings we perceive how intensely he felt about what he read and what he wrote. His correspondence and (especially for the earlier years) his poems provide a connecting link for many of his early efforts: indeed, until the works begin to pour forth from the printing presses after 1500, the letters and poems must be read in order to perceive the warp and woof of his development. But the early writings must be interpreted with care, and that is the purpose of the chapter on interpretation.

Erasmus grandescens: 'Erasmus growing' – it was not only that the number of his works multiplied. Much more important is the fact that those works grew in conception and scope, and that Erasmus himself grew in mind and spirituality.

The second epigraph from St. Augustine illuminates this conception of growth and contrasts the growth in mind with a merely physical growth of the belly, leading to a glowing in the heart. The growth of Erasmus can be studied in stages: the conventional schoolboy to scholar, yes, but with Erasmus this is complicated yet enriched by his development in the monastery of Steyn with the Canons Regular of St. Augustine – examined in Part III – and by his immersion into the complex world of a fifteenth-century bishop and his court – examined in Part IV, where the concept of liminality will be brought to bear upon the enlarging structures of Erasmus' world.

Erasmus peregrinus: Erasmus the wanderer everywhere. A constant and characteristic feature of Erasmus' life after the age of about 25 is his urge to travel and a constant restlessness. This feature is the more striking in that it surfaced after a number of years – perhaps seven – in a monastery. There is a remarkable parallel in Petrarch (whom we know Erasmus admired), who may in turn have been following the model of Augustine whom both Petrarch and Erasmus read passionately, though their reasons were evidently different and their modes of expression distinctly individual. Yet the comment of Nicholas Mann on Petrarch's journeying bears quotation and can serve for reflection at this point for its applicability to and appropriateness for Erasmus:

> This trait, of which Petrarch was fully aware (he called himself *peregrinus ubique*: a wanderer, or pilgrim, everywhere) was to structure his daily life by imposing constant patterns of movement upon it, while also reflecting a profound aspect of his psychology: something between curiosity, the quest for the new, and a deep dissatisfaction, an unwillingness to settle down and define himself and his deepest concerns (*Petrarch* [1984], p. 5).

This calls to mind the reinforcing comment of Peter Brown on St. Augustine: 'Augustine was finding in it all that he had always valued in his intellectual activity – hard labour, the excitement of discovery, and the prospect of endless movement in a philosopher's quest for Wisdom.' (*Augustine* [1979], p. 263). Journeying can of course be viewed as a purely physical activity, but for Augustine, Petrarch and Erasmus there was the much more exciting journeying of the mind and spirit: the *itinerarium mentis* familiar to medieval philosophers and mystics, like Bonaventura, among others.

Not all of the movement in Erasmus' career was entirely voluntary, and for some of the travels he was dependent on the invitations of patrons; and one thinks that there were some trips not taken, like a pilgrimage to the Holy Land that Erasmus never made. But the pattern of travel is there, and one must see the significance of that pattern for understanding the personality of Erasmus.

While there have been many biographies of him, none has achieved recognition as *the* standard life of the great Dutch humanist. Part of the difficulty has been that most biographies have focused upon only a single aspect of Erasmus, or have attempted to portray him in a single light, whether as a precursor of Voltaire or foil to Luther, or whatever. Perhaps the two sanest treatments have been those of Preserved Smith and Johan Huizinga. With Smith, whose biography was published in 1923, the role of humanism is subordinated, or not understood in its fullness of context as has generally been the case with other biographies. With Huizinga, whose life was first published in English translation in 1924, we have an interpretation of his fellow Dutchman as a tolerant and civilized person, but much necessarily is left out in a biography of fewer than 200 pages. There are similar qualifications to be made about other more recent biographies, including some in which there are often unfortunate and serious errors in citing and translating Erasmus' Latin.

Too many historians and critics have tended to dismiss Erasmus the man and to concentrate upon his writings – thus to lose sight of Erasmus as a person in the quest for concepts in those writings. The worst side of that tendency is crystallized in the witty but unjust quip that Erasmus was descended from a long line of maiden aunts. A better effort is made by those who have tried to recognize one part of Erasmus' achievement – whether the religious or the humanistic – but have too much stressed his not taking a public stance in the historic debates and religious conflicts after 1517. But Erasmus as a person can be seen, and indeed must he be seen, behind his writings; there was a man of courage and a friend capable of great efforts for friendship. Part of my purpose has been to consider Erasmus the man, as well as to study the humanist, the scholar and theologian, and to offer an interpretation which emphasizes the remarkable growth of Erasmus as a scholar and writer: Erasmus growing (*Erasmus grandescens*) indeed.

There is another reason, it must be said, for a major biographical study of Erasmus at this time. The tidal conflicts of Protestant and Roman Catholic controversies have largely subsided now in the second half of the twentieth century, and one may now attempt to view with a less strained objectivity the place of Erasmus in that turbulent age; it is time to clear the air of many misunderstandings still current concerning Erasmus' relations to both the Roman Catholic and the Protestant reformers. Still further, there is the side of Erasmus the humanist which must be understood if one is to understand all of Erasmus; and only in the last half-century of humanistic scholarship – and I stress the contributions of P. O. Kristeller, Eugenio Garin, J.-C. Margolin among others – can the biographer of Erasmus draw upon a firmly established consensus of scholarship concerning Renaissance humanism. It is now firmly agreed that it was not essentially secular, *pace* nearly all nineteenth (and some twentieth) century secularist scholars; and it is to be accepted that one of the limitations of Burckhardt, for example, was his failure to consider the force of religious ideas and institutions in his fascinating and influential portrait of the Renaissance in Italy. Thus tribute must be paid to scholars like L.-E. Halkin and C. Augustijn who have endeavoured to focus upon the religious core of Erasmian thought and spirituality.

Yet in attempting to view Erasmus as one of the lights of the Renaissance, a humanist with an international reputation and even public identity, and a scholar of prodigious productivity, I shall not attempt to cover the flaw and blemishes. Like Montaigne in his autobiographical *Essais*, I shall try to present an Erasmus 'in his simple, natural and everyday dress, without strain or artifice ... with all his imperfections.'

There are older models for biographies of scholars, such as Bernays' splendid nineteenth-century biography of the sixteenth-century classical scholar J. J. Scaliger and Mark Pattison's of Scaliger's contemporary Casaubon, and both are appropriate to the casting of a model for an Erasmian biography in that both Bernays and Pattison studied classical scholars of the late sixteenth and early seventeenth centuries. But the role of Erasmus was far greater, and more public, and a fuller rendering of the raw material is needed to interpret so complex a Renaissance scholar to our own age; much more is needed of context, in the way that we have learned from the vision and historical understanding of a Ladurie or a Braudel.

The more than 1600 letters by Erasmus in the much larger correspondence (of more than 3000 letters) provide an astonishingly rich resource for his biographer as well as for the historian (a point discussed in the essay on the letters). (Myron P. Gilmore called the correspondence of Erasmus 'perhaps the greatest single source for the intellectual history of his age.') But it must be recognized that each letter had its own context, which both illuminates and restricts our modern reading and interpretation of it (and therefore our use of it for larger purposes), and due attention will be paid to context in each discussion of a letter. Here I can only call attention to my own literary theory that no literary work or document exists in a vacuum and that it both springs from and contributes to its milieu (as I have discussed the principle in my monographic *Intertextuality and Renaissance Texts*). Where I have occasionally resorted to paraphrase (usually to compress a lengthy passage), I have usually given the key passage or phrase in Latin in the notes. Paraphrase alone will not serve us in a work of intellectual history or biography (as Michael Richter has recently argued cogently in *EHR* xcix 1984), for the method of paraphrase 'has the danger of guiding the reading towards the (modern) author's implicit attitudes. A paraphrase can never stand for the original.'

It should be added that the outpouring of contemporary twentieth-century scholarship dealing with Erasmus has been prodigious. There are now three volumes in the eminently comprehensive bibliography of J.-C. Margolin, and they manifest the accelerating pace of Erasmian scholarship, for which years of reading are necessary, and a compass not only of the originals of a considerable bulk of Neo-Latin writings (for which see J. IJsewijn, *Companion to Neo-*

Latin), but also of the several languages of European scholarship. The Selective Bibliography attempts to provide the basic tools for scholarly study of Erasmus.

Not least, one who essays to write a life of Erasmus must have a sense of humor in order to catch the play of wit, irony and humor in what are sometimes the unlikeliest of places, as in a rhetorical handbook where he provides formulas for greeting an expectant mother, including one that wishes that the little one may come out as easily as he slipped in. I can only hope that the reader will become aware of the play of wit and humor in some of the pages that follow.

Among the questions which I have asked myself in writing of Erasmus are questions which bridge his importance in his own age to the problems of our age. How did a humanist of the early sixteenth century, a humanist of Western Europe, understand the world that was changing around him? How – to borrow from William G. Bowen – 'did he invest it with meaning, and infuse it with emotion?'

Erasmus was involved in both the Renaissance and the Reformation; and his humanism, first of all, provides a key for our understanding of each as well as of the links between the two. Finally, therefore, Erasmus was (in his correspondence especially) a bridge between nationalities and special interests, and for our age that will have to establish better bridges to the East and to the Third World the humanism and civility of Erasmus and his patient and unceasing irenic efforts will offer a vital mode of understanding of and models for our age and that challenging unknown one that shall follow.

R. J. Schoeck

Toronto – Washington – Boulder – Wolfenbuttël – Trier
1967-1987

LIST OF ABBREVIATIONS

Allen, OE	P.S. Allen, H.M. Allen, and H.W. Garrod, eds. Opus Epistolarum Des. Erasmi Roterodami (Oxford: Clarendon Press, 1906-1958)
ARG	Archiv für Reformationgeschichte (Leipzig/Gütersloh, 1903 ff.)
ARW	Archiv für Religionswissenschaft (Freiburg i. Br./Tübingen, 1898 ff.)
ASD	Opera Omnia Desiderii Erasmi Roterodami (Amsterdam: North-Holland, 1969-. In progress)
BHR	Bibliothèque d'Humanisme et Renaissance (Genève, 1938 ff.)
BR	Contemporaries of Erasmus: A Biographical Register of the Renaissance and Reformation. 3 vols. ed. P.G. Bietenholz, T.B. Deutscher (Toronto: University of Toronto Press, 1985-1987)
CSEL	Corpus scriptorum ecclesiasticorum latinorum (Wien, 1866 ff.)
CWE	Collected Works of Erasmus (Toronto: University of Toronto Press, 1974-. In progress)
DACL	Dictionnaire d'archéologie chrétienne et de liturgie, ed. F. Cabrol and H. Leclercq (Paris, 1924 ff.)
DHGE	Dictionnaire d'histoire et de géographie ecclésiastique, ed. A. Baudrillart et al. (Paris, 1912 ff.)
DSAM	Dictionnaire de Spiritualité ascétique et mystique. ed. M. Viller (Paris, 1932 ff.)
DTC	Dictionnaire de théologie catholique. ed. A. Vacant et al. (Paris, 1930 ff.)
EHR	English Historical Review (London, 1886 ff.)
EB	Encyclopedia Britannica – edition quoted is cited.
ELN	English Language Notes (Boulder, Colorado, 1963-)
ELR	English Literary Renaissance (Amherst, Mass., 1970 ff.)
Hain	L. Hain, Repertorium bibliographicum, 4 vols. (Stuttgart & Paris, 1826-1838); rptd. 1903. Suppl. W.A. Copinger, 3 vols. (London, 1895-1902)

IANLS	International Association for Neo-Latin Studies
JWCI	Journal of the Warburg and Courtaud Institutes (London, 1937)
LB	J. Leclerc, ed. Desiderii Erasmi Roterodami Opera Omnia, 10 vols. (Leiden, 1703-1706)
LexThK	Lexicon für Theologie und Kirche, ed. J. Höfer and K. Rahner (Freiburg, 1957; 1986). 14 vols.
MedSt	Mediaeval Studies (Toronto, 1938 ff.)
NCE	New Catholic Encyclopedia, vols. (New York and Washington, 1967)
Opuscula	W. K. Ferguson, ed. Erasmi Opuscula (The Hague: Martinus Nijhoff, 1933)
PL	Patrogia Latina, ed. J. P. Migne, 217 vols. (Paris, 1878-90)
Reedijk	C. Reedijk, ed. Poems of Desiderius Erasmus (Leiden: Brill, 1956)
RenQ	Renaissance Quarterly (New York, 1947 ff.)
RHE	Revue d'histoire ecclésiastique (Leuven, 1900 ff.)
Sandys	J. E. Sandys, History of classical scholarship, 3 vols. (Cambridge: Cambridge U.P., 1903-1908)
Spec	Speculum: A Journal of Medieval Studies (Cambridge, Mass., 1926 ff.)
STC	Short-title Catalogue of Books printed in England ... 1475–1640 2nd ed. (London: Bibliographical Society, 1976–86).
StudRen	Studies in the Renaissance (New York, 1963 ff.)
ZHTh	Zeitschrift für die historische Theologie (Leipzig, 1832-1875)

Give him the darkest inch your shelf allows,
Hide him in lonely garrets, if you will —
But his hard, human pulse is throbbing still
With the sure strength that fearless truth
Endows.
...
Whether or not we read him, we can feel
From time to time the vigor of his name
Against us like a finger for the shame
And emptiness of what our souls reveal
In books that are as altars where we kneel
To consecrate the flicker, not the flame.

Edwin Arlington Robinson

PART I

THE PLACE OF ERASMUS TODAY[1]

I want to begin with a little verse fable by R. P. Blackmur that has a bearing on Erasmus, and perhaps for all teachers today:

> ... he cast himself a role
> that needed ancestors and children to play;
> behind / ahead; dragon slaying dragon.
> Folly is more acceptable if played
> half by memory / half expectation /
> and violence loses unreality.[2]

And to build towards what the epigraph carries as a burden of meaning for me, I start from positions already prepared.

Erasmus has been much dealt with in recent years, and we might reflect on the sheer bulk of scholarly industry. The current literature on Erasmus is a formidable mass: in the fourteen years from 1936 to 1949 there were nearly 1200 items; in the twelve years from 1950 to 1961 (reflecting the World War II drop-off of research), still more than 500; and for the years from 1962 to 1970, only an eight-year period, there were 1996 items – clearly a marked acceleration in published research on Erasmus.[3]

What has been the evaluation, the picture of Erasmus in all of this? As would be expected, he has always been the target of extremists on both sides. In his own *Compendium vitae* of early 1524 (than a man of about 57), he himself tells us that 'the Lutheran tragedy had burdened him with unbearable ill will' and that 'he was torn apart by each faction, while he sought to serve the best interests of each.' And in the same year he wrote to John Fisher, the holy and learned bishop of Rochester who was a good friend of Erasmus as he was of More: 'Indeed, I war on three fronts: against these pagan Romans, who are meanly jealous of me; against certain theologians and friars, who use every stone at hand to bring me down; against some rabid Lutherans, who snarl at me because – so they say – I alone delay their own triumphs.'[4] And he saw still another dimension in his role: 'I am a Ghibelline for the Guelphs and a Guelph for the Ghibellines.' Little wonder that the problem of evaluating Erasmus' place in history continues to be as complex. Preserved Smith (in 1923) viewed Erasmus as a rationalist heralding the Enlightenment and the Liberal Age, and Van Gelder has largely continued in that view. (In his *Bridge of Criticism*, Peter Gay played Erasmus against Lucian and Voltaire and pictured Erasmus as less than sympathetic to the Enlightenment.) Huizinga presented a most attractive and influential view in 1924 of Erasmus as anti-hero: not the champion of any great cause, he was 'the man who is too sensible and moderate for the heroic.' In 1949, Margaret Mann Phillips enlarged that view to offer a man of sincerity and humor and common sense, a Christian humanist and reformer, but who followed a middle way between Catholic and Protestant, between the mind and the heart. There have been many others, obviously, and we can mention but one further interpretation: that of Renaudet who in his *Etudes érasmiennes* (1939) had concentrated upon the crucial Basle years from 1521 to 1529 and applied to Erasmus' biblical and religious thought the term *modernisme* which he borrowed from the stormy early 20th-century movement; and in 1954 in *Erasme et l'Italie* Renaudet developed this earlier view of Erasmus into a thesis that claimed him as wanting a *troisième Eglise*, the Roman Church 'profoundly reformed, renewed, modernized'; and for this he based much upon Erasmus' own statement that, 'I will bear with this Church (meaning the Roman Catholic Church) until I see a better one.' But Margolin and Olin have since challenged that part of Renaudet's thesis and have stressed the fact that the crucial statement just quoted is prefaced by Erasmus' declaration: 'I have never defected from the Catholic Church'; further, Renaudet failed to complete the full original sentence, which should go on to read: 'I will bear with this Church until I see a better one, and it must bear with me until I become better.'[5] More and more scholars are reading all of Erasmus, and what has been emerging in Erasmian scholarship of recent years – and here we are laid under debt to the work of Bataillon, Bouyer, de Lubac especially – is the image of an Erasmus who was fully orthodox (let us not forget that he died before Trent began, so that we do not try to make him conform to the defensive orthodoxies of Trent), deeply religious (in his fashion), fully committed.[6] He was faithful to the patristic tradition (and we can never forget how large a part of his working life was devoted to the editing of St. Jerome and a number of other fathers); he never lost sight of the centrality of the Scriptures to the Christian life (for he regarded his editing of the New Testament and the writing of the Paraphrases as his major life-work); and the balance and humanity of his *philosophia Christi* give us the main thrust of nearly all of his popular writings. We can here take the testimony of his good friend Thomas More in this light. 'Nor surely,' More wrote, 'can the faith of Erasmus be obscure, a faith adorned by so many labors, so many vigils, so many dangers, so many troubles, all sustained for the sake of Sacred Letters, the very storehouse of faith.' And so it seems to me that Erasmian studies of the 1980s and beyond are going to deepen our understanding of the interrelationship of theological and scriptural studies with his humanism. In my own recent lectures and papers I endeavored to establish the view that Erasmus' sense of tradition as a living dynamic was consistent in theology, law, scripture studies and literature; and I shall return to his re-discovery of tradition.

In point of fact, we have begun to walk all the way around the traditional literary or historical view of Erasmus – as though around the free-standing statue of him in Rotterdam[7] – and to see him more nearly in the round. We are beginning to recognize that he was no mere skeptic, no rationalist; that he was not (as one wit would have him) a descendant of a long line of maiden aunts, for he was engagé and tough: a humanist and a man in holy orders, he could ask of a Benedictine abbot (one Paul Volz), 'for what is the city but a great monastery?'[8] (And I would suggest that such a question was no less revolutionary in 1518 than it is today, if addressed to any administrator of a religious institution in an inner city of North America.)

He may well be regarded as an ancestor of the intellectual *clerc*, in the sense of Julien Benda, whose descendants no longer kept up the fight, of whose *trahison* Benda could write so persuasively – indeed, it is worth recalling that Benda calls Erasmus (along with Goethe and a few others) one who was a great patrician of the mind. Beyond observing that linguistically *tradition* and *trahison* are cognate, and that an *Ueberblick* of western culture could find countless examples of tradition that became betrayal, when it was either handed over to the enemy without a fight to keep it alive or put into so guarded and fortified a position that it petrified and thus became only a relic of real tradition – beyond observing, then, that there are many ways to betray tradition – I would nail up to the wall the thesis that it is the special responsibility of us *clercs* to keep tradition alive.

What I have been doing for the past few minutes, is nothing less than an exercise in tradition. One begins by questioning what is essential and viable, but one cannot end there. (In the spirit and manner of Renaissance intertextuality, Montaigne a half-century later than Erasmus would quote Dante: 'For doubt, not less than knowledge, pleases me.') One works (especially if he is a teacher of humanities) towards transmittal, through the students who will in turn question and carry on; but he must himself have begun questioning and have continued by evaluating – provisionally, to be sure, but with serious commitment.

First we have to mark Erasmus as a man whose work is today condemned to fragmentation, for we are compelled to read it in separated contexts and unrelated approaches; a man who becomes – as the burden of the past tends to harden inherited views and judgements of him by scholars whose sense of the whole of past tradition tends to diminish – a man who becomes, that is to say, progressively more difficult to understand. Even the commendable essay by Olin attempting to put Erasmus into a place in history suffers from a departmentalized approach: it is the judgement only of previous historians, and it proceeds only by the conventional techniques of historians. With Huizinga we do have a widening of the nets: they are woven with different strands, and they are cast more widely; but it is not until Bouyer and de Lubac begin to relate theology with scripture, and secondarily humanism, that the larger whole of Erasmus begins to emerge. There are gains from specialization, but we pay a high price for those gains: a point which I think needs our patient study and very full reflection. Erasmus stands above both the departmentalization of modern history and the problematics of a modern Benda, yet in the modern university we contribute to misunderstanding by setting up walls to prevent the reading of Erasmus' writings as a whole:

> How many graduate students in literature have read more than the *Praise of Folly* (and that in translation, of course)? This is no dilletantish point, for unless one follows (what weak translations cannot give) the subtle gradation of tone which structures the irony, to move ultimately to the folly of Christ, one misses much.
>
> How many graduate students in French, who read Rabelais, have dug into the deep Erasmian roots of Rabelais' thought on marriage and scripture?
>
> In scripture studies today very little attention is paid to sixteenth-century work in Scripture, yet how much of the force and the directions of Reformation movements can be understood without an understanding of how they read the Bible? How many have read all of Erasmus' influential preface to the New Testament, and the enlarged *Paraclesis*?
>
> How many theologians have read that profound work, *Ratio Verae Theologiae*? Or preachers, the *Paraclesis*; or historians of ecclesiastical institutions considered the hint on monastery/city in the prefatory letter to Volz?
>
> Historians of education will refer to the *Education of a Christian Prince*, and the *Ciceronianus* is printed in the series of a teacher's college; but how many educational historians relate these significantly to Erasmus' humanism, and to the profound influence in the history of education of the *Colloquies* and *Adages*?[9]

One could go on, but I trust that my point has been made. At a time when some scholars are beginning to walk around the statue of Erasmus and to see it whole and in the round, their students are allowed to view it from one departmental window only.

Yet the historical importance of Erasmus is well-nigh incalculable. I cannot think of his counterpart in the history of modern European thought and letters — not even Voltaire, whose philosophical influence was perhaps greater, but his literary influence surely less, and whose range is simply not anything like that of Erasmus. There have been something like 2000 editions of Erasmus' works, among which we must stress the *New Testament* and the *Adagia*, each of which in the 16th century passed through nearly a hundred authorized and unauthorized editions; and these were widely scattered in the Low Countries, France and Switzerland especially (much less so in Italy, or Spain) — but even these data do not fully or accurately measure his influence, for there were many translations, adaptations, borrowings, attacks and replies, and a still wider indirect influence.[10]

Let us ask whether departmental structures do not need scrutiny when we are confronted with the fact of our neglect of so great a writer. Given the accident of his birth — a real accident — we cannot leave Erasmus to that rarest of Phoenixes, a department of Nederlandsche literature. We should insure that an occasional course in Erasmus will make his thought and writings *as a whole*, in a body, available to specialists from literature, theology, history, etc. I would not argue against departmental structures (provided that there is flexibility), for they are needed for discipline; and we must grant that there can be only a smattering and scattering of ignorance in a student who has 'done' all Western Civilization in one or even two years — *grant*? Indeed, we *must* assume it, both in such an undergraduate and perhaps also in his instructor. But we cannot be absolute; there must also be provisions at both the undergraduate and the graduate levels for inter- and trans-disciplinary work. This has been a digression, but it is a needed one; both for the present subject, and for the present-day considerations of roles, functions and structures of the modern university.

I return then to the place of Erasmus today.

To speak in large terms, the age of Erasmus was one in which tradition had hardened: in the universities at the end of the fifteenth century, scholastic curricula were deeply intrenched and textbooks were, by and large, centuries-old. Witness More's trenchant *caveat* that 'a conviction that is first handed on by stupid teachers and then strengthened in the course of years is extremely capable of perverting the judgement of even sound minds.'[11] Hence the well-nigh universal attack by humanists on scholastic logic, in fact upon a wide swath of medieval habits of thought — More in his *Utopia*, Rabelais — the list would grow quickly. In areas of faith and belief, the fierce wars on heresy had won patterns and modes of conformity by 1500, but at a great expense both of institutional freedom (witness the lamentable state of things in late 15th-century Oxford) and of individual conscience. Pico's fresh, and dangerous, enthusiasm for the freedom of the individual must be seen in this context, as well as Thomas More's fight for the freedom of individual conscience, extolled in Roper's saints-life of a lawyer with a superlatively developed conscience; and the entire career of Erasmus, I urge, must be so viewed. For in an era in which tradition had long hardened, Erasmus fought for a sense of freedom, of development, of the possibility of organic change. Nearly every book of his is a sign of it, for Erasmus was the first master of the growing book, and the prime example is the *Adagia* with many editions that not only multiplied adages: 818 proverbs in 1500 grows to 3260 in 1508, and these grew and were regrouped again in 1515, 1520, 1523, 1526, 1528, and 1533. But the *Adages* also developed the thought, as Erasmus wrote in a 1523 letter:

> Well, just as we spend our life seeking to make ourselves better, so we shall not cease to make our writings richer and more accurate until we ourselves cease to live.

Thus there is a double sense in the term *grandescens*: not only an increase in number and size, but also an enlargement of scope.

Like More, and alongside More, Erasmus defended humanism against the attack of narrow-minded young theologians like Dorp, of ossified institutions like the faculty of theology at the University of Paris, of calcified disciplines like logic and dialectic; and the position defended against Dorp and others (in massive epistles, apologia, and other writings) is consistent with the position of the *Ratio Verae Theologiae*, the Preface to his New Testament of 1516, which was expanded and published separately in 1519. One finds worked out in the *Ratio* what Erasmus had put as a question in the *Enchiridion*:

> Quid igitur faciet Christianus? Negliget ecclesiae mandata? contemnet honestas maiorum traditiones? damnabit pias consuetudines? Immo si informus est, servabit ut necessarias, sin firmus et perfectus ...

For the Erasmian position on tradition is everywhere consistent: namely, that there is a *consensus omnium*, a living and growing body which the individual must approach humbly, through study, and to which he then gives his individual acceptance or assent: that is, there is an obligation, but there must be the self-giving.[12]

I have already spoken of the closeness of More and Erasmus in their early years, and their collaborative friendship needs no emphasis today. But here I would contrast the More of the 1520s and early 1530s – that is, the More in his 40's and 50's – in order to give a measure of Erasmus' essential balance and consistency.

I ask you to look not at the author of the early poems, the translator of epigrams and the life of Pico, or the author of the *Utopia*, but the later More, during his years from about 45 to his death at 58. And looking at the More of the polemical works, I am led to ask this question: 'how are we to understand or judge the sense of tradition, of living tradition, in a man who in his *Responsio ad Lutherum* attacked Luther so uniformly and totally, so rigorously – I would say, indeed, savagely – finding nothing to praise and apparently nothing to take up for consideration in the reform of the Church?' To ask such a question is to look for factors that could explain the widening gap between More and Erasmus in this area – I repeat, *in this* area, for in so many other areas More would have been as consistent as Erasmus and the two would have enjoyed a continuation, *mutatis mutandis*, of their intimate and cooperative relationship.

Thomas More was about 46 in 1523, the year which I take to delineate the change, but he had been unofficially in the King's service half a dozen years, unofficially nearly ten since his trade mission to the Low Countries in 1515. More's election as Speaker of Parliament in 1523 further underscores his ambiguous position (his growing involvement in public policy, both publicly and psychologically): for although More was a spokesman for parliament (and his address in 1523 is a noble document in the history of freedom of speech), he had of course been a member of the King's Council since 1517-18, and under-treasurer and knight since 1521![3]

I would here emphasize the probability that More was drawn into the examination of heretics in some official or quasi-official capacity quite early in his public career, perhaps by virtue of his office as under-sheriff of London (which he was from 3 September 1510 onward). But certainly he was deeply enough involved in the celebrated affair of Richard Hunne, which lasted from 1511 until Hunne's death in 1514 and his posthumous burning as a heretic, and continued to figure in the Standish-Kidderminister debate over Criminous Clerks in 1515, which occupied parliament, the King's Council, and many of the learned common and canon lawyers of England throughout 1515; that affair then rose again to the surface of polemics in 1529, and More tried to defend both canon law and the handling of the Hunne affair by the hierarchy in his writing from 1529 to 1533![4] In More's *Dialogue Concerning Heresies, Confutation, Apology*, and *Debellation*, there is again and again indication of involvement in matters concerning heresy long before he became Lord Chancellor in 1529. I could not say at what point his primary judgement in this category became essentially legalistic, but I would insist that before 1523 (the date of the publication of the *Responsio*) he had begun to think this way. Let us recall too the moving anecdote in Roper's *Life of More*: of More's prayers for William Roper at the time of his son-in-law's commitment to Lutheranism, probably just after his marriage to More's beloved daughter Margaret – i.e., in 1521 or shortly afterward, Roper became a Lutheran but later returned to the Catholic faith. Given More's deep and special fondness for his daughter this incident might help to explain his hatred of the influence of Lutheranism. (By contrast, during this period Erasmus was corresponding with a number of the Reformers.)

The fact remains that in 1523 his *Responsio* tries to counter Luther on every point – *tota in toto et tota in qualibet parte*, as C.S. Lewis comments: 'that the reader, whatever page he lights upon, should find there all that he needs for refutation of the enemy'; and it does so with extraordinary vulgarity (even for his times), and a total lack of charity. One example must suffice:

> But meanwhile, for as long as your reverend paternity will be determined to tell these shameless lies, others will be permitted, on behalf of his English majesty, to throw back into your paternity's shitty mouth, truly the shit-pool of all shit, all the muck and shit which your damnable rottenness has vomitted up, and to empty out all the sewers and privies onto your crown divested of the dignity of the priestly crown, against which no less than against the kingly crown you have determined to play the buffoon.

More, it is abundantly clear, read Luther — or more likely considered some of his teachings by second-hand information and report — as having no possible relation with the living development of Christian doctrine. An idea that is not orthodox was ipso facto to More heretical and to be condemned; this is the logic of More's rhetorical strategies, and the theological thrust is an ever-greater insistence on more and more inclusive and explicit orthodoxy. The contrast with Erasmus could not be more obvious: 'I speak of these things more freely.' he could write in 1519 to Albert of Brandenburg, 'because I am not involved in any way in the cause of Reuchlin and Luther'; and in 1518, in the Prefatory letter to Abbot Voltz for a new edition of the *Handbook of the Militant Christian*, Erasmus wrote: 'Let this book lead to a theological life rather than theological disputations.' And though he engaged in much controversy and debate in the 1520's, there is nothing I know of that stoops so low as More's *Responsio*.

The outbreak of peasant uprisings in the Schwartzwald during June, 1524 — which spread quickly and widely through Swabia, Franconia, Thuringia and into the Rhineland, and reports of which circulated in England with considerable exaggerations of the facts — for More these events would have confirmed for the sphere of the political order his fears concerning the dangerous effects of Lutheranism in the spiritual order.

Yet, even if all that I say concerning reasons for More's fierceness towards heretics be so, can we accept such fears as sufficient explanation for his violent reaction to Tyndale, St. German, and others from 1528 to 1533, in writings which I would characterize as theological overkill? From the date of the authorization by Tunstall, Bishop of London, for More to read Protestant books in order to refute them in English — 7 March 1528, and given so legal a mind as More's, a mind so alert to potential dangers, is it not possible that it might have been issued at More's request? — from 1528 to 1533, More wrote several thousand pages of polemics, in which there is but rarely the notion that anything from the reformers might conceivably be valid, might contribute to the desperately needed reform of the Church and Christian society (which he himself had proclaimed in *Utopia*). Indeed by the time of the *Debellatiort* (1533), the inescapable conclusion, it seems to me, is that tradition is no longer dynamic for More: it is now a repository which must be safeguarded. To use his own metaphor from greener days, it has become an established treasure, a deposit behind walls, which must be defended against the enemy – and it is worth considering the extent and force of military and *para*-military metaphors that run from the titles of the *Confutation* and *Debellation* and into the works themselves.

The contrast between More and Erasmus from 1517 to 1523 is striking enough, and it becomes the greater after 1523; and it would seem that Erasmus is not only trying to walk the middle of the road – and that metaphor, while superior to expressions of valueless neutrality, is really unsatisfactory. Erasmus was trying to keep the lines of communication open to stay in touch with, to continue to make meaningful contact with, the younger and sometimes militant generations. Erasmus was trying to preserve the possibilities of true dialogue, so beloved to generations of humanistic effort, so essential to their principles and values. Years earlier More had written the *Utopia* as dialogue, but there is little enough dialogue in More's polemical writings after 1520 (not until More himself is in the Tower are we again given dialogue with compassion in *The Dialogue of Comfort*). Even in theological debates like Erasmus' strenuous one with Dolet, there is nothing that approaches the vituperative violences of More's *Responsio*.

On the crucial subject of heresy, Erasmus comes through admirably, and one could cite a number of passages in the letters, the *Paraclesis*, the *Ratio*, and elsewhere. But the 1519 letter to Albert of Brandenburg will serve again, and two brief passages must suffice:

> Besides, while the proper task of theologians is to instruct, I now observe that many do nothing but constrain or destroy and extinguish, though Augustine, even in the case of the Donatists, who were not only heretics but also savage brigands, does not approve of those who only use force and do not instruct. Men, whom gentleness especially becomes, seem to thirst for nothing except human blood, and they eagerly desire only that Luther be seized and destroyed. But this is to play the part of the executioner, not the theologian ...

And, further,

> At one time the heretic was heard respectfully, and he was absolved if he made amends; but if he persisted in his heresy after his conviction, the extreme penalty was his exclusion from communion with the Church. Now the crime of heresy is a different matter, and yet for any trifling reason the cry is immediately raised ... I admit that the charge of a corrupted faith is grave, but it is not necessary to turn everything into a question of faith ...

Yet I would not want to over-simplify the complexities of history (nor to fail to recognize that More had responsibilities as Lord Chancellor which Erasmus as an essentially private citizen did not); and one must recognize too that Erasmus' attitude changed significantly in 1520, both after the papal condemnations and still more, I think, after Luther's several treatises of that year. As Gilmore has formulated the situation:

> He feared the consequences of what he now saw to be a revolution, and he deplored Luther's appeal to the general public. As the Lutheran movement took shape and the gap between Rome and Wittenberg widened, Erasmus's position became increasingly uncomfortable ...![17]

The *Inquisitio de fide* (so ably edited by Craig Thompson) must indeed be read not only, or not simply, as a theological tract in its abstractive structure, but as a characteristically Erasmian effort 'to explore in a dialogue the implications of the religious division.' And there is a significant shift from this dialogic effort to the definition of position in his treatise on the freedom of the will, a shift from dialogue to tract, from exploration to separating definition. The *Hyperaspistes*, while they are of course elaborations of Erasmus' original argument, are also confessions that the possibility of dialogue is diminishing: here Erasmus is forced closer to the polemic spirit and techniques of More.

But the dialogue spirit in Erasmus returns and continues in the late *Colloquies*, and it is in these that I would see one of the marks of Erasmus' greatness as a humanist. For it is one thing to write dialogues in the halcyon years before 1516 — that was a time for summer humanists — it is quite another thing to write dialogues as Erasmus did in the winter years from 1522 to 1534. One must recognize, nay celebrate, the greatness of More's achievement in the *Dialogue of Comfort,* written during his imprisonment in the Tower, 1534-35; yet there is relatively little in this work to indicate any readiness on More's part to enter into dialogue with reformers. There is compassion, but only for his co-religionists, whom he foresaw as poised on the brink of disaster; the dialogue renders his towering powers of intellect and faith and will, but it does not engender fraternal charity towards the reformers. I would take nothing away from this great *consolatio* — one of the great works after Boethius in this genre that has its share of literary masterpieces — but there is little in it to change what I have said concerning More as against Erasmus on the point of tradition.

'Like all life,' Curtius writes, 'tradition is a vast passing away and renewal.'[18] To the humanist scholar (and Richard Schlatter has spoken eloquently of his offices in an ACLS paper on 'Humanist Scholarship in the U.S.'), the gathering and preservation and evaluation of tradition has been a vital part of his whole effort, scarcely to be separated from his enjoyment of good letters. It is one of the responsibilities of the literary critic continually to make the effort to repossess the past. For, as we have been shown by a number of critics beginning with Matthew Arnold — but new generations of students seem not to have learned the lesson — that for his own work the critic has to be both involved in his age and detached from it. This double quality of experiencing our own time to the full and yet being able to weigh it in relation to other times is what the humanist as critic must strive for, if he is to be able to discern and demand the works of art that we need most.

> ... he cast himself a role
> that needed ancestors and children to play
> behind / ahead ...

But our burden is still larger. Literature is but a part of the humanities, and I must speak of the burden of the teacher and scholar in the humanities, for it is here that Erasmus has still larger place today. Without its bases of tradition, mankind is like an individual without memory. 'Memory is a dynamic principle,' the great Russian critic Ivanov wrote, and he went on to remind that 'forgetting is weariness and interruption of movement, descent and return to the condition of a relative inertness.'[19] As it is with the individual man, so is it with a people or a race: a culture that turns its back upon tradition is forgetting and interrupting its organic movement. It is, however, a travesty of tradition to erect walls that halt movement, for tradition is not that which is safeguarded in a vault or behind barriers: for that would be to harden the thing which tradition is keeping alive into a doctrine that cannot long live by itself, into a fixed and unchallengeable choice of canonical books. Ironically enough, it was More, in an early writing, who used the figure of the locked chest at one point for such a concept. Living tradition is process, not product, and an imaginative transmittal of what has been inherited can always bring life, indeed is necessary to sustain institutional life.

The Thomas More who defended humanism then under attack in his celebrated 1517 letter to Oxford University — he knew this, as did the Erasmus who praised with such beautiful irony the folly that would destroy tradition and, with consummately managed gradation of tone, allows his irony to deepen and embrace the folly and simplicity of Christ and his followers.[20] But after 1523 I would look to Erasmus for the one who kept viable a sense of tradition, not More. Let me read an extended passage from one of the adages which Erasmus added to the 1526 edition, for it is a splendid statement by Erasmus on the new and the old.[21]

> On the other hand, if the older men were ready to accept (with civility and fairness) what are really not newcomers and strangers, but guests of old days returning to claim their right of citizenship, they would find the addition of these things was far from useless, and lets in new light not negligible at all. As it is, they wage irreconcilable war on old friends, as if they were

enemies. They call 'new' the things that are the oldest of all, and they call 'old' what is really new. It is something new (with boys who are to learn grammar) to stuff them with *modus significandi*, and read them crazy lists of words which teach nothing but to speak faultily. It is something new to accept a youth as a student in Philosophy, Law, Medicine or Theology, who can understand nothing in the ancient authors owing to his ignorance of the language they speak. It is something new, to exclude from the Holy of Holies of Theology anyone who has not sweated for years over Averroës and Aristotle. It is something new to stuff young men, who are reading for a degree in Philosophy, with Sophistical nonsense and fabricated problems, mere brainteasers (*meras ingeniorum cruces*). It is something new in the public teaching of the Schools, for the answers to differ according to the methods of Thomists or Scotists, Nominalists or Realists. It is something new to exclude any arguments which are brought from the sources of Holy Scripture, and only accept those which are taken from Aristotle, from the Decretals, from the determinations of the Schoolmen, from the glosses of the professors of papal law, or from precedents (inane for the most part) distorted from Roman law. If we are to be offended by what is new, these are the really new things. If we approve of what is old, the oldest things of all are what are being brought forward now. Unless, maybe, 'new' means coming from the century of Origen, and 'old' means what started up three hundred years ago and has gone from bad to worse ever since. The only course left to us now, therefore, is this: that the study of language and of good letters, coming back to take their place amongst us and spring up again from the roots, as it were, should courteously and peaceably work their way into the company of those disciplines which have held sway for so many centuries in the universities, and without disparaging anyone's particular study, should be of use to the studies of all ... Let them warn, and help, and correct [Erasmus concludes with an evocation of the Psalm that figures in the Office], as a conscientious maidservant warns, and helps, and corrects her mistress.

For us today there are a few final reflections. From the past, much remains — and can we blame young students who at times feel too much? Young artists, young citizens, young lovers who feel too heavily on their backs the burden of history, of all that is inherited? Yet it is the continuing task of the historical critic to study that past, continuously to re-evaluate it (let us admit: we must resolve to do this more rigorously than we have done in practice), to test its relevance to our own values and needs, but remembering that such a test is always only provisional, only a moment or stage in an ever-changing development. Therefore as humanist (I return to modify our epigraph), each should cast himself a role that needs ancestors and children to play: *behind / ahead* ... One last thing:

as perhaps the greatest of the great humanists of the Renaissance, Erasmus never lost sight either of the essentiality of enjoyment as part of the process in or of relevance to the good life as the end of learning. If those new barbarians, our students, to whom we devote our lives as teachers, do not understand that tradition must always be re-discovered − and that it is worth the effort − then we shall have failed as teachers and lovers of the humanities. *Saint Erasmus*, we can indeed say with humanistic piety, *pray for us*.

1   Originally presented to the Royal Society of Canada (and published in that form in the *Transactions of the Royal Society of Canada*, Series IV, vol. VIII [1970], 287-98), and later published in revised form in a volume of Erasmus studies edited by Richard L. DeMolen, *Erasmus of Rotterdam: A Quincentennial Symposium* (New York: Twayne, 1971).
2   R.P. Blackmur, *The Good European, and Other Poems*.
3   See the three volumes of *Bibliographies Érasmiennes*, ed. J.-C. Margolin, covering the years since 1936.
4   P.S. Allen, ed. *Opus Epistolarum Des. Erasmi Roterdami* (= Allen, *OE*), IV, 537 (no.1489). Cf. *OE* VI, 76 (to Celio Calcagnini).
5   Huizinga has neatly pulled together two separate Erasmian quotations: ' "Neither death nor life shall draw me from the communion of the Catholic Church," he writes in 1522, and in the *Hyperaspistes* in 1526: "I have never been an apostate from the Catholic Church. I know that in this Church, which you call the Papist Church, there are many who displease me, but such I also see in your Church. One bears more easily the evils to which one is accustomed. Therefore I bear with this Church, until I shall see a better, and it cannot help bearing with me, until I shall myself be better. And he does not sail badly who steers a middle course between two several evils." ...' J. Huizinga, *Erasmus of Rotterdam*, trans. F. Hopman (New York: Garden City Books, 1952), p. 165.
6   See esp. L.-E. Halkin, 'La piété d'Érasme,' *Revue d'histoire ecclésiastique*, 79 (1984), 671-708.
7   On the statues of Erasmus erected in Rotterdam since the 16th century, see the recent discussion in *Erasmus in English*.
8   Allen, *OE* III, 376/561 (Ep. 858); 'if we are moved by splendid names, what else, I ask you, is a city than a great monastery?' (*CWE* 6: 89/593-4.
9   The issue is not a simple one, for the canon − whether that of theology or of literature − cannot be expanded *ad infinitum*. Yet precisely for that reason there must be a continuous revision of the canon (but not a renunciation of it): those figures whose achievements are now seen to be of prime importance, both historically and to our problems today, must be read and understood in the fullness of their work. There are as well other reasons than that of economy for the continous revising of the canon (see the studies cited below).
  A second consideration is that of context − a term often bandied about like a cliché − and I have tried to discuss context within a theory of literature that allows for tradition: in *Intertextuality and Renaissance Texts* (Bamberg: H. Kaiser, 1984), esp. p. 16; and 'Erasmus in England: *Translatio Studii* and *Studia Humanitatis*,' *Classical and Modern Literature*, VII (1987), 269-83, and esp. 283.
10   On the influence of Erasmus, see my essay reprinted in Part VII below.
11   Q. from Thomas More, *Selected Letters*, ed. Elizabeth F. Rogers (New Haven, Conn.: Yale Univ. Press, 1961).
12   I have outlined a theory of tradition in *Intertextuality and Renaissance Texts*, ch. 1, and I have developed it in a number of other essays.
13   See my monograph on *The Achievement of Thomas More: Aspects of His Life and Work* (Victoria, B.C.: English Literary Studies, University of Victoria, 1976).
14   I have discussed the Hunne affair in *Proceedings of the IV Congress of Medieval Canon Law, Strasburg 1968* (Rome, 1971) and in *St. Thomas More: Action and Contemplation*, ed. R. S. Sylvester (New Haven, Conn.: Yale Univ. Press, 1970).
15   *The Complete Works of St. Thomas More − Responsio ad Lutherum*, ed. John M. Headley (New Haven, Conn.: Yale Univ. Press, 1969), V, 311.
16   *CWE* 7: 110/40-1.

17 Myron P. Gilmore, 'Erasmus,' in *New Catholic Encyclopedia* (New York and Washington: McGraw Hill, 1967).
18 Ernst Robert Curtius, *European Literature and the Latin Middle Ages*, trans. Willard Trask from *Europäische Literatur und lateinisches Mittelalter* (1948) – Bollingen Series XXXVI (New York: Bollingen/Pantheon, 1953), p. 395.
19 Ibid.
20 See now M. A. Screech, *Ecstasy and the Praise of Folly* (London: Duckworth, 1980).
21 Margaret Mann Phillips, *The Adages of Erasmus* (Cambridge: Cambridge Univ. Press, 1964), pp. 376-8.

PART II

THE EARLY ERASMUS

The biographer and historical critic must both deal with the problematics of Erasmus' date of birth, his family, and his place of birth: these are important in themselves and in their casting long shadows upon Erasmus' sensibilities; but they must be dealt with responsibly and sensitively in scholarly biographical investigation.

Here I have chosen two studies which focus on questions which are also of prime importance for our understanding of the early Erasmus, yet both too involved and necessarily discursive for inclusion in a biography proper. The first deals with the Brethren of Common Life and touches certain aspects of his schooling, though in the biography I shall deal with that whole matter in greater detail; it pulls in the deeper questions of the values and teachings of those individuals who were Brethren, or schooled by them, and with whom Erasmus came into some kind or degree of significant relationship. The second deals with Rudolph Agricola and his bearing upon Erasmus, and it involves the background of northern humanism. These two are by no means the only problem-questions concerning the early years of Erasmus; but they are two without clear answers to which no clear understanding of Erasmus' remarkable growth as a student can be understood, and obviously both must be subsumed in the more complex question of Erasmus' religious vocation and spiritual development.

A. The *Devotio moderna* and the Brethren of the Common

Although the two movements of the *Devotio moderna* and the Brethren of the Common Life were intimately connected, it is best to consider them separately; for there is a great deal of controversy concerning each movement and *a fortiori* the relationship of each to the other and to Erasmus. The appended bibliography calls attention to the major lines of scholarly investigation, and it must be regarded as a necessary tool for further study.

(1) Devotio moderna

The term *devotio*, one may first observe, has classical, patristic and medieval roots (see *DOS* III, cols. 703 ff.). While throughout the Middle Ages the word *devotio* carried forward the double sense of both exterior and interior devotion, there is a more or less explicit reference as well to the liturgical ceremonies and their observance, but with these ceremonies having their principal source in charity and their purpose in the service of God (*DOS* 709). *Modernus* meant primarily 'present-day' or 'now,' and only indirectly our 20th-c. sense of 'new' (as I stress in my discussion elsewhere).

The *Devotio moderna* ('present-day devotion,' or 'piety for now'), then, was a religious movement which rose in the Low Countries during the fourteenth century and lasted into the sixteenth. Its immediate roots are to be found in medieval *devotio* (especially that of the 12th-c. Paris School of St. Victor.[2]) and in the mysticism of the Rhineland, where the spiritual teachings of Meister Eckhart, Sister Hadewych and Jan van Ruysbroeck had created a fervor that moved out of religious institutions and into the houses of the laity.[3] In the spiritual writings of the founders and teachers of the *Devotio moderna* movement, one finds a stress on the teachings of St. Bernard, St. Bonaventure, and Jean Gerson,[4] and a fervent desire to reestablish the sanctity and the austerity of the religious life by other forms, spiritualities and structures than was thought to be offered by the rules and traditions of the older orders, especially the monastic ones. *Devotio moderna* can be most simply described as a conservative and ascetic Christianity that emphasized a faithfulness to the example of Christ while living communally, but without vows, in the world.

The most inspiring figure of the *Devotio moderna* and one thought of as its *pater et origo*, though the movement had begun earlier, was Gerart Grote (or in Latin, Gerardus Magnus, 1340-1384), whose preaching and example of pious living — devoted to a combination of moral action with spiritual communion and the development of the interior life taught by the mystics of the Church and by the Stoics (especially Seneca) — gave direction to the thought and work of his followers in the fifteenth and early sixteenth centuries. It was one Henry Pomerius, who in writing of the mystic Jan van Ruysbroeck, gave the title to Grote and the name to the movement: he calls Grote 'the *fons et origo Modernae Devotionis*, the fount and origin of the Modern Devotion' (writing in the years between 1414 and 1421). Although to some extent triggered by the examples of the Beguines in the Southern Low Countries[5] and by the Rhineland mystics, like Ruysbroeck (whose teachings on the sacraments and the nature of man, involving consequently grace and free will, were at times unorthodox and even eccentric), Grote's *Devotio moderna* was in part also a reaction against some of the unorthodoxies of those groups; and there were among the Devotionalists as well positive connections with the teachings of Pierre d'Ailly and Nikolaus von Kues (Cusa), together with certain of the implications in the realist thought of Ockham.[6] It was, however, Jan van Ruysbroeck who inspired Gerart Grote in one of his sermons and who transformed him from a rather worldly man into a powerful reformer of men[7] — a pattern repeated in another who had been schooled by the Brethren, Ignatius Loyola. Various forms of the *Devotio moderna* shared a common stress upon austerity and the strict observance of habits of prayer, meditation, communal readings or chant, and work. Devotionalists thus nearly all stressed a practical piety, a following of the example of Christ,[8] and an emphasis upon pastoral work and teaching.

Among Devotionalists can be named the following: Grote and his successor, Florens Radewijn (c. 1350-1400), Thomas à Kempis (d. 1471), whose *Imitatio Christi* is the most popular by far of the many writings of the Devotionalists; and such now lesser-known but then significant figures as Gerard Zerbolt of Zutphen (1367-98), Gerlach Peters (1378-1411), and Hendrik Mande (1360-1431) – with Gerlach and Hendrik taking us into the congregation of Windesheim (discussed below).

The influence of the *Devotio* movement as a whole – conceiving it as a large movement that embraced two or three main lines of development – can be traced not only in the Low Countries and through the Rhineland but also into northern France, Switzerland and even, at least among individuals, in Italy and Spain. Thus, Loyola's reading of the *Imitatio Christi* was a key influence in his sudden conversion into a soldier of Christ. Other key figures, who were members of or influenced by the Brothers of the Common Life, are listed in (2) below.

Bibliography:
[Many of works listed present divergent or even opposing interpretations, and I have indicated in each section those which argue for extreme points of view.]
P. Mestwerdt, *Die Anfänge des Erasmus, Humanismus und Devotio Moderna*, 2 vols. (Leipzig 1917) ... (again described and criticized in detail by Post, pp. 1-8).
A. Hyma, *The Christian Renaissance, a history of the Devotio Moderna* (Grand Rapids, Mich.: The Reformed Press, 1924) ... but this work makes the *Devotio Moderna* the source of northern humanism and indeed the locus of all piety and inward meditation (see the critique of Post, pp. 16-7).
P. Debongnie, *Jean Mombaer de Bruxelles, abbé de Livry, ses écrits et ses réformes* (Louvain 1928).
J. M. E. Dols, *Bibliographie der Moderne Devotio* (Nijmegen: 1941).
St. Axters, *Geschiedenis van de vroomheid in de Nederlanden* (Antwerpen 1956).
R. R. Post, *The Modern Devotion*: Confrontation with Reformation and Humanism (Leiden: E. J. Brill, 1968).
Dictionnaire de Spiritualité.

(2) The Brethren of the Common Life

In Grote, a man of deep devotion and of wide and perhaps even scholarly learning (despite his rejection of the contemporary scholasticism that dominated late fourteenth-century universities), his followers found an inspiration: he was indeed *pater et origo Devotionae modernis*. There are several early lives of Gerart, including a life, *Vita Gerardi Magni*, by Thomas à Kempis, which interestingly forms an integral part of the *Dialogi Noviciorum* (of which it comprises the greater part of the *Liber Secundus*). These lives are much like the medieval lives of the saints, the *vitae sanctorum* which were *legenda*: that is, to be read, and to serve as models for living in this world. Even during the lifetime of Gerart there was a development from individual to communal living under his guidance, and thus the first Brethren of the Common Life began to shape their special mode of living, studying, working and praying. Towards the end of Gerart's life, Florens Radewijn (d. 1400) was named as rector of a group of laymen and religious who had begun to live together, and he was accepted as the successor of Grote. The first community of *fraters* – it is to be noted that they were brothers, not priests – began to develop in the 1380s at Zwolle in the north. The expansion moved energetically under Radewijn with Zwolle at the center: to Deventer (where the schools in which brothers taught became famous), and to other cities like Hoorn, Münster (which became the center of a group of houses in Westphalia and the Rhineland), Liège, and so to many other places, from Trier and Tübingen into Switzerland. Apart from prayer and the sharing of religious observances, the Brethren occupied themselves with the tasks of copying and illuminating books, preaching, and serving as spiritual directors to individuals (particularly to schoolboys and the Sisters), and to providing board and lodgings, and sometimes teaching, for schoolboys.[9] One must therefore be cautious in speaking (as has sometimes been done) of schools 'run by' the Brethren: in nearly every case one should rather speak of the schools in which individual brothers may have taught. Further, there was a kind of anti-intellectualism as well as anti-scholasticism: when the community wished certain of the Fraters to become priests, they were (according to Post, p. 208) ordained without any higher theological training and they 'never sent [one of their members to] university.'[10]

Brethren of the Common Life
Bibliography:
J. Busch, *Chronicon Windeshemense und Liber de Reformatione monasteriorum*, ed. K. Grube in *Der Augustiner Propst, Johannes Busch*, Geschichtsquellen der Provinz Sachsen, vol. 19 (Halle, 1886) ... a most important primary source.
E. Barnikol, *Studien zur Geschichte der Brüder vom gemeinsamen Leben* (Tübingen: Mohr 1917).
Thomas à Kempis [Thomas Hemerken a Kempis], *Opera Omnia*, ed. M. J. Pohl, 7 vols. (Fribourg, 1902-22).
William Spoelhof, *Concepts of religious nonconformity and religious toleration as developed by the Brethren of the Common Life in the Netherlands, 1374-1489*. Unpubl. doct. diss., University of Michigan, 1946.
C. van der Wansem, *Het ontstaan en de geschiedenis der Broederschap van het gemene leven tot 1400* (Löwen, 1958).
R. R. Post, *The Modern Devotion* [cited above].

(3) The Windesheim Congregation

Houses of the Brethren and the Sisters of the Common Life spread rapidly through the cities and towns of the Low Countries and Germany, and into northern France and Switzerland; and these constituted a major part of the history of the *Devotio moderna*. Another development is marked by their movement at certain moments into monastic institutions, and the most notable achievement was the formation of the Windesheim congregation (near Zwolle, that home of the Brethren), about 1386 or 1387. In 1394 and 1395 four monasteries, including that of Windesheim, then united to form the congregation of Windesheim; and the reformation of monasteries became, in the view of the fifteenth-century historian of the congregation, Johannes Busch, the mainspring of Windesheim's activities.[11] Early in the fifteenth century they adopted the Rule of St. Augustine, in order to have a more strict observance, and thus they became known as Canons Regular of St. Augustine (discussed in the chapter on Erasmus and Augustinianism); this adoption of the Augustinian Rule was followed by a number of houses of the Sisters of the Common Life, who had been tertiaries of the Third Rule of St. Francis, perhaps the most widespread and most numerous of the third orders of women religious.

Throughout the fifteenth century the Windesheim congregation flourished; at its peak there were more than 80 houses for men and 13 for women, and it entered into a decline only after about 1500. So much of their special sense of vocation resided in their work as copyists of manuscripts, and *a fortiori* of the Bible, that it is not to be wondered, that the advent of printing and the great production of printed Bibles should have diminished the Windesheimers' sense of unique purpose, as well as deprived them of a prime source of income. But other factors were operative as well, of course: the implosion of the Reformation upon the closed world of the monasteries could only have produced deep and riving shock-waves in the communities and within individuals. Above all there was a diminution of vocations, always a threat to monastic congregations and to this one which had expected continuing growth and in any event depended like all others upon a certain critical mass to preserve the vitality of its central liturgical and other communal functions.[12]

The Windesheim community produced such powerful figures as Thomas à Kempis (c. 1379-1471), Johannes Busch (1399-c. 1480), and a number of others. As Post observes, 'it is to such persons that the Windesheim congregation owed its greatness. Not only did they promote its increase and expansion, they also enhanced the quality of its spiritual life, rendering it attractive for the devout men of the fifteenth century.'[13] As early as the Council of Constance (1414-1417), the Windesheim congregation and its scattered monasteries won support and privileges through the approval and strong support of such reform-minded leaders of the Church as Pierre d'Ailly and Jean Gerson; and elsewhere I have provided a discussion of the remarkable proposal of the Duchess of Burgundy that Windesheimers lead the reform of monasteries in France.

(4) Erasmus and the Brothers of the Common Life

It is not a simple matter to describe Erasmus' relationship with the *Devotio moderna* and with the Brothers of the Common Life, for the nature of the schools he attended is not beyond dispute, and with some of the individuals involved the question of the degree of their commitment to the *Devotio moderna* has yet to be studied definitely for their thought and writings.

For the period of Erasmus' schooling at Deventer (c. 1478-83) there is little question: we know that he studied there some time, and that he studied under John Synthen and during the first year of the headmastership of Alexander Hegius (on both of whom, see below). The role of Agricola — who in 1484 employed the formula *philosophia Christi* (see below) — must be studied also in the light of his schooling by Brethren of the Common Life as well. Synthen was a Brother who taught in the *domus pauperum* (or hostel) during Erasmus' school years at Deventer, and we can be certain that Synthen taught Erasmus. But Hegius, though he had been a pupil of the school at Zwolle himself, seems not to have been a Brother, however sympathetic to their values and aims he may have been. It must be stressed, *pace* Hyma, that St. Lebuin's school at Deventer was not run by the Brethren of the Common Life![14] Rather, there were individual teachers in that school who were Brothers. During the years 1485 to 1487 Erasmus stayed with the Brothers in their hostel at 's-Hertogenbosch, but he seems to have studied closely with only one individual among the Brethren, and he had a poor opinion of the other![15]

Yet the influence of the *Devotio moderna* and of the Brothers of the Common Life upon Erasmus cannot be reduced to a curricular matter only — that is, what courses did he take, and with whom — and it cannot be left at such a negative conclusion (as some historians have proposed); in the chapter on Erasmus in the monastery I shall argue for the importance of Thomas à Kempis for Erasmus. The general spirit of the *Devotio moderna* provided the atmosphere, if not the specifics of doctrine, of the *philosophia Christi*. Erasmus' commitment to lifelong study and to service to Christian learning owes much, it can be seen, to the emphasis by the Brothers upon work. The influence of the *Devotio moderna* is pronounced in the *Enchiridion* — for nearly every theme or motif of this work can be traced to the writings of Thomas à Kempis — and it is still present (as Guttman has shown) in the *Colloquia*.

One must also note that the following friends or colleagues of Erasmus had been schooled by the Brethren: Josse Bade, Hermann Buschius, Jacob Faber, Cornelius Gerard of Gouda, Gerard of Kloster, Gerard Geldenhower, Conrad

Goclenius, Gozewijn (Goswin) of Halen, William Hermans, Jan Koechman of Zwolle, Gerardus Listrius, Georgius Macropedius, and others. Further, of these men, Gerard of Kloster and Cornelius Gerard were also canons regular of St. Augustine (Gerard of Kloster at St. Agnietenberg, which had been the house of Thomas à Kempis); Gozewijn had entered the house of the Brethren at Groningen, and Hermans was schooled under Hegius at St. Lebuin's school and was a canon with Erasmus at Steyn. Koechman too was a member of the Brethren's community at Zwolle and in 1490 became rector; Listrius attented St. Lebuin's while Hegius was still alive and was closely associated with Koechman: the list is far from complete, but it calls attention to the number of Erasmus' relationships with former students of the Brethren.[16] Without assuming that 'any pupil from the schools of Deventer or Zwolle who achieved something in later life was a product of the Brothers' (thus Post, p. 676), one must recognize that among the friends and associates of Erasmus and by virtue of their friendship, the Brethren exercised a continuing influence of some kind or degree![17]

Erasmus himself became a canon regular of St. Augustine, an order deeply imbued with the values and goals of the *Devotio moderna*. Having been exposed to several figures active in the *Devotio moderna* and to individual Brothers of the Common Life he became a member of the community of canons regular at Steyn, which was a dependent house of Windesheim. It is important to note that even at the time he lamented that he did not find true piety at Steyn;[18] this lament is not so much a profession of a lack of piety on his part or a state of boredom — or even necessarily a blanket indictment of Steyn when that most loyal Busch was critical or monasteries that fell short of an ideal (see below), as it is a sign of his higher ideals. It is difficult to estimate the size of the community at Steyn during Erasmus' stay there, but the size matters: there is a certain critical mass necessary for the continuing vitality of communal spiritual life, not below a certain number (at least a dozen, one would think, together with a steady flow of postulants and novices). Many other monasteries were suffering from a reduction in numbers at about this time (as Knowles has shown in his study of Religious Houses).

But we may follow Halkin in declaring that Erasmus was an heir of the *Devotio moderna* — perhaps even without his full realization — and from it and its flowering glory, the *Imitatio Christi*, he was able to channel his task for a vigorous spirituality of the interior life, one neither exclusively intellectual nor rigidly formalist.[19] And the emphasis of the Brethren upon working — whether copying or studying — reinforced Erasmus' largely self-motivated dedication to study.

In spite of and in opposition to the charge in the influential *Dictionnaire de Théologie Catholique*, and other summary treatments, it must now be seen that Erasmus was and remained a priest with a vocation;[20] but it was no longer the conventual vocation (in both senses of the word 'conventual'): he remained faithful to his priestly vows — even according to his private interpretation to his vows as an Augustinian canon. But in place of the monastery and its demands (see Part III), Erasmus kept his commitment to a life of piety; his was an Augustinian vocation that was faithful to the spirit, if not the letter, of the Augustinian Rule. His was a piety early nurtured by the Brothers of the Common Life, then reformed by humanist teachings, and it became his unique *Philosophia Christi.*

Bibliography on Erasmus and Devotio moderna and Brethren of the Common Life.

Paul Mestwerdt, *Die Anfänge des Erasmus, Humanismus und 'Devotio Moderna,'* (Leipzig, Studien zur Kultur und Geschichte der Reformation 2, 1917).
Richard L. DeMolen, 'Erasmus' Commitment to the Canons Regular of St. Augustine,' *Ren Q*, xxvi (1973), 437-43.
Robert Stupperich, 'Zur Biographie des Erasmus von Rotterdam. Zwei Untersuchungen,' *Archiv für Reformationsgeschichte* 65 (1974), 18-36.
Charles Trinkaus, 'Humanism, Religion, Society: Concepts and Motivations of Some Recent Studies,' *Ren Q*, xxix (1976), 676-713.
L.-E. Halkin, 'La piété d'Erasme,' *Revue d'Histoire Ecclésiastique*, LXXIX (1974), 671-708.
L.-E. Halkin, 'La Devotio Moderna et l'humanisme,' *Réforme et humanisme*, Actes du IVe *Colloque* (Montpellier, 1977), 103-112.
Cornelis Augustijn, *Erasmus* (Ambo/Baarn, 1986), esp. ch. III, 'Jeugd en studietijd.'

1 In the Benedictine Rule there is the meaning of vow (chs. 18/24), and the term *devotio* could also mean obedience or loyalty during the Middle Ages, as well as a pious deed, and even graciousness: see Niermeyer, *Mediae Latinitatis Lexicon Minus.*
2 The School of St. Victor in Paris – notably Hugh (d. 1141) and Richard (d. 1173) of St. Victor – regarded *fervor* and *devotio* as the gift of God and they taught methods of prayer and contemplation, always striving to unite intelligence with love, that led to a love of God and His place to joy, and even ecstasy. The history is fully narrated by Fourier Bonnard, *Histoire de l'abbaye des chanoines réguliers de St.-Victor de Paris*, 2 vols. (Paris, 1904-7). Love, as Pelikan has remarked, was 'more central to the Augustinian system than faith' and faith was seen as 'faith formed by love' [*fides charitate formata*]: Pelikan, *Reformation of Church and Dogma*, p. 253, q. Galatians 5:6: In *Vulg.* reads 'fides quae per caritatem operatur.'
   Hugh of St. Victor, who also wrote an *Expositio in regulam Sancti Augustini*, was deeply influenced by the teaching of St. Augustine, to which he added concepts of St. Bernard on the ascent of the soul to God: *cogitatio, meditatio,* and *contemplatio* were the three stages described by Hugh; and in this teaching Hugh gave a great stress in theological doctrine to inner experience.
   The question of Erasmus' connections with the Abbey and School of St. Victor in Paris is as yet somewhat obscure; but certain elements can be identified and stressed. The Abbey of St. Victor was a house of the canons regular of St Augustine, and thus it had many connections at the end of the 15th c. with the Dutch houses. One may cite the mission of 1497, which was intended to assist in the reform of St. Victor's, in which Erasmus' close friend Cornelis Gerard was one of the leaders. Erasmus, we know, visited St. Victor's during his Paris years.
3 On the mysticism of the medieval mystics, one might first begin with the general studies of Evelyn Underhill, *Mysticism* rev. ed. (NY: Dutton, 1930) and David Knowles, *The English mystics* (London, 1927). Two recent studies are: F.-W. Wentzlaff-Eggebert, *Deutsche Mystik Zwischen Mittelalter und Neuzeit: Einheit und Wandlung ihrer Erscheinungsformen,* 3 ed. (Berlin: de Gruyter, 1969) esp. pp. 1-21: and Alois M. Haas, *Sermo Mysticus: Studien zu Theologie und Sprache der deutschen Mystik* (Freiburg/ Schweiz: Universitäts-Verlag, 1979), esp. 1-36. Yves Congar has discussed the

paradox of the medieval mystics — in the world, but not of the world — and its relation to lay spirituality in *Der Laie — Entwurf einer Theologie des Laientums* (Stuttgart: 1957), pp. 652 ff.

4   For a summary placing of the *devotio moderna* in the larger context of medieval devotion, see *DOS* III, 714-6, and the survey of R. R. Post, cited in the bibliography above. For the connections with Meister Eckhart et al., see Maria Alberta Lücker, *Meister Eckhard und die Devotio Moderna* (Leiden: E. J. Brill, 1950).

On the philosophical thought of these medieval masters, Bernard of Clairvaux (1090-1153) and Bonaventure (1217/8-1274), see E. Gilson, *History of Christian Philosophy in the Middle Ages* (London: Sheed and Ward, 1955), and further *Die Mystik des Heiligen Bernhard von Clairvaux* (Wittlich: 1936). On Gerson (1363-1429), see André A. Combes, *Essai sur la critique de Ruysbroeck par Gerson*, [I: *Introduction critique et dossier documentaire*] (Paris: Vrin, 1945) and *La théologie mystique de Gerson: Profil de son évolution*, II (Rome: 1964).

5   The Beguines developed in what is now southern Belgium towards the end of the 12th c., as a result of a number of social and religious causes. Although the women were not bound by permanent vows, they lived a communal life and wore a religious habit. Beguines were generally praised for their holy living and their devotion to caring for children and the sick. See E. W. McDonnell, *The Beguines and Beghards in Medieval Culture* (New Brunswick, N.J.: Rutgers University Press, 1954).

6   The doctrinal development in which Ockham's thought can be placed is described by Jaroslav Pelikan, *The Christian Tradition: A History of the Development of Doctrine: 4. Reformation of Church and Dogma (1300-1700)* (Chicago: University of Chicago Press, 1984); and the philosophical significance is treated in N. Kretzmann et al., eds., *The Cambridge History of Later Medieval Philosophy ... 1100-1600* (Cambridge: Cambridge University Press, 1982). Heiko Oberman has interpreted nominalism in *The Harvest of Medieval Theology* (Cambridge, Mass.: Harvard University Press, 1963) and *Masters of the Reformation* (Cambridge, Mass.: Harvard University Press, 1981).

7   See Dieter Kanduth, 'Die Windesheimer Augustiner-Chorherrenkongregation,' in *Thomas von Kempen — Beiträge zum 500. Todesjahr* (Kempen, 1971), p. 9 (9-13): '... der durch eine Predigt des Johannes Ruysbroeck von einem ziemlich weltlichen Menschen zu einem sehr religiösen geformt wurde, war denn der große Erneuer auf religiösem Gebiet.'

Ruysbroeck (1293-1381) was the first prior of the Augustinian monastery of Groenendaal, which Erasmus later visited while in the service of the Bishop of Cambrai (see above).

8   The seminal work is the 'imitation' or 'following' (the *Imitatio Christi*) of Thomas à Kempis, a canon of the Windesheim Congregation. This work, for many generations second in popularity and influence only to the Bible and 'in fact, one of the most widely read books of all time' (Pelikan, op. cit., p. 36), expresses the teaching of Grote and its form and style provided a microcosm of the teaching of the Brothers of the Common Life. In his first book of the *Imitatio*, Thomas makes clear that 'the imitation of Christ was not a substitute for redemption through his cross and the infusion of merit, and yet the primary emphasis lay on following the example of Christ in his passion, as this was made possible by the forgiveness of sins.' (see Pelikan, p. 37).

Many of the themes of Erasmus' *philosophia Christi* are to be found in the *Imitatio* — such as the contempt of the world (*De contemptu mundi*), the importance of communal life, prayer, study and work — see the final section of §A of this part.

The word 'imitatio' (as Sudbrack has observed) comes only in the title of later collections of the four books of Thomas à Kempis; and he further notes that 'Die Imitatio aber übersteigt die Schrift; jetzt ist der Mensch in Gottes Hand das Buch' — Josef Sudbrack, S. J., 'Das geistliche Gesicht der vier Bücher von der Nachfolge Christi,' in *Thomas von Kempen — Beiträge zum 500. Todesjahr, 1471-1971* (Kempen, 1971).

See further A. Ampe on *imitatio* in *Dict. de Spiritualité*.

9   Post, p. 244.
10 Post, p. 209.
11 Based upon Post's account, pp. 310-11.
12 More systematic study of such data as the number of professions needs to be made; but Post is surely too conservative in counting its decline as from 1525 (cf. p. 640). However, the question is not simply a quantitative matter; and even at the end of the 15th c. that loyal Windesheimer Busch, considering the production of the Windesheim copyists, writes, 'When we consider all this, then

it is no wonder that we complain today of the neglectful and lukewarm spirit of the present times' (Post, p. 308, q. from Busch, p. 313).
13   Post, p. 504.
14   See Post, op. cit., p. 578.
15   Post, p. 398.

Erasmus was now at an age where individual tutelage would have been far more important than attendance in classes; and it is conceivable that his work in epitomizing Valla's *Elegantiae* began during this period, perhaps at the suggestion of one of the two Brethren indicated, perhaps of some other.

16   This list is drawn from *BR*, only two volumes of which have as yet been published at the time of writing.

17   Post writes that 'Erasmus had no dealings with them [the masters of the 's-Hertogenbosch school] since he had already completed or nearly completed in Deventer all the classes which the school in 's-Hertogenbosch had to offer' (p. 398): but, again, that may not have been the case. For it seems obvious that Erasmus may well have had dealings with them even without enrolling in classes.

The influence of the Brethren is certainly to be found also in the interest for Erasmus of the following: Agricola (on whom see above), and Wessel Gansfort (1419-1489), some of whose books Erasmus owned (see *BR*). Not least, the influence of Thomas à Kempis upon Erasmus remains to be studied in full, although Erasmus does not quote or allude overtly to Thomas.

18   See Ep 11 – Allen, I, 50, line 90 (*Interea, tametsi adolescens, sensit quam non esset illic vera pietas*). One must weigh Erasmus' statement to Servatius Rogers in April 1506: 'For myself, I am deeply preoccupied with pondering how I can wholly devote to religion and to Christ whatever life remains to me' (*CWE* 2: 111/7-8, Ep 189).

19   L.-E. Halkin, 'La piété d'Erasme,' *Revue d'Histoire Ecclésiastique*, LXXIX (1984), 671-708. See also 'Le Devotio Moderna et l'humanisme,' in *Réforme et humanisme, Actes du IVe-Colloque* (Montpellier, 1977), 103-12.

20   See R. L. DeMolen, 'Erasmus' Commitment to the Canons Regular of St. Augustine,' *Ren Q*, xxvi (1973), 437-43, which stresses that 'Erasmus continued to be a member of the Austin Canons, subject to its rules and under obedience to its religious superiors' (p. 442).

B. Agricola and Erasmus: Erasmus' Inheritance of Northern Humanism

The full story of Erasmus' inheritance of Northern humanism has yet to be told in full, but it is clear that Rudolph Agricola was the *fons et origo* for Erasmus. In this paper I propose to examine that part of Erasmus' heritage and to attempt to appraise the debt to Agricola.*

In the 1480s Rudolph Agricola was esteemed as something of a prodigy by his countrymen, and on his visits home from his humanistic studies in Pavia he personified the glamour and the lure of Quattrocento humanism. It is clear that there was an Agricola circle in Deventer, and prominent among those who met regularly at the abbey of Aduard were Wessel Gansfort, Alexander Hegius (see Appendix), Antoon Vrije, Synthen, and the printer Richard Pafraet, at whose house Hegius lived and where Agricola visited in 1484. A boy of about 14, as Erasmus was at the time of Agricola's visit, could not have known all of this, not at the time, although he seems to have been conscious of the high esteem

* To be published in the Proceedings of the Rudolf Agricola Conference (1985), ed. F. Akkerman (1988).

in which Agricola was held by his schoolmasters. There is the contemporary testimony of one who (I follow P. S. Allen here) 'was a friend of Erasmus and Dorp, and who had been present in the school at Deventer when Hegius read out with great emotion a letter containing the news of Agricola's death.'[1] It would appear that for the young Erasmus Agricola became the personification of the Dutch humanist who was privileged to go to Italy for humanistic studies. For Agricola had studied with Battista Guarino, son of the famous Guarino da Verona, as well as with Ludovico Carbone and Titus Strozzi, and he had also twice represented Groningen at the Court of Maximilian at Brussels, then the most splendid court of Europe. All of this was part of the fame of Agricola.[2]

Later legend would embroider on the 'passing sight' that Erasmus had had of Agricola, and Melanchthon and others would represent Agricola as prophesying a bright future for the young Dutch boy. It was, quite certainly, only a passing sight, and in such case one could scarcely speak of Agricola's 'personal encouragement' of the young Erasmus;[3] but it may well have been something even stronger than encouragement: it seems to have been an inspiration. For Synthen and Hegius were both friends and in some sense disciples of Agricola and would have shared some of his humanist enthusiasms. This view would explain Erasmus' later statement that the two schoolmasters were the intellectual sons of Agricola, and he, through them, the grandson. Both Synthen and Hegius were heads of the school that Erasmus attended in Deventer. First there was Johannes Synthen, who had some degree of understanding classical antiquity in the new light.[4] Second there was Alexander Hegius, a man older than Agricola but willing to take Greek lessons from Agricola on one of his return visits to Deventer, probably in 1474.[5] Both schoolmasters were active in the publication of schooltexts, and the texts of both were in the areas of grammar as well as the new humanism.[6] Yet at Deventer, we have been reminded by Koch, more books in the classics were published during the 1490s than were published in Paris during the same period.[7]

The context in which Erasmus had his view of Agricola was likely an assembly of all the students, for on festal days the rector gave his oration to all of the pupils; it would seem probable that it was on such an occasion that Agricola addressed the schoolboys. For once, and apparently only once, the celebrated Agricola spoke to the entire school. But that occasion alone could not account for the many references to Agricola in later life; as we know, Erasmus continued to read Agricola, seems to have known some of his unpublished papers, and praised him very highly on all but one point.[8]

One instance of such praise is to be found in Erasmus' celebration of Agricola in the adage *Quid cani et balneo* (Adag., I, iv. xxxix). For in this recollection by Erasmus of Rudolph's assertion that putting a theologian to teaching children was 'as out of place as a dog in a bath,' we find the core of much of Erasmus' later views about the need to keep theologians to the teaching of theology, that literary education was more than merely a preparation for scholastic theology, and that Latin should be learned for a larger purpose than equipping a student for the dialectic of the schools.[9] In this adage Erasmus called Rudolph Agricola the first to bring the breath of good letters from Italy.

Erasmus praised Agricola in a number of epistles (numbers 23, 480, 1237, 2073) and in the *Ciceronianus*,[10] and he cited Agricola in that earliest of works, the *De Contemptu Mundi*.[11] Further, as van Leijenhorst has conveniently summarized in the essay on Agricola in *Contemporaries of Erasmus*, Erasmus 'purchased a number of his [Agricola's] works, keeping several of these in his library until he died.'[12] Finally, Erasmus used Agricola's profuse annotations in his personal copy of the edition of Seneca which had been printed by Bernard of Cologne at Treviso in 1478, an annotated copy which included many corrections of the text. Through a young Frisian named Haio Hermann – a kinsman of Agricola married to a daughter of the Frisian merchant Pompeius Occo, who had a neglected collection of Agricola's papers in Amsterdam – Erasmus received a loan of Agricola's Seneca, which Erasmus returned with due acknowledgments both to Agricola and to his young kinsman in the preface.[13] In that preface Erasmus wrote of Agricola: 'It was incredible how many good guesses were made by that remarkable man, *quam multa divinarit vir ille plane divinus.*'[14] At least twice, we know that Erasmus used Agricola's translations from the Greek, but he denied using Agricola in translating Sophocles.[15]

The biographical and bibliographical evidence is overwhelming: Erasmus knew the writings of Agricola early in life, and he continued to admire and make use of Agricola until his old age.

But what is even more important is Erasmus' indebtedness to Agricola for concepts and values in humanism and theology, and I shall try to analyze certain key concepts. The term *Northern humanism* is too large and vague to be very useful here for analysis,[16] and I propose to begin with a summary of the central concerns of the Brethren of the Common Life, to take up the role of rhetoric in both Agricola and Erasmus, and then to move briefly to the concept of *philosophia Christi*.

We cannot follow Albert Hyma in attributing the genius of the Northern Renaissance nearly totally to the work of the Brethren of the Common Life, important – indeed, vital – though that work was. But we must accept the work of the *Devotio Moderna* as one of the essential elements of – theirs may well have been the major contribution to – the development and spread of humanism along the Rhine and down into Hessia and Wurtemberg, as well as throughout a large part of the Netherlands. Their work in establishing schools, hospices for poor students in university towns and cities, and printing presses, cannot be minimized, and through some of its students – Cusanus, Agricola, Celtis, Mutianus, Wessel Gansfort, Erasmus, and Luther – that influence of the Brethren widened still further.[17]

What one does not find among these products of the schools of the Brethren is the new Platonism of the Florentine Academy, even though the personal influence of Ficino among northern scholars was great![18] There is in fact little interest in the occult and in astral influence among Agricola, Erasmus and their circles; nor is there an appreciable following of Ficino's development of the Platonic concept of love (as in Ficino's Commentary on the *Symposium*). In fine, neither Rudolph Agricola nor Erasmus is much touched by Florentine Platonism, and it is to be noted that Hegius wrote against the Platonists (see Appendix). And among German humanists, as Spitz has observed, 'no German humanist so seriously cultivated the theme of the natural and essential goodness, wisdom, and dignity of man as did Pico in his *Oration* or various theses.'[19] What Erasmus did have in common with Agricola was a high regard for rhetoric and a fondness for the humanistic forms of dialogue and epistle.

For Agricola, language was the indispensable medium of the *studia humanitatis*, and not surprisingly Cicero was extolled as the expression of ideal wisdom.[20] Behind Agricola we find such less well-known figures as Peter Luder — who had studied, Classen reminds us, with the older Guarino, and who taught at Heidelberg and Erfurt — and Albrecht von Eyb, author in 1459 of the widely read *Margarita poetica*. Luder, von Eyb, and others like Publicius (Rufus), were all involved in what might be called the Ciceronian revival of the fifteenth century: the study of Cicero's orations and the theoretical discussions of the role of rhetoric — even, the reaches of rhetoric as a path to wisdom.[21] By virtue of Agricola's work and example, and through the mediating teaching of Synthen and Hegius, Erasmus was enabled to respond (while in the monastery of Steyn in the 1480s) directly to Valla's *Elegantiae* and to make it at once a part of his personal program of studies: first Valla, then Poliziano and that later generation of Italian humanistic philologists. After 1500 there was everywhere a flood of new energy in a range of writings on rhetoric, which included commentaries on the *De Oratore* of Cicero, especially as Classen has recently noted in studying the context and achievement of rhetorical scholarship north of the Alps and emphasizing Luder, v. Eyb and Agricola in the 15th and early 16th centuries:

> Schon vorher liess er eine Ausgabe von Ciceros Reden für Archias und Marvellus cum argumentis, coloribus et rhetoricae partibus, wie er im Widmungsbrief an Christoph von Knoringen sagt, 1494 in Reutlingen drucken.[22]

Erasmus' great and enduring interest in Cicero, and his emphasis on the rhetorical tradition, must be seen in the light of his inheritance of the Agricolan devotion to rhetoric, which was itself part of a larger pattern of rhetorical studies and publications in the Low Countries and Germany. (One notes that a number of Erasmus' rhetorical works were during the sixteenth century printed or bound with copies of Agricola's *De reformando studio, de usu locorum communiae,* and his first Pavian oration.)[23] Closer comparative studies of the rhetorical writings and orations of Agricola with parallel works of Erasmus would, I urge, be most rewarding. Another point is that Agricola provides a valuable and much needed linkage with traditions of medieval rhetoric, as in his borrowing 'his mode of classifying the material to be deployed in eloquent discourse from medieval arts of preaching' (as Terence Cave has observed in his valuable work on *The Cornucopia* Text [1979]).

The larger question of Erasmus' indebtedness to Agricola for theological concepts demands much fuller treatment than is possible on this occasion. Agricola's *De formando studio* (1484) is significant in this context for its employment of the formula *philosophia Christi*, echoed so often and so richly by Erasmus, as an all-embracing title for a system of thought and values which mediated between classical wisdom and Christian faith: there was for Agricola little tension between the two.

Agricola seems to have been largely dependent upon the basic line of thought of such Italian humanists as Leonardo Bruni in his *De studiis et literis*, both for the genre of a treatise on the nature and direction of studies and for the concept of service for the humanist. Yet Agricola, while he served briefly as *scriba et orator* for Groningen, does not appear to have developed quite so fully the concept of civic humanism (in the terms of Hans Baron[24]); for, although he was less than completely content with his position at Groningen – and it must be asked whether it was so much the location as it was the position of town secretary – he waited to move until in 1482 he had received the offer from his old friend and fellow-student at Pavia, Johann von Dalberg, now bishop of Worms, to come to Heidelberg. He arrived there in 1484 to lecture, participate in disputations, and write. *De formando studio* is a product of that brief period at Heidelberg, and it is in the form of a letter to a friend, Jacobus Barbirianus, defending humanistic studies.

Like Erasmus a product of the schools where the Brethren of the Common Life taught – Agricola in Groningen, Erasmus in Deventer and 's-Hertogenbosch – Agricola expressed a view of man and a concept of learning which had deep roots in the piety and non-speculative non-scholastic thought and spirituality of the Brethren, among whom Seneca was a favorite author, as he had been for the author of their foundational text, *The Following of Christ*. From that part of his heritage Agricola developed a stoical-moralistic emphasis, as did Erasmus. And finally, the two shared a reasonably critical attitude towards Aristotle – one of respect without veneration – and this was balanced by their shared non-Platonism.

We can now see how much of the *philosophia Christi* of Erasmus – whether it was modelled directly upon the teaching of Agricola or came, at least in part, through such intermediaries as Hegius – was in fact probably both inspired and guided by Agricola's unique fusion of the teaching of the *Devotio Moderna* with that of his pious Italian masters.[25] For there was in both Erasmus and Agricola a basically non-speculative interest in philosophy and theology, an emphasis upon the practical with a strongly moralistic (and, to a considerable degree, Stoic) emphasis on the essential business of living in this world. The *philosophia Christi* was simple, but not easy; it was moralistic, but not puritanical; and it valued the role of classical learning and especially rhetoric, as embodied in Cicero, in teaching wisdom.

Yet there was also in both men a commitment to the study of the Christian Scriptures and a deep and abiding love of Christ and complete acceptance of the fact, of the actuality, of Christianity, however much one might criticize the abuses of the clergy; in both there was an essential commitment in matters of faith and to a life of study. The weight of the parallels and correspondences is very great, and the differences between them — such as the pure ultramontanism of Agricola, which Erasmus never shared — remarkably few. The lasting influence of Rudolph Agricola upon Erasmus cannot be doubted, and it is reflected in Erasmus' great loyalty to Agricola.

An Appendix Note: Alexander Hegius (i)

From about 1481 the schoolrector at Deventer was Alexander Hegius (c. 1433-1498), who resided in the house of Richard Pafraet, the first printer of Deventer, which was then becoming one of the major centers of printing in Europe. It was largely through the work of Pafraet that, as Koch has reminded us, 'more classical texts ... came from the presses of Deventer than from Paris' in the last decade of the fifteenth century.[26]

Hegius was a decade older than Agricola, and it is a mistake therefore to speak of him simply as a student of Agricola's. But it is accurate to say that Agricola instructed Hegius in Greek, and that this probably took place in 1474 on one of Agricola's extended returns from Pavia to visit his father. What is remarkable, nonetheless, is that Hegius was forty years old when he received that instruction in Greek from the younger Agricola. 'When a man of forty I came to young Agricola,' Hegius confessed, 'and from him I have learned all that I know, or rather all that others think I know.'[27] He wept when he announced Agricola's death to his students, and it is to be noted that the first publication of any new writing by Agricola after his death was in 1503, by Jacob Faber of Deventer, who added two letters (the one from Hegius and the other Agricola's reply) to a volume of Hegius's poems.[28]

For Hegius, as Spitz has remarked, 'metaphysics was still the "*praestantissima omnium scientiarum*," high above grammar and rhetoric, and alone deserving the name of wisdom; and in his work directed against skepticism, the *De Scientia et de eo quod scitur,* he argued that Aristotle was basic to a knowledge of the *res naturales* and to metaphysics as well and expressly polemicized against Plato and Platonists'[29] – but a humanist might be an Aristotelian as well as a Platonist. When we turn to Hegius's *Farrago* (1496), we find intimations of humanism – e.g., his dialogue on rhetoric, and his striking 'Against Those Who Believe that the Knowledge of Modes of Significance is Necessary to Grammar' – but we also find him writing on John of Garland and dialectic. The quality of his Latin is far from sophisticated, and his own *Carmina* are undistinguished.[30]

1 P.S. Allen. 'The Letters of Rudolph Agricola,' *EHR* xxi (1906), 303 (pp. 302-17). (Hereafter cited as Allen, 'Letters'.)
2 See C.G. van Leijenhorst in *Contemporaries of Erasmus*, vol. 1 (Toronto, Collected Works of Erasmus, 1985), pp. 15, 17. (Hereafter cited as van Leijenhorst, *Contemporaries*.) In his unpublished IANLS paper (Wolfenbüttel, 1985), Prof. C.J. Classen notes that Carbone was 'wiederum einen Ciceroherausgeber.' It is now thought more probable that the father of Erasmus also studied under Guarino.
3 As does M.M. Phillips in her otherwise excellent survey article on Erasmus in the volume *Erasmus*, ed. by T.A. Dorey (London, 1970), p. 3. (Hereafter cited as Phillips, *Erasmus*.)
4 See P.S. Allen, *Erasmi Epistolae*, I, 48, where it is noted that in conjunction with Hegius he wrote commentaries on the *Doctrinale* of Alexander, the first of which he had printed at Deventer (R. Pafraet) in 1488. There were as well other works of grammar: among these were a *Composita Verborum* (1485), *Verba deponentialia* (1499), and *Aequivoca* (1486). In that Deventer school at the time Erasmus was a student, then, there was considerable scholarly activity – not in humanism so much as in pedagogical work based on medieval grammar and logic.
5 Cf. Agricola's letters of 1470 (in Allen, 'Letters', p. 310); and from his letters it seems clear that Agricola himself was still studying Greek in 1475 (ibid., p. 311).
6 See n. 4, above.
7 See A.C.F. Koch in *Post-Incunabula and their Publishers*, ed. Hendrik D.L. Vervliet (The Haque, 1978), p. 122.
8 The one exception is in *Spongia* (LB x, 1666A), where he remarked that he owed nothing to Agricola; but that was a passing remark, and the context does not support any larger application.
9 Cf. Phillips, *Erasmus*, p. 3.
10 *Ciceronianus, ASD* 1-2, 682-3.
11 *De Contemptu Mundi, ASD* V-I, 56.
12 *Contemporaries*, I, 16: Epp. 174, 184, 311.
13 See Allen, 'Letters', pp. 307-8.
14 Q. Phillips, *Erasmus*, p. 16.
15 *Contemporaries*, I, 16; on the charge that Erasmus published Agricola's translations as his own, see Allen, *Erasmi Epistolae*, I, 365 n.
16 The introduction by Lewis W. Spitz to his studies of *The Religious Renaissance of the German Humanists* (Cambridge, Mass., 1963), pp. 1-19, will serve to indicate the many problems inherent in the term. The recent work by A.G. Dickens and John M. Tonkin, *The Reformation in Historical Thought* (Cambridge: Harvard University Press, 1985), does not appear to discuss either the term 'Northern Humanism' or the work of Albert Hyma.
17 See R.R. Post, *The Modern Devotion. Confrontation with Reformation and Humanism* (Leiden, 1968). I agree with Spitz's summary statement that Hyma was one of the revisionists 'who held to the autochthonous nature of Northern humanism and its continuous development out of the medieval past,' attributing 'the Northern Renaissance fundamentally to the work of the Brethren of the Common Life': thus Spitz, op. cit., p. 3, commenting on Hyma's *The Christian Renaissance* (New York, 1924).

18   On the influence of Ficino north of the Alps, see P. O. Kristeller, 'The European Diffusion of Italian Humanism,' in *Renaissance Thought II: Papers on Humanism and the Arts* (New York, 1965), pp. 69-88; and 'Ficino' in *Eight Philosophers of the Italian Renaissance* (1965), ch. 3 (and the works of Festugière and Moench cited on p. 172). See also the following: A. Della Torre, *Storia dell' Academia Platonica di Firenze* (Firenze, 1902); N. Robb, *Neoplatonism of the Italian Renaissance* (London, 1935); and Sears Jayne, *John Colet and Marsilio Ficino* (Oxford, 1963). Ficino's first letters were published in 1495 and his correspondents included − to name one Northern humanist − Reuchlin, but not, apparently, Rudolf Agricola, and not Erasmus.
19   Spitz, *Religious Renaissance*, p. 16.
20   This interpretation of the force of language in the studia humanitatis was first vigorously presented by Ernesto Grassi in *Verteidigung des individuellen Lebens* (Bern, 1946), and the role of rhetoric has been even more vigorously argued in his *Rhetoric as Philosophy* (University Park, Pa.: Penn. State Univ. Press, 1980).
21   See C. J. Classen, unpublished paper given at the IANLS Congress (Wolfenbüttel, 1985), and Ernesto Grassi, *Philosophy as Wisdom*. I am grateful to Prof. Classen for being able to read his address.
22   Classen, loc. cit.
23   C. G. van Leijenhorst has noted Erasmus' publishing of Agricola's first Pavia oration with the *De pronuntiatione* and the *Ciceronianus* (1528) − see *Contemporaries*, I, 16.
24   See Hans Baron, *The Crisis of the Early Italian Renaissance* ... 1-vol. ed. (Princeton: Princeton Univ. Press, 1966); and *From Petrarch to Leonardo Bruni: Studies in Humanistic and Political Literature* (Chicago: Univ. Chicago Press, 1968).
25   In her excellent paper on 'La "Philosophia Christi" reflétée dans les "Adages" d'Erasme,' − in *Courants Religieux et Humanisme à la Fin du XVe et au Debut du SVIe Siecle,* Colloque de Strassbourg 1957 (Paris, 1959), pp. 53-71 − M.M. Phillips has extended the discussion of *philosophia Christi* into the learned yet popular, immensely influential *Adages*, with which Erasmus was deeply and continuously concerned throughout his life after 1500.
26   See n. 7, above.
27   Cf. Spitz, op. cit., p. 39.
28   Allen, "Letters," p. 304.
29   Spitz, op. cit., p. 132.
30   I have here commented on Hegius as a link between Agricola and Erasmus; Hegius is vital in this respect, but there were others; and I shall discuss the question more fully in my future biography of Erasmus.

PART III

THE MONASTERY YEARS

A. Augustinian Erasmus (1487-1492)

Radix studii tui et speculum vitae sint primo evangelium Christi: quia ibi est vita Christi.

Vita domini Florentii, 'De Sacris Libris studendis'

Quanto magis se ipsum quis vincit et defectus suos emendat:
Tanto plus amor Dei in eo crescit:
et carnis effectus marcescit et decrescit.

THOMAS À KEMPIS, *Libellus de discipline claustralium*

Today we have many questions about Erasmus and Christianity, but those must remain for a later and larger synthesis to attempt to resolve, though many efforts have already been made.[1] Vital to any effort to understand that very large question of Erasmus' ever-developing Christianity − the *philosophia Christi*[2] − must be a closer study of his years in an Augustinian monastery and his spiritual formation there as an Augustinian canon. It is therefore the purpose of this paper to attempt to clarify the interpretation of what evidence we have, and to offer conclusions about his spiritual formation at the time that he left the monastery at Steyn in about 1492.[3] Many of the particular questions that must be raised are prompted in part by our knowledge of Erasmus' growing antimonasticism in later years (but even 'anti-monasticism' must be qualified), and stimulated in large part by a general twentieth-century ignorance concerning the monastic life in general and that way of life at the end of the fifteenth century in particular. Some understanding of monastic life is necessary, therefore, and we need to know the kind of monastery that Steyn was and to begin to comprehend the kind of spiritual and intellectual life that Erasmus found there. These are questions that are vital to our deepening understanding of Erasmus, of course, but they are also significant in the history of Augustinian spirituality in the Low Countries, and on the eve of the Reformation more generally.

There are some questions which now seem to be beyond the reach of the modern historian, such as, what kind of prior was at Steyn at the time of Erasmus' entrance? Was he in favor of 'good letters' and likely to be sympathetic to the humanistic ambitions of such a promising young novice? And we want to know much more about his friends and contemporaries in the monasteries. Some of these questions can at least be addressed, for we can suggest a line of interpretation which will at least point towards probable answers; but we know all too little about Erasmus' profession of vows and of his inner life at the time of ordination, and still less about his decision to seek ordination as a priest in such a community. Finally, there is a conspicuous lapse in Erasmus' otherwise massive volume of correspondence between about 1487 and some time in 1493, and significantly it was at the end of this period that Erasmus left the monastery at Steyn to become secretary to the Bishop of Cambrai in the spring of 1492.[4]

The sequence of ordination and leaving the monastery – to begin with a fundamental question of chronology – is by no means certain. P.S. Allen has discussed the evidence along with the problems of interpretation; but I do not agree with his suggestion that 'the whole period with the Bishop was not more than a year'.[5] The authoritative account by Beatus Rhenanus (a very close friend to Erasmus in his later years) that Erasmus was ordained before joining the Bishop of Cambrai would appear to be contradicted by the implication in the extraordinary Letter to Grunnius of 1516 that he was ordained after joining the Bishop.[6] But we do know that he was ordained on the 25th of April 1492, and the probability is that he left Steyn shortly afterwards.[7]

The modern student of Erasmus must guard against the assumption that monasticism was everywhere regarded as imperfect (as apparently by Chaucer in his satiric though ironic *Canterbury Tales*), or that the image of monasticism was tarnished before the Reformation as it was seen to be after 1520 by the Reformers. As Giles Constable has justly written in his splendid essay on 'Petrarch and Monasticism,'

> That so perceptive an observer of his own times as Petrarch had nothing but good to say about monks and monasteries, considered the monastic life the most perfect form of Christian life on earth, and regarded his own failure to become a monk as a spiritual weakness is striking testimony to the continued presence and attraction of monastic ideals and institutions in the fourteenth century.[8]

It is not improbable that only a century later, and in a part of Christendom where such things were changing more slowly, Erasmus found a monasticism in Holland that was not greatly different in its ideals from the monasticism Petrarch knew in the mid-fourteenth century, for the *Devotio Moderna* in general and the Windesheim community in particular were deeply concerned with reform and with a strict observance of the rules and ideals of the movement.

Evidence from the Letters

The letter from Erasmus to Elisabeth, a nun, written about this time, is therefore precious evidence for his biography (Epistle 2). We are certain of neither place nor date, but Allen has suggested Gouda and the year 1487, with question marks. The place is likely enough, but the year is conjectural indeed: not knowing, we may mark the date a year or two earlier than 1487, for we are not certain of the date of his entering the monastery, nor are we certain of the reasons for supposing that the letter was 'written during the period of uncertainty and depression before he entered the monastery' (*CWE* 1:3). However, Allen's suggestion that Elisabeth may have been one of the daughters of Berta de Heyen (on whom see below) is most reasonable, for Berta's surviving daughters belonged to one of Gouda's four convents of Augustinian nuns, and this letter may have been addressed to one of them.[9] This suggestion is most plausible, and it fits neatly into the jig-saw puzzle that begins to take shape of Erasmus' status and of his state of mind.

Yet the letter does not sound like one written from a monastery, particularly by a young novice or postulant. For it turns about Erasmus' sense of his own misfortune – I think it most unlikely therefore that it was written after the death of Berta, c. 1489 (when Erasmus' *Oratio funebris in funere Bertae de Heyen* ... and the two epitaphs Erasmus wrote for her, were probably written): it would have been inappropriate to write the daughter immediately after her mother's death and to talk only about his own misfortune – and he writes, but without specifics, 'in my present misfortune' (line 7). Next he alludes to Fortune's wheel and quotes Ovid on the change of attitudes in fair-weather friends when the winds of Fortune change and the poet feels shipwrecked.[10] While Erasmus' letter is full of friendship and Christian love, it says nothing which specifically relates the writer to a monastic vocation. It may well be connected with a 'period of uncertainty and depression before he entered the monastery' (*CWE* I:3), but it is striking that in writing to a friend who is a nun he should not speak of spiritual aspects of his mental condition. It is possible, further, that by reference to 'misfortune' Erasmus is referring to difficulties over acceptance into the monastery: it is possible too that the letter of dispensation from the bishop was slow in arriving.

On second reading, one feels that this letter is almost deliberately not personal, and perhaps this is why Erasmus felt free to include it in his later collection of his own early letters. One further note: along with the preceding letter, Ep. 1 to Pieter Winckel (also placed at Gouda by Allen and dated as probably the end of 1484) this letter marks an early attraction to Ovid![1] All in all, the letter is very much the mood of one of Erasmus' early poems, his *Elegia de Collatione doloris et leticiae* (dated by Reedijk as probably 1487), with its Vergilian echoes; in this poem, after glancing at care and sorrow, the young poet concludes with 'Leticia ingenium clarius esse solet' (through joy, beauty is greater and the spirit brighter).

Both the epistle to Elisabeth and the early poems of Erasmus are tantalizing for us in the effort to establish the personality of the young Erasmus; both also point up the perils of using too literally the early writings as evidence, especially when there has been a circularity of argument in supposing that there was depression before entrance into the monastery on the basis of a letter like Ep. 2, and then dating the letter because it must have been written before entering the monastery. Erasmus was troubled, no doubt, but the letters and early poems do not provide us with anything more than a general sense of his state of mind and cannot be used to establish the more precise chronology that of course we would like to have.

The degree of conventionality in the letters is at first reading a troubling question, and after further reading that reaction becomes less troubling. But one cannot allow the quicksilver question to slip through our fingers. In 1521, in his preface to his own *Epistolae ad Diversos*, Erasmus informs us, his readers, that,

> Although when I was a young man, and also in the age of my manhood, I wrote very many letters, yet I hardly wrote any for publication. I practised my style, I beguiled my leisure, I trifled with my friends, I gave way to my displeasure – indeed I did nothing more than amuse myself as it were, expecting nothing less than that my friends should copy out and preserve such trifles ...

This letter to Beatus Rhenanus,[2] is filled with self-evident contradictions, not least in the final clause: these are such trifles, but I expect nothing less than that they should be copied out and preserved ...

Erasmus felt that all about him there was at that time little effort towards clarity and little reaching for classical style: this is itself both a criticism of the current standards of writing (which produced either much bad or careless writing, or the overstrivings of the *Florida Venustas* of the derivative Latinate), and also a calling for classical standards. The efforts of Erasmus to write with control, clarity and true style must be seen as a swimming against the stream; and the stream continued to flow. For writing towards the end of the sixteenth century Montaigne provides a splendid image of writing in an unruly age (not unlike the Low Countries of the 1470s and 1480s): 'L'escrivaillerie semble estre quelque simptome d'un siècle desborde'[13]; and this image fits the period of Erasmus' youth and the years before he became twenty-one as admirably as it does Montaigne's age. Erasmus too railed against the bad writing and fuzzy thinking of his contemporaries, and he also felt (like T. S. Eliot in *The Four Quartets*[14]) that writing could be a raid on the inarticulate. Elsewhere I shall discuss the development of Erasmus' style in his letters and other writings.

By the time of Epistle 3 to his brother Pieter, and this pretty certainly is in 1487 and written from Steyn, Erasmus had entered the monastery, and the mood of this letter becomes both warm and playful; overall we are on firm ground in seeing an affection between the two brothers. In his statement that 'we are denied each other's actual presence' (3/29) we have an indication that there is some strictness in the mode of life, for Pieter's monastery at Sion near Delft was only a few miles from Erasmus' monastery at Steyn, which was near Gouda. By some date in 1487, then, Erasmus had entered the monastery of the Augustinian canons regular, and if it was in the latter part of 1487 (as seems most plausible) then Erasmus was about twenty years old.[15] Pieter was already a monk at Sion, a community which was the head of the congregation of which Steyn was a priory. The writing of letters asking for replies was conventional enough, and there are examples in the treatises of Aeneas Sylvius and Mario Filelfo;[16] but Erasmus goes beyond the conventions in not only requesting a reply but also developing his feelings of love for his brother, and the closing touch of asking Pieter to lend Servatius Rogerus his small copy of Juvenal's satires is characteristically Erasmian — for as he was later to write in the first adage (I.i.1) *Amicorum communia omnia* (between friends all is common).

In later years Erasmus argued that he had entered the monastery under pressure and that he entered the religious life at too early an age — see esp. Ep. 466 to Leo X and Ep. 447 to Grunnius (and the comment in *CWE* 4:2). But these arguments were put forth to press Erasmus' request for papal dispensation, and today one must feel that Erasmus was pressing very hard indeed upon a slender reed — that in fact he exaggerated greatly, for the age of twenty was scarcely too young. As Koch has made clear, the period of Erasmus' requesting papal dispensation of his vows is a period of chronological inconsistencies on Erasmus' part: that inconsistency too was part of his rhetorical strategy.

Spiritual formation

Little is now known of the instruction Erasmus received as a novice, yet a certain amount is known about the Augustinian spirituality at that time, about the Hildesheim community, and about the teaching and ideals of the *Devotio moderna* (to which the life at Steyn was closely related). It is worth our examining each of these spheres. We can then examine the question of Erasmus' attitude towards monasticism contained in the *De contemptu mundi* while recalling his own statement in the epistolary catalogue of his works written at Basel 30 January 1523, where he declared that he was scarcely twenty — that is, about the year 1487 — when he wrote *Laudem monasticae*:

> Sed admodum iuvenex vix annos nati viginti scripsimus in eodem genere Laudem vitae monasticae, hoc est solitariae, in gratiam amici cuiusdam, qui nepotem venabatur proselytum quem in nassam pelliceret![17]

But even this *Laudem*, it is clear from the context ('in gratium amici cuiusdam'), had something of another motive besides the praising of monasticism itself; at any event, this allusion would date the work at about 1487, which would appear to be if not during the first year of his admission to the monastery, certainly early on at the monastery.

It may therefore be profitable to pause here for consideration of a fellow Canon Regular of the Augustinians whose work Erasmus is most likely to have known and who in any case offers us a glimpse into the counseling for spiritual formation during the fifteenth century: I refer to the collection of sermons to novices ('sermones ad novicios regulores') of Thomas à Kempis![18] Even if these sermons were not repeated or drawn upon by the novice-master at Steyn in 1487-88, and even if Erasmus did not read them — though the statement in the *prologus* that Thomas is offering them to be read (*ad legendum*, which surely meant to be read aloud, as in the *legends*[19] of the saints) must be given weight — these *Sermones ad novicios regulares* provide a remarkable view of what such sermons to novices would have covered, and what the tone or style might be: what the goals of spiritual formation of this community were at that time. It cannot be argued that Erasmus must necessarily have heard these sermons by Thomas repeated in whatever form. But as a novice he would have heard many such sermons, and these may serve us as way-markings in our effort to understand the spiritual formation of the young Erasmus.

Thus we find in the *Sermones* the treatment of such familiar themes in novice-instruction as the good of the community and love among the brethren, of obedience of and respect for superiors, as well as the love and praise of God, Of Jesus, and of the Blessed Virgin Mary. Going back to the *Regula ad servos Dei*, Augustinians emphasized charity as the foundation of spiritual perfection; and we find again and again in the *Sermones* a stress on charity.[20] Most valuable for us is the approach in the instructions for novices upon the cultivation of the interior life and the value of Augustinian spirituality: Erasmus was schooled in the monastery of a reformed community of the canons regular of St. Augustine, and the importance of his training as such a novice cannot be neglected or underestimated. The sermons, further, are richly grounded upon Scriptures, and on nearly every page there are two or three quotations from or allusions to the Old Testament as well as the New, and other allusions, as to the *O salutaris hostia* in the final sermon.[21]

A final point: in the two sermons on the spiritual warfare against vice and the battles and dangers of this life (XVIII & XIX), we may indeed perceive the roots of Erasmus' *Enchiridion*, which was published in 1503, about ten years after his leaving the monastery.

Out of the papal reforms of the eleventh century – that great reform movement known as the Gregorian Reform – had come a movement to regularize all clergy who were not monks (in the strict, canonical sense of the term: that is, followers of the Rule of St. Benedict in one or another of the orders of traditional monasticism). Those non-monastic clergy were then subjected to the Rule of St. Augustine, a rule not directly composed by Bishop Augustine of Hippo in the fifth century but developed from his principles of living for communities of men and women. This rule was practical and flexible, yet oriented towards spirituality, and it carried the prestige of the name of the great Father of the Church, Augustine.[22] Less strict than the Benedictine Rule, the Rule of St. Augustine 'left rather more scope for the development of good works' – an element or directing force which was important for the spirituality of the Brethren of the Common Life. The spirit of the Augustinian rule is founded in the charity of the Gospel, and it stressed a governance with kindness, austerity without rigidity, and observance of the rule without narrowness. Father L. Hertling, S.J., has observed that the union of the monastic ideal of the earlier fathers with sacerdotal activity is the creation of St. Augustine, a willed and personal creation that remains living and fruitful.[23]

In the Low Countries there were monks who followed the Rule of St. Benedict; there were also the many communities of the canons regular, Augustinian and Premonstratensian, and later the Dominican and Austin Friars and the Franciscans to a much lesser extent. We note that Erasmus was drawn to a community of the canons regular of the Augustinian order. He was therefore strictly speaking not a monk: more accurately (if technically to the modern), he was an Augustinian canon as he indeed signed himself in his letter of November 1496 to the Bishop of Cambrai (Ep. 49) and as he had been addressed by Robert Gaguin in October 1495 (Ep. 46).[24]

The Augustinians of the fourteenth century had been notable in their loyalty to the Holy See, and a number of Augustinians figured prominently in the fierce controversies of theologians and canonists over the validity of the election of Boniface VIII and the claims of papal power. We mark the answer by Augustinus Triumphus of Ancona to Marsiglio of Padua's imperialistic *Defensor Pacis*, his *Summa de Ecclesiastica Potestate*; and Alexander of St. Elpidio (d. 1326) wrote his *De Eccesiastica Potestate* and *De Jurisdictione Imperii* against Lewis of Bavaria. There were others as well who expressed devotion to the Holy See and unwavering loyalty. While we do not know all of the reading or the instruction of Erasmus during his monastic period, it is well to consider the traditions of the Augustinians of the preceding century and to weigh within the tradition of loyalty to the Holy See that was inculcated in the intellectual traditions of the order[25] Erasmus' later refusal to attack the papacy directly.

The typical day of a medieval monk or cloistered canon like Erasmus can be quickly outlined. The monk is enjoined to model all outward and inner exercises on the example and the doctrine of Our Lord Jesus Christ.

> Then follows how the monastic must begin, live and end his day: Rise, pious thoughts, preparation for Matins; sleep, reject all imaginings and also all good thoughts (for it is time to sleep); do not singularize yourself when eating, act normally and remember that it is for your salvation. Then follows the reading, which must conduce to prayer and reflection (meditation); after this the *scriptura*, writing, that is the work of the hands.[26]

I follow the outline of the *Breviloquium* of Gerlach Peters, one of many representatives of the *Devotio moderna* (1378 to 1411, just a century older than Erasmus), who attended school in Deventer and became a canon of Windesheim.[27] For it is not clear whether the canons of Windesheim, or the canons regular of Steyn, followed as rigid a monastic rule and life as did some of the monks of the Benedictine and other orders; and this rather simple formulation by Gerlach Peters will serve to capture the essences of their daily life.

In the Low Countries the Augustinians were one of the dominant religious orders at the end of the fifteenth century. During the fourteenth and fifteenth centuries there had been a new flowering of the order through the reform congregations that arose in other countries as well as in the Low Countries. There it was the Congregation of Windesheim that led the reform movement, and it is notable that Erasmus chose to enter a house of the Congregation of Windesheim[28] and to become a canon regular of St. Augustine.

By some date in 1487 – and it is not impossible that it was as much as a year earlier – Erasmus entered the monastery of the Augustinian Canons regular at Steyn, near Gouda; we may with confidence say that this step can be considered as sharing in the spirit of the *Devotio Moderna*.[29] Following the argument for dating his birth in the year 1467, we would thus make Erasmus nearly twenty at entrance into the monastery and twenty-one at the time of his profession, with ordination following four years later at the age of twenty-five. Old enough, no doubt, at that time, but perhaps still a *faute de mieux* choice of profession *if* he were only an ambitious young Erasmus (as some modern biographers imply): however, we cannot read back into his youth those later attitudes and values which became so strongly anti-monastic. There is no reason for believing that in 1487 Erasmus was not utterly sincere in his profession of vows.

Yet let us bear in mind that his brother, Pieter Gerard, who was two or three years older, was already a monk at Sion, near Delft, which was the head of the congregation of which Steyn was a priory. This house was within a mile of Gouda (a familiar place to Erasmus), situated in the parish of Haastrecht on the 'other' side of the Yssel River and known as Emmaus. Founded in 1419, it too modelled its statutes on those of the Chapter of Windesheim, a congregation headed by the Augustinian convent of Windesheim, near Zwolle. On 11 April 1486 – about a year before Erasmus' entrance – Pope Innocent VIII had granted the privileges of the Lateran congregation to the congregation of Windesheim; but it is not clear what the full implications of this action were.[30] Whatever else, the papal granting of privileges must have been regarded as a token of recognition for the important work of the congregation, which earlier had received the vigorous support of Pierre d'Ailly. Besides, Erasmus knew former schoolmates at Steyn, and on his earlier visit he had doubtless visited the library; and we believe that some of his father's manuscripts and books were in the library there – no small attraction, doubtless, for Erasmus.[31]

At the time of Erasmus' entrance, Steyn had as its prior – only its fifth in about seventy-five years (a mark of stability) – one John, son of Christian; but we know little about him. Van Leijenhorst writes in *Contemporaries of Erasmus* that the *Christianus* so passingly referred to in Epistle I is not likely to have been Jan Christiaanse the prior (d. 8 August 1496), for 'one would expect Erasmus to refer to the prior with greater reverence'.[32] Perhaps.

From the earlier letters images emerge of Erasmus secretly reading at night, alone and with friends. Writing from Steyn about 1489 – to an unnamed friend, obviously a married man who had shown him kindness (Ep. 31) – Erasmus provides this lovely picture of his own reading-habits:

> I consider as lovers of books, not those who keep their books hidden in their store-chests and never handle them, but those who, by nightly as well as daily use, thumb them, batter them, wear them out (*sordidant, corrugant, conterunt*), who fill up all the margins with annotations of many kinds, and who prefer the marks of a fault they have erased to a neat copy full of faults (*CWE* 1:58/35-9).

Perhaps one of the reasons that the early 'monastery letters' are so filled with the excitement of that nocturnal reading and not his novitiate studies is precisely that they were so very much his own, and so very much extracurricular, and yet not necessarily in violation of the disciplinary rules of the monastery, for presumably they were condoned. What emerges, too, is the conviction (as Febvre has expressed it[33]) that the nascent humanism was for the young Erasmus no literary game or mere formal effort towards the perfection of letters: it was a light that dispelled the darkness. At this point we can profitably appropriate Brian Stock's concept of 'textual community'[34] and apply it to Erasmus in the monastery. For him there was during the day a participation in one kind of textual community, in those prescribed texts which were a part of the formation of the

Augustinian novice and preserved as the Augustinian canon; and at night there was the secret sharing of key texts — canonical in a very different sense, that of the humanism that was spreading across Europe — with, as we gather from those early letters, Erasmus taking a lead in enlivening and bonding that little community of his friends, which slowly but steadily began to widen.

Tradition

It is important to speak of tradition, for it mattered greatly to the Brethren of the Common Life and to Erasmus himself. But his concept of tradition was not precisely that of the Brethren, and it is necessary to distinguish them.

Traditio involves a handing over, a continuing of a process; but the very use of the word 'tradition' is (as Michael Platt has perceptively observed recently[35])

> a sign that we do not possess the thing it [the word] tries to name. Those who live wholly within the spiritual dwelling they were born and raised in do not speak of their way of life as traditional. They would not even say 'the old is the good' for that is a theoretical statement. Instead they would speak of 'our way' or 'the right way.'

And the Brethren spoke in just this manner: one finds the phrases 'our way' and the like in the fifteenth-century writings of Thomas à Kempis and others. For them 'the way' was the unquestioning following of something old that had been received, and the charge of their community was seen as the copying of those texts (from an exemplar of undisputed authority) and of following that 'way' without questioning. There was no textual criticism — there could be none, if there were no questioning of the sources — and one was expected at Steyn simply to follow. (One may read Erasmus' words about 'a neat copy full of faults' as a comment upon the exemplars in the library at Steyn.)

The books available in Steyn

The monastery of Steyn was destroyed by fire in 1549, but remnants of the library survived, and there were lists drawn up in 1599 and 1631 (of the books kept by the last two surviving monks).[36] We find there several copies of the Bible, thirteen works of Augustine, nine of Chrysostom and two of Jerome, as well as works of Origen, Bede, Basil, Gregory, Anthony, Boethius, and Bernard. Although they are apparently not listed, one would expect that there had been at least some Aquinas and Bonaventure from the range of Scholastic writers: perhaps for some special reason these did not survive. These two listings of books compare to a similar list of the library of the monastery of Windesheim.

Of the classics, the following had been part of the library at Steyn: Terence (three times mentioned), Euripides, Aesop, Cicero, Sallust, Pliny the Younger, Valerius Maximus, Justinus, and Aulus Gellius — not a distinguished list, but not altogether mean.

There were apparently humanists represented, for the names of Poliziano, Ficino, Reuchlin are found — but not those of Valla or Poggio, who were considered either irreligious or hostile to the Church.

Altogether, the library at Steyn would seem to be little more scholarly than that of the Brethren of the Common Life at Zwolle (Hyma, 135) which apparently had rather more of Scholastic works and of works for serious study of the Bible. The Windesheim library (at the monastery of the Canons Regular outside Zwolle) contained a manuscript which was thought to have been compiled from that of Jerome, and they accepted this attribution in complete trust:

> For them this was the end of the affair. They had the correct Vulgate text in their possession and they had copied it. From henceforth it was forbidden to the fathers to alter one jot or tittle of the text, not even in the choir books, if these conflicted with the emended text. In this way they brought scholarly investigations to a halt. The matter was now concluded. The highest ideal had been attained! No more study in this field was necessary ... (Post, 307).

Even the punctuation marks carefully placed and preserved in the text of the Bible are there for reciting in a traditional manner:

> The text served not as the basis for a scholarly study of the Bible, but ensured that the tone adopted in reading aloud should be the same in the various houses. The Canons Regular employed the same methods of comparison and correction to obtain their own text of the four great church Fathers [Gregory, Ambrose, Jerome and Augustine] and of other orthodox Fathers; of the sermons, homilies, books and treatises. They also achieved their optimum text by comparison with the best models. They never reveal, however, just why a particular model is considered superior. These pieces too will have been read aloud in the choir service and in the refectory ... (Post, 307).

As the work of Busch's *Chronicon Windeshemense* celebrates, this was a great achievement: correcting all of the books of the divine office, the Bible, and the many volumes of the major authorities of the Church, and (Busch proudly added) they have written them in various sorts of script, punctuated them, accented them according to the spelling, and bound and annotated the choir books. ... All this they have brought to a good end, labouring for the honour and love of God, for the communal good of the brothers (Canons) and for the harmonious uniformity of the entire chapter.[37]

According to the Letter to Grunnius, Erasmus (under the name of Florentius) had been told of the fine library at Steyn: Cantelius 'repeatedly dwelt on the abundance of books that were to be had there, and what opportunity for study; for he well knew the bait by which the mind of the boy might be caught. ...'[38] But allowance must be made for the rhetorical exaggerations of the Letter to Grunnius.

It would appear, however, that the library at Steyn was far from fine, and that little study in depth could be undertaken on the Fathers of the Church, or indeed on the Bible, as compared, let us say, with the riches available in the library of the Abbey of St. Victor in Paris. There is at this time, not surprisingly then, only occasional reference by Erasmus to serious reading of Jerome, Augustine and Ambrose.

One text has not been named, one which surely must have been present in the library at Steyn: that is the *Imitatio Christi*. But it is possible that monks possessed their own copies of this, as they would likely have possessed their own copies of the New Testament. In itself the *Imitatio* was a microcosm of much wider reading, for it fused traditions of vulgar and of the official Church Latin (the rhythmic Latin of the Curia), of Patristic Latin, scholastic Latin, and certain key classical authors, notably Seneca, Cicero and Aristotle.[39]

The library reveals few treasures from the classics, yet Erasmus was able to engage in nightly and secret reading:

> For Florentius frequently and secretly by night would read to him a whole comedy of Terence, so that in a few months, as a result of their secret nocturnal sessions, they had finished the principal authors, but with a great risk – Erasmus adds in the Grunnius letter – to the boy's delicate constitution.[40]

It is especially in the letters to Cornelis Gerard that we find a sense of the secret textual community of the classics and of humanistic writings: 'our favourite Horace' (Ep. 15, *CWE* 1:20/29); and allusions to or quotations from him and Virgil and Ovid crowd the pages of these letters. Most notably Erasmus wrote in 1489 (Ep. 20): 'My authorities in poetry are Virgil, Horace, Ovid, Juvenal, Statius, Martial, Claudian, Persius, Lucan, Tibullus, and Propertius; in prose, Cicero, Quintilian, Sallust, and Terence' (*CWE* 1:31/97-99). Somehow he was able to lay his hands on these texts, and he arrived at an extraordinarily well-defined, and canonical, sense of the major authors.

Again and again Erasmus speaks of his respect for Lorenzo Valla: 'again, in the niceties of style I rely on Lorenzo Valla above all' (Ep. 20, *CWE* 1 : 31/99-100) – see also Ep. 23, which cites Filelfo, Aeneas Silvius, Agostino Dati, Guarino, Poggio, and Gasparino in the next breath (*CWE* 1 : 39/77-8).

Upon examination, then, the secret and nocturnal textual community seems to have dominated Erasmus' intellectual world during these years at Steyn, and the lack of serious attention to Biblical scholarship or to the study of the Church Fathers would have to be repaired later by the studies at Paris after 1495 and by the counsel of new friends like John Colet. Little wonder that there is so little of this later scriptural or patristic interest in his Steyn letters.

It is so important to recognize that Valla's *Elegantiae* which became so much of a stylistic *vade mecum* for Erasmus (and which he had epitomized before entering Steyn) was a work that was at best unpopular among the monks and friars: some condemned all of the writings by the author of the *De Falsa credita et ementita Constantini declamatio* (which was, in effect, a document that attacked papal claims to temporal power) and the *De voluptate* (which apparently was read as a deeply irreligious work). And often monks and friars treated Valla's attacks on Priscian and medieval grammarians as heretical – but according to Salutati, there were theologians of his day who despised even Augustine's *City of God* because Augustine had quoted Virgil and other classical poets.[41]

Vocation

Upon reflection from our distance in time and from our secular world, too much stress can be put upon the unique personal motivation of a single individual vocation at the end of the Middle Ages, even if that were only the center of interest. In the late 1480s, an intellectual young man could have thought neither of the waning of the Middle Ages nor – to give a more literal translation of Huizinga's title – the harvest. It would now seem that the religion of Christianity would have been conceived as a moral and social as well as ecclesiological system, with a necessary set of beliefs articulated by the teaching authority of the hierarchical Church through the dioceses and their parishes, and enforced by the disciplinary norms of that Church. There were, to be sure, disputes over the peripheral matters and the diaphora that were largely contained within a professional and Latin-speaking body of clerics; however, only a small part of this world of disputation is likely to have percolated down to the ordinary Christians, even in the cities and monastic centers. Consequently, the articulation in ever-increasing detail of one or another of the set of beliefs defining that moral-social-ecclesiological system – over which there was, to the modern eye, such an extraordinary outpouring of disputatious energy and emotional commitment –

came only a generation later, after 1520 in the storms of Reformation and Counter-Reformation, and still partly in Latin but now increasingly in the vernacular and made vastly more widely available through the new instrumentality of printing.[42]

'The Church' for Erasmus in his early years was necessarily, therefore, hierarchical, authoritative, conservative – but not necessarily and certainly not essentially non-spiritual (though the concentrations of power and wealth at the top of the structure led to abuses and to the ever-present tendency of power to corrupt).[43] It was operated by a small army of bishops and their staffs, of parish priests, and of monks and nuns in the most of monasteries and convents.[44] A vital legal system, that of the canon law, and much of the educational system were staffed by priests and monks, together with many in minor orders.[45] In the Low Countries there was only one university, Louvain, but the young religious and many laymen went to other universities as well: from Groningen and the east especially, to Heidelberg and Cologne; from the main part of Holland and the regions to the south, often to the University of Paris. Only a few were enabled by the support of willing bishops or well-to-do parents to travel to and study in Italy (as was done for Rudolph Agricola).

But for the most part theology as a discipline and its faculty still dominated the universities; and the liberal arts were in theory seen as propadeutic to the study of Scriptures and theology. In theory the *divina lectura* was supreme, and the study of the Bible was conceived as the highest reach of study; but this ideal seems to have been better practised in the monasteries than in the universities, and even in monasteries the reading of the Bible was too often piecemeal or, as we see in the example of Hildesheim, quite rigidly restricted to the single purpose of reading and chanting.[46] Medicine was still far down the list of professional options, and a doctorate in law (*utriusque iuris*) was a long and expensive route, though it led to a number of rewarding careers in the Church and with monarchs, and often to great wealth. Small wonder that intelligent and ambitious young men – often to be sure, younger sons – turned to the Church for a range of reasons (which too often did not include spiritual vocations, though of course these were by no means excluded) and for a range of vocational possibilities. There was some provision for ecclesiastical support for future parish priests, which was no small argument for that choice, especially to parents with several children.[47]

Religion was not only an indissoluble part of the sociology and economics of the fifteenth century, it provided much of its poetry, and the Church hierarchy patronized much of the art and music. While concerned with the human condition – which in the main it taught was a transient thing, meaningless in the light of the eternal scheme – religion often gave Christianity in the world great beauty and rich meaning. The anonymous English play *Everyman* of about 1495 was based upon an earlier Dutch play, *Elckerlijck*, and on the title page of the English we read, 'Here begynnyth the treatyse how ye hye Fader of Heven sendeth Deth of somon every Creature to come and give account of theyr lyves in this Worlde, and is in maner of a Morall play.' Such themes of stewardship and accountability are rich in fifteenth-century sermons and other literature.[48]

Ordination

When we think of two younger contemporaries of Erasmus who were monks or friars extraordinarily different from each other as well as each from Erasmus – Luther and Rabelais – we realize how dangerous it can be to generalize too facilely about monks, friars and the monastic life of this period. There was one spectrum of belief concerning humanism and scholasticism, as well as that spectrum concerning reform; another concerning the authority of the church – one might be to the right on one line and to the left on another.[49] But we do not do an injustice either to those elements of human nature which are relatively unchanging or to those conditions shaped by the immediate society if we think it normal for Erasmus to have sought and accepted ordination at the age of 24, which was Erasmus' age in April, 1492, when he was ordained a priest by the Bishop of Utrecht on 25 April 1492.[50] Although the times were somewhat different, and Aeneas Sylvius Piccolomini was much older, we might consider the letter of Aeneas Sylvius upon his deciding to enter the priesthood, after training as a humanist and much activity in humanistic writing: on 8 March 1446 Aeneas wrote a friend:

> He must be a miserable and graceless man who does not at last return to his better self, enter into his own heart, and amend his life: who does not consider what will come in the other world after this. Ah! John, I have done enough and too much evil! I have come to myself; oh, may it not be too late![51]

And within the month Aeneas was ordained priest at Vienna.

David, Bishop of Utrecht

Born around 1427, David van Bourgondië was one of the numerous bastard sons of Philip the Good (1396-1467), the third Valois Duke of Burgundy. David matriculated at Louvain before 1453 and was named bishop of Thérouanne in 1451, having apparently been coadjutor of Cambrai for a few years previously.[52] In September 1457 he was transferred to Utrecht, the see of which his predecessor, Ghisbrecht de Bréderode, was forced to resign to David after only two years as its bishop. In 1477 there was an insurrection in Utrecht following the death of Charles the Rash, and David had to flee, returning only in 1492.[53]

For Erasmus the see of Utrecht had special meaning, for his birthplace (whether Gouda or Rotterdam) lay in that diocese; and it was Bishop David who ordained him on 25 April 1492, not long after his return to Utrecht, where he died 16 April 1496. The 25th of April, one may remark, was the feast of St. Marcus, but it cannot be said whether the date was chosen by Erasmus.

Bishop David for Erasmus was a bishop of peace and learning. In the *Ecclesiastes* (in a passage outlining Erasmus' view of the episcopate), Erasmus made note of the bishop's theological examination of his clergy and of his dismissing those not qualified.[54] Erasmus appears to have composed poems in honor of the bishop (Ep. 28), but these are not extant; and after David's death he did compose two epitaphs for him (Reedijk, 41 & 42), praising his love of peace (though he had engaged in military conflicts in order to centralize political power) and his love of *patria*. Erasmus kept with some pride a cap worn by David and a valuable ring of David's that was given him by Philip of Burgundy, a later bishop of Utrecht.[55]

Yet another connection between Erasmus and the household of David is to be noted: the bishop was patient and patron of Wessel Gansfort.[56] Inevitably in trying to distance himself from Steyn, Erasmus effected a widening gap with the bishop of Utrecht, who died in 1496 while Erasmus was beginning his studies at Paris.[57]

De contemptu mundi

Although Erasmus' treatise entitled *De contemptu mundi* was not published until 1521, when it appeared at Louvain in an edition by Th. Martens, it appears that it was most likely written about 1488-89, not long after Erasmus had become a member of the community at Steyn and taken his vows. For in the preface Erasmus refers to himself as barely twenty years of age ('olim vix annos natur viginti') at the date of writing the work; and in his epistolary catalogue of his works written at Basle 30 January 1523, Erasmus again declared that he was scarcely twenty when he wrote *Laudem vitae monasticae*, which is another title for the *De contemptu mundi*. The form of the *De contemptu mundi* is that of an epistle, and it purports to be written from an uncle to a nephew – but *nepos* could mean cousin as well as nephew, and the view that the more probable candidate for the addressee is Servatius Rogerius of Rotterdam seems most likely.[58]

The *De contemptu mundi* is both a contempt of the world and a praise of the monastic life. Although in his later years Erasmus was uncomfortable or unwilling to be seen as an advocate of the monastic way of life – he did, however, praise monks in his last years – it must be recognized that the thirty years between the writing of the work and its publication encompassed not only changes in Erasmus himself but also in the acceptance of humanism in the Low Countries and, it must be further acknowledged, some decline in the rigor of the monastic life and a greater readiness for reform of many ecclesiastical institutions.[59]

Still further, it should be observed that in the *De contemptu mundi* three movements in which Erasmus from an early age was personally involved and which he experienced with intensity, come together in a complex, somewhat fluid, but deeply demanding system of thought and belief: the traditions of the Brethren of the Common Life, the larger traditions of late medieval piety and spirituality, and traditions of medieval learning.[60]

That Erasmus chose to write a treatise in a well-defined medieval convention is notable. A celebration of the 'contempt of the world' *topos* had been given authoritative form in the treatise of that name attributed to St. Bernard of Clairvaux in the twelfth century, extolling a contempt of the world and of all its glories. Before he became pope, Innocent III wrote a treatise under the same title with a similar theme, and this treatise circulated widely. Even Petrarch, we are reminded, did not fail at the dawn of the Renaissance to warn his readers 'that the world was to be despised if one wished to achieve his eternal goal': an early work of Petrarch, and one which Erasmus does appear to have known, to be sure, and it is indicative of the currency of the thought.[61] At the closing of the Middle Ages the *Imitatio Christi* appeared, the first chapter of which bears the title 'Of the imitation or following of Christ and of the despising of all vanities of the world' ('et contemptu omnium vanitatum mundi') – a work which Erasmus almost certainly would have read and heard read aloud many times, certainly in the communities of the Brethren of the Common Life and very likely at Steyn as well.[62]

What is clear is that the *De contemptu mundi* of Erasmus was written by an earnest young monk within the seclusion of an Augustinian monastery – one guided by the spirituality of Augustine and Augustinianism, by the special emphases of the Windesheim community, and (in a less direct way) by the teachings and ideals of the *Devotio moderna*. Erasmus' treatise shares much of the emphases and the ideals of the Brethren: like them, Erasmus remained essentially orthodox in the light of the essential teachings of the Church and steadfast in his loyalty to the Church (if not always the papacy); and he followed 'their approach to religion [which] emphasized greater individualism in one's personal devotion, an approach which manifested a distrust of philosophy and assumed at times an antirationalist attitude.'[63]

For a work in such a tradition as the *De contemptu mundi* is to be located, the recourse to the fruits of reading – and, in fact, the stress upon reading itself – is striking. Sacred studies, the *studia sacra*, are never out of sight, for the youthful Erasmus quotes frequently from the Gospels, especially St. Paul, and his spiritual authors include St. Jerome and St. Bernard of Clairvaux especially.

One passage stands out in this respect, in which he suggests a reading list for the young religious who will find time for reading in the monastery:

> For if they luste to drynke out of the fyrste fountaynes,[64] than they resort to volumes of the olde and new testament. If that verite, of it selfe honestely arayd, and hyghted with the fresshe garments of eloquence, dothe delyte them, they renne to saynt Hieronyme, saynte Augustine, saynt Ambrose, Cypriane and suche other. If those be nat eloquente inoughe to thy minde, and haste a luste to here some christen Cicero: take and put Lactantius Firmianus in thy bosome. And in case that thou canste be contente with lesse costlye apparayle and sobre fare, than then take in thy hande Thomas, Alberte, and suche lyke bokes.[65]

Immediately afterwards, Erasmus goes on to wider ranging:

> Lo, thus thou hast the secrete and many volumes of holy scripture, thou haste the monumentis of the holy prophetes, of the apostles, of theyr interpretours, and of the doctours, thou haste the wrytynges of the phylosophers and poetes, the whiche shulde nat be eschewed of hym, that knoweth howe to chose the holsome herbes among those that are venomous. (PAYNELL ed. p. 159)

I do not know when – or even, if – Thomas More read Erasmus' *De contemptu mundi*, but the correspondence between the thought of his work and More's *Four Last Things*, a work of the early 1520s (though it too may have been a revising of much earlier writing), is remarkably close. More would have approved of virtually everything in the Erasmian *De contemptu mundi*, one feels: the centrality of the Scriptures, the allocation of the Church Fathers, and the doctrine as well. To be sure, there were available to More somewhat different avenues to the *de contemptu* theme, for he too had known the monastic life; but the spirituality of the Carthusians is to be charted a little differently from that of the Augustinians. The essential point is that there is much of this theme in More's own spiritual life and his later writings.[66]

It must be emphasized that the 1521 version of the *De contemptu mundi* adds chapter xii, like the preface;[67] and in this additional material there is a sharp criticism of the monastic vocation and way of life that undercuts, indeed even contradicts, all of the rest of the work. Unlike many of the early letters – which are at times playful, at times deliberately and obviously adopting an attitude – the tone of the treatise is consistently serious throughout; it is in its first eleven chapters an earnest advocating of the advantages of a monastic life. Not only was Erasmus in 1488 or 1489 writing in this vein to a friend (or cousin), he was also expressing his own feelings about monasticism at the age of twenty-one or thereabouts, and during his first year (as we think) of his own monastic career. Most scholars agree with Hyma that the eleventh chapter with its praise of the monastery as the best place for study and friendship concludes the treatise as it had been written at Steyn. Not only is the tone consistent from beginning to the end of chapter eleven, but the values are consistent as well.

The twelfth chapter was added without a title, but the tone has radically changed – as indeed the times had changed from 1489 to 1521 – and Erasmus decries the monastic life. 'Many monasteries are worldly; here discipline has relaxed; they are nothing but seminaries of impiety, where it is impossible to be pure and upright.' We may well ask why Erasmus added such an about-face chapter to an earlier piece of writing, for not only must he have recognized the flagrant contradictory position but he must have expected an intelligent reader to see this as well.

Hyma judges that Erasmus had moved 'rapidly away from the principles of the *Devotio Moderna*,' and that he had become selfish and self-seeking.[68] It is difficult to fathom Erasmus' reasons for publishing the *De contemptu mundi* in 1521, after the Lutheran revolt had begun: what must be observed is that he apparently had left the work unrevised, and we can only conclude that Erasmus felt in 1521 that it fairly represented his earlier thinking about monasticism. What the addition of chapter twelve does is to frame that earlier picture in a more sober or objective view of the reality of monasticism as a socio-ecclesiological institution, for Erasmus now had other monasteries to compare with Steyn and had other institutions to compare with monasticism. In 1521 he finds monasticism wanting. Instead of sharing too readily Hyma's view that Erasmus had moved away from the principles of the *Devotio moderna*, may we not equally see that Erasmus was now judging monasticism by higher standards than it was itself practising at that time?

Friendship

In one of his monastery letters Erasmus wrote to a friend, at the age of twenty or twenty-one, that 'there is nothing on earth more pleasant or sweeter than loving and being loved' (*CWE* 1:17/3-4): this occurs in one of the nine letters to Servatius Rogers, a young man whom Erasmus met shortly after entering Steyn and about whom Erasmus had written to his brother (Ep. 3) that he was 'a youth of beautiful disposition and very agreeable personality and a devoted student in those branches of learning which have given the greatest delight to us both from our boyhood onwards' (*CWE* 1:5/37-40). These letters are difficult to interpret, for at face value they would indicate that Erasmus formed an emotional attachment to Servatius which at first was reciprocated; but then Servatius seems to have withdrawn. At first (Ep. 4) Erasmus complained about the discipline that apparently kept them from frequent meetings; then (Ep. 9) it would seem that they were not often permitted to talk face to face: perhaps their superiors observed and wanted to limit the closeness of their relationship. The tone of intimacy in these letters is paralleled by four early poems (Reedijk nos. 5-8), one or two of which may also have been addressed to Rogers. But one must question whether these letters and poems can be taken at face value, for they are heavily rhetorical and obviously mannered. Further, it has been argued that a motivating force in these poems and letters is the imitation of a well-understood tradition of monastic rhetoric in the writing of letters.[69]

The fact remains that these early letters constitute a celebration of friendship, and in forging the bonds of friendship letters were vital for Erasmus. Thus, as he writes Cornelis Gerard in about 1489, 'Everything about that letter, indeed, has a ring of love and kindness, a flavour of affection and of longing' (*CWE* 1:24/27-8). And on the theme of friends separated by great distances, he wrote (Ep. 23 to Cornelis Gerard, c. June 1489): 'It was by such means [the exchange of letters] that the two famous Fathers of the Church, Jerome and Augustine, prevented as they were by temporal and spatial distances from being together and enjoying each other's embrace as they would have wished, still managed never to lack each other's presence; and each was ever aware of the other's feelings of good will' (Ep. 23, *CWE* 1:36/15-20).

In his life Erasmus cultivated friendship like a living plant: generally he stayed in touch with his friends over the years and across the miles, and in his last years he wrote that half his days was spent in correspondence.[70]

Among Erasmus' oldest friends was Cornelis Gerard, who came from Gouda and had been a childhood friend; their extant correspondence begins with Ep. 17, probably written 1489 from Steyn. He was a kinsman, likely an uncle, of Willem Hermans, who was also a childhood friend of Erasmus (see Ep. 33). Cornelis and Erasmus remained friends and kept in touch with each other until about 1499; after that, for whatever reasons, they apparently drifted apart. But in the Steyn years theirs was a close relationship, and their letters are marked by an openness and a sharing of ideas and ideals. As well as Cornelis' relation Willem Hermans, there were mutual friends, such as Reyner Snoy of Gouda.

Willem Hermans of Gouda had also been a pupil of Alexander Hegius at Deventer and had become a monk at Steyn: they shared much, and Erasmus made him one of the speakers in the dialogue *Antibarbari* (see Ep. 30). The bond of friendship evidently connected Hermans and Gerard directly, and there are interesting exchanges between the two (cf. Ep. 36) and between Hermans and Jacob Batt, with whom Erasmus became a friend at about the time that he entered the service of the bishop of Cambrai. *The friend of one was the friend of all.* Often these letters speak about Erasmus and his work. Erasmus welcomed new friends. There are the interesting letters to Franciscus Theodoricus, who was probably a monk at Sion (where he would have known Pieter, the brother of

Erasmus); and Erasmus exchanged letters in later years, until his death in 1514 (see Eps 168 and 296). Many of the friends were not clerics – there was a growing number of laymen and laywomen, beginning with Ep. 31 to a married man who had shown kindness to Erasmus (c. 1489), and Ep. 32 to Jacob Canter, the learned younger son in a learned family of Frisians. It is fitting that in the very first of his Adages he wrote of one friend being the friend of all. When he moved to Paris in 1495 there were new friends as well as the forging of new bonds of friendship with some old acquaintances from the Low Countries, and these in turn created Erasmian circles in their own lands.

'If you, Colet, can love a man of this sort, if you consider him worthy of your friendship, then pray stamp Erasmus as the most securely yours of all your possessions,' Erasmus was to write in October 1499 (Ep. 107) when he made two of the deepest friendships of his life, with Colet and Thomas More (*CWE* 1:201/57-9). Erasmus' concepts of true friendship were eminently Ciceronian: there had to be a mutual estimation of worthiness, there had to be a sharing of virtue and like goals, and there had to be generosity flowing between the friends. If Erasmus at times cooled in some of his friendships, it was because that friendship no longer met the ideals: criticism to another person was a sign of lack of faith, and Erasmus himself – who spoke of generosity in one of the letters to Cornelis Gerard (Ep. 18, *CWE* 1:25/34-6), 'I should be the most ungrateful man alive if I did not try my utmost to feel the highest degree of gratitude to one who pursues me with such endless kindnesses, and also to repay those when I have a chance' – is celebrated by his friend for his lofty ideals (see Ep. 35, *CWE* 166:12-14) and for his generosity.

Although there are no letters from Erasmus to Berta Heyen, her role as friend and almost foster-mother must be mentioned. She was indeed a *moeder* to the hospital of St. Elisabeth at Gouda, and Erasmus and his fellow monks sat regularly at her table. Van Leijenhorst continues: 'it seems that she had been particularly fond of Erasmus from his childhood and after the death of his parents accorded him her motherly affection. Erasmus praised her courage when one of her daughters, Margareta Honora Heyen, died.'[71] It is likely that one of her daughters was the nun to whom Erasmus wrote Epistle 2, and Erasmus wrote both an *Oratio funebris in funere Bertae de Heyen* and two epitaphs.[72]

Augustinian Rule

One can declare that the canons regular at Steyn were bound by the Augustinian rule, but the exact formulation cannot be precisely stated. For the textual history is most complicated, 'un véritable maquis', in the words of the modern editor.[73] There was more than one rule, and manuscripts rarely presented the whole series; it is not surprising, therefore, that in the 1520s when Erasmus was preparing his edition of the works of St. Augustine and came upon the three Rules, he raised the question of their authenticity. Further, he could not imagine that men could have submitted themselves to the constraints of such strict regulations.[74]

Sacrae litterae

The canons regular of St. Augustine stood a little to the side of the main stream of Biblical studies that we find among the Eremites de Saint Augustin by virtue of their closeness to the Brethren of the Common Life. To the BCL and the *Devotio Moderna* (and Windesheim was a spiritual descendant of the DM) the canons regular were indebted during the fifteenth century for their devotion to the exact text of Scripture that derived from their traditional work as copyists; at Windesheim their faith in tradition was anchored in their possession of a manuscript they believed went back to Jerome himself and from which not the slightest deviation[75] was to be countenanced.

Further, the canons regular were strongly influenced by the non-intellectual attitude of the Devotionalists: Post has stressed their tradition of ordaining without special theological training and of not sending their men to universities as a general rule.[76] By contrast, the superior of the order of St. Augustine from 1507 to 1517, Giles of Viterbo, wrote in 1514 requesting good books that he might study in his free hours (*DdeS*, 991).

Erasmus may not have perceived how closed an intellectual system the monks of Steyn had developed concerning Biblical studies, but later at Paris and *a fortiori* in his discussions with Colet in 1499 his world suddenly was enlarged. And it may be that such an enlargement produced a new view of the limitations of the monastery, and if so that would explain the severe criticism of the monastic way of life that we find in the chapter added years later to the *De contemptu mundi*.

Novice

First Erasmus was a postulant, and his spirit had to be tested (*probetur spiritus ejus*). Next he became a novice, and once admitted the novice was entrusted to the master of novices, and he remained a novice for a year and a day. At this stage he was likely introduced to the *Sermones ad novicios* of Thomas a Kempis, indirectly by his novice-master who surely would have known them, or directly, through repetition of them. Those *Sermones* stressed charity, and this was to be comprehended in Augustinian terms: if the communal life is the foundation of monastic society, fraternal charity is its soul. As well as charity, obedience was stressed; and in the communities of the Hermits the Rule was read in all communities each week.

It is at this stage that the spiritual formation of the postulant-novice ideally was supposed to take on the character of the order. After his profession the new religious divided his day between the practices required by the liturgical rites (*les actes du culte*) and sacred studies. For Augustinians generally, and not less for the canons regular, sacred studies were centered upon the Bible. In the Oxford letters of 1499 we observe the closeness of Erasmus' reading of the New Testament and the clarity and firmness of his meditations upon its meaning.[77] Commentaries on both the Old and the New Testament were part of the Augustinian tradition; *The Song of Songs* was explicated mystically by Gilles, and we shall later note the preservation of the mystical explication in the Biblical writings of Erasmus.[78] But this reading was not for the Augustinians an end in itself, however important: the study of sacred letters was enjoined as a means of sanctification, both for the person himself and for his neighbor.

Augustinian spirituality

In the larger Augustinian tradition — and are we not right in feeling that Erasmus, surely, would have sought the optimum or maximum, rather than the minimum or weakest, in his religious reading and studies?[79] — the thought of Saint Augustine flowed strongly: from his works directly,[80] and through such masters of the Augustinian tradition as Gilles of Rome (d. 1316[81]), and still more with Gregory of Rimini (d. 1358) and Hugolin d'Orvieto (d. 1373).

Characteristic of the Augustinian school was an insistence on the need for curative or cleansing grace: by original sin man had been deprived of grace and was vulnerable in his human nature alone. It follows that for them, one's spiritual life finds its principle in seeking and receiving of divine grace, and divine action is essential, man's role one of cooperation. [1004] Hence the Augustinian dictum: *amor meus pondus meum* (my love is my balance or constancy).

Always in these theological doctrines the influence of Saint Augustine is steady and undeniable. Thus from Augustine's *De natura et gratia* (70, 84) this text is well understood: *caritas inchoata, inchoata justitia est; caritas provecta, provecta justitia est; caritas magna, magna justitia est; caritas perfecta, perfecta justitia*; and it is repeated by the theologians of the Augustinian school in order to make more clear the essence of Augustinian spirituality and to define the degrees of perfection, with the primacy residing in charity: charity towards God and one's neighbor. It is from this essential charity that all other virtues flow. [1004]

With the hindsight of history one can understand how different roads might lead from fifteenth-century Augustinianism: the central lines of Augustinian teaching through St. Thomas de Villeneuve and Seripando, but other paths also — equally, in their unique ways, Augustinian — through Erasmus and Luther.

Erasmus at 25: Leaving the monastery

Ordained, as we have already discussed, in April 1492 at the age of about twenty-four, Erasmus was also becoming known as a poet and as a Latinist. There is a gap in the letters of Erasmus after 1489 and until the letter from Willem Hermans, which Allen has provisionally dated 1493: thus a period of silence after both Erasmus' ordination and the decision to leave the monastery and join the Bishop of Cambrai. In this zone of silence we know nothing from external evidence about the ordination or the steps which led to Erasmus' joining Hendrik van Bergen. It may well be that Erasmus felt he had to keep the intended departure from Steyn a secret until permission from the Bishop of Utrecht had been secured and the formal invitation came.[82]

It appears most likely that the Bishop of Cambrai preferred a priest as his Latin secretary, both to accompany him to Rome (in that frustrated expectation of receiving a Cardinal's hat[83]) and also to handle official correspondence and other duties as a member of his household. All lines of interpretation converge on a sense of Erasmus' eagerness to leave the monastery and to join the Bishop of Cambrai.

But questions still remain about Erasmus during the period of his life up to 1492 and his leaving Steyn, and the answers to those questions are colored by the fact that the evidence is drawn, very largely, from later writings. Let us take up the questions that Post has formulated, for they are heuristic:

> Did Erasmus, in his formative years in Deventer and 's-Hertogenbosch, and during his first years in the monastery, come into contact with and absorb the combination of, devotion and humanism, enriching both and deriving from them an individual outlook on life which may perhaps be characterized with the general term *philosophia Christi*? Or did Erasmus absorb the principles or the spirit of the devotion in Deventer, Zwolle and Stein, later adding to these the humanism which scarcely existed in these circles, but which entered the Netherlands as a new culture, to some extent supplementing the existing school training? Must we assume that Erasmus, by his own efforts and utilizing what he already knew from the school, assimilated the new culture, afterwards developing it considerably, moulding it into a coherent system of thought, the *philosophia Christi*? ... He may indeed have gained the humanistic culture, as it was revealed in the Netherlands of this period, through his own great mental efforts and exceptional talent, and developed it without any fusion with the devo-

tion which had been more or less imposed upon him in the early period ...[84]

One's conceptualizing of the intellectual and spiritual development of Erasmus depends upon the answers to these questions. A strong intellectual independence marks Erasmus from a quite early time (from as early as Epistle 1): may we not also think that there was also a strong spiritual independence? If we follow the interpretation of Post, there was a parallel development by Erasmus of the intellectual and the spiritual, but little fusion until during his nine months' stay in England from May 1499 to February 1500. Yet the example – or, as the term now has it, the rôle models – of Alexander Hegius and Rudolph Agricola must be given due weight. Particularly in the years immediately following his school days in Deventer, Erasmus thought highly of Hegius, and he never lost admiration of Agricola. For in these two men Erasmus sensed a combination of humanistic culture and a piety that was essentially that of the *Devotio Moderna*.[85] In his early *De contemptu mundi* there is a celebration by Erasmus of human intellectual activity, but it is not raised above humility and mortification, characteristic monastic values.[86] And in the *Antibarbari* Erasmus goes beyond a mere attack upon the 'barbarians' – ignorant schoolmasters, prejudiced mendicants and theologians – and offers a view of humanism that harmonizes with Christianity.

To be sure, Erasmus had not yet crystallized his individual sense of vocation in studying the Bible under the aegis of a learned piety and a humanistic theology: that inspiration would come in England during 1499 under the guidance of John Colet and with the exampling of Ficino's effort to create a *prisca theologia* that fused Platonism and Christianity. We do indeed perceive that a sense of that vocation grows clearer and firmer after 1500. But in 1495 Erasmus was not necessarily less 'religious' or spiritually motivated: only he felt frustration at Steyn more and more, and he yearned for the opportunity to grow and to utilize his talents. He was both dissatisfied with the atmosphere at Steyn that for him had become distasteful and oppressive, and also eager to move to the opportunities and challenges of a university. Some of the deeper themes of Erasmian scholarship and humanism are notable even in this early work: the exhortation to go to the 'fyrste fountaynes' (cf. the humanist's cry *ad fontes*)[87] and the concern for eloquence that is so much a part of the reading of the Church Fathers. In the allusion to Cicero there is perhaps an implied criticism (or it could be so construed) that he is not Christian, as well as the stress on Lactantius for his Ciceronian rhetoric: but these implications will be made far more clearly and strongly by Erasmus in more mature writings. A final point: there is here an acceptance of the worth of Thomas Aquinas and Albertus Magnus at a certain level of study: nothing yet of the later attack on the lesser Scholastics of the late fourteenth and fifteenth centuries.[88]

In leaving the monastery at Steyn Erasmus did not cease to be an Augustinian canon, and his spirituality and thought remained profoundly Augustinian.

1 The scholarship on theological and related questions in the life and works of Erasmus is very large indeed. One may begin by remarking that the studies of Erasmian religious thought made after World War II have gradually dissipated prejudices of long standing against Erasmus, both in Rome and north of the Alps; and especially one notes Louis Bouyer's pioneering *Autour d'Erasme* (Paris, 1955) for its sensitive reading of Erasmus. To that one may add the following: J. Etienne, *Spiritualisme Erasmien et les Théologiens Louvanistes* (Louvain, 1956); K. Oelrich, *Der späte Erasmus und die Reformation* (Münster, 1961); and, among a number of recent biographies, that of C. Augustijn (Amsterdam, 1986). In a number of valuable studies in scholarly journals, L.-E. Halkin has examined a number of particular problems; a biography by Halkin is promised for the near future — see 'Bio-bibliographie de Léon-E. Halkin', par J.-P. Massaut et A. Willicot, *Bulletin de L'Institut Historique Belge de Rome*, fasc. LV-LVI (1985-1986), 3-32.
2 See Halkin, 'La piété d'Erasme', *Revue d'histoire ecclésiastique*, 79 (1984), 671-708.
3 Too many modern biographers of Erasmus, and others, have put a contemporary reading on this action, and they have chosen to stress what they therefore see as a desire by Erasmus to break away from his vows. One notable exception is Richard DeMolen in *Renaissance Quarterly*.
4 Here it is well to state that in this study and in my forthcoming biography I accept the dating of 1467 as the year of Erasmus' birth for the reasons and arguments put forward most lucidly and succinctly by A. F. C. Koch, *The year of Erasmus' birth* ... (Utrecht, 1969).

On this point of a gap in the epistolary evidence, see among others, J. K. Sowards, 'The Two Lost Years of Erasmus,' *Stud Ren.,* IX (1962), esp. p. 163-4, n. 7, and my Discussion of 'The Early Letters of Erasmus' following.
5 P. S. Allen et al., *Opus Epistolarum Des. Erasmi Roterodami*, (Oxford, 1906-1958), I, Appendix V, 587-90 (hereafter = Allen, *OE*).
6 On the Letter to Grunnius — a highly rhetorical, and therefore necessary to be interpreted carefully, letter that was part of his 'campaign' for a Papal Dispensation of larger scope than his earlier one — see the *Collected Works of Erasmus* (= *CWE*) (Toronto, 1974 and in progress), IV, 21/497.
7 See Allen *OE*, I, 588.
8 Constable in *Francesco Petrarca — Citizen of the World*, ed. Aldo S. Bernardo (Albany 1980), p. 99.

Erasmus' knowledge of Petrarch has been well argued by Margolin (see below); but his *De contemptu mundi* differs in aim from nearly all of Petrarch's works that contain references to or discussions of monasticism (adds Constable): it is rather a work that might have been written by Petrarch's brother Gerard, who 'entered the Carthusian monastery of Montreux, a few miles north of Toulon, on April 1343, when he was thirty-five or thirty-six years old and Petrarch was thirty-eight' ('Petrarch and Monasticism,' p. 61).
9 C. Reedijk, *The Poems of Desiderius Erasmus* (Leiden, 1956), p. 19, 59; Allen, *OE*, I, 74.
10 In his *Penitential Psalms* and elsewhere Petrarch described himself as a shipwrecked sailor and appealed to God; there are other correspondences or affinities between Erasmus and Petrarch — such as the closeness of the two on *meditatio mortis*, but one must consider how two such individualistic writers employ these *topoi*.
11 Here is Erasmus's quotation from the *Epistulae ex Ponto* II. 3. 25-8: Erewhile with many a friend encompassed / When following breezes all my sails did fill: / Now waves do swell, and clouds lower overhead, / Shipwrecked am I, and lost, 'mid waters chill.
12 Pref. to *Epistolae ad diversos* (Basel, 1521), q. by J. W. Binns, 'The letters of Erasmus,' in *Erasmus*, ed. T. A. Dorey, pp. 57-8.
13 *Essais* III, ix — Pléiade ed., p. 946.
14 And every phrase / And sentence that is right ... / The word neither diffident nor ostentatious, / An easy commerce of the old and new, / The common word exact without vulgarity, / The formal word precise but not pedantic ... / 'Little Gidding,' V.

15   For discussion of the arguments for and against taking 1467 as the year of Erasmus' birth, see Koch, cited in n. 4 above.
16   The letters of Aeneas Sylvius Piccolomini (Pope Pius II) were printed as early as 1473. Mario Filelfo's widely-known *Epistolare* was printed at Paris in 1482, and again at Milan in 1484. Both treatises-complications on the epistle were therefore available to Erasmus by 1487.
17   This letter to Johannes Botzheim is in Allen *OE*, I, 18/16-9.
18   There was a printing of Thomas' work c. 1473, and numerous manuscripts were circulating: see Thomas Hemerken à Kempis, *Opera omnia*, ed. J.J. Pohl. Vol IV (Fribourg, 1918).

Further, it is most likely that some of the older monks at Steyn would have heard Thomas à Kempis speak (for he died in 1471). Zwolle is only a few miles from Steyn (perhaps 50 miles on the roads at that time), and there were many lines of communication between the two houses of the same community. We know in point of fact, that Gerard Groote, founder of the Brothers of the Common Life, preached in Gouda: *Praedicavit autem ... In Hollandia partibus Leydis Delfi Goudae ...* (cf. Thomas' *Vita Gerardi Magni*, in *Opera Omnia*, VII, p. 75).
19   See my introduction to H. Delehaye, *The Legends of the Saints* (Notre Dame, Ind.: University of Notre Dame Press, 1961), p. iv.
20   For an admirable setting of the development of Augustinian communities into a larger framework, see G. B. Ladner, *The Idea of Reform: Its Impact on Christian Thought and Action in the Age of the Fathers* (1959), pp. 356 ff.; and on the role of the *Regula ad servos Dei*, see J.C. Dickinson, *The Origins of the Austin Canons and Their Introduction Into England* (1950), appendices i and ii. See also *Dictionnaire de Spiritualité* on Augustinian spirituality and on charity. (= *DDS*).
21   Some of the themes and motifs and nearly all of the values of Thomas à Kempis are continued in the teaching of his disciples: see e.g. the *vita domini Florentii* (Thomas à Kempis, *Opera*, VII, 31 ff.).
22   I follow the convenient summary of Christopher Brooke in his *Monasteries of the World – The Rise and Development of the Monastic Tradition* (New York, 1982) [first published in the U.K. under the title of *The Monastic World* (1974)] pp. 125-6. In the monographic article by Giles Constable, 'Petrarch and Monasticism,' in *Francesco Petrarca – Citizen of the World*, ed. Aldo S. Bernardo (Padova: Editrice Antenore; Albany: State University of New York Press, 1980), 53-99, one may find both a convenient index to studies of medieval monasticism and a pioneering examination of the monasticism of the fourteenth century with respect to Petrarch.
23   'Kanoniker, Augustinusregel und Augustinusorden,' in *Zeitschrift f. katholische Theologie*, (1930), p. 359.
24   Robert Gaguin himself was minister general of the Trinitarian Order (a mendicant order founded in the late twelfth century and approved 1198 by Innocent III [see *New Catholic Encyclopedia*]); and he was a canonist, who after 1483 was elected dean of the faculty of canon law at Paris. He knew the difference between a monk and a canon, and he addressed Erasmus as *canon* (Allen *OE*, I, 153).
25   See A. C. Shannon, 'Augustinians,' in *NCE*, and also the article of R. P. Russell on Augustinian spirituality in *NCE*, as well as the studies of Ullmann, Kantorowicz, Post, and others, cited in the Bibliography. On Augustinian canons the following are relevant: J.C. Dickinson, *The origins of the Austin canons and their introduction into England* (London: 1950), provides an introduction for the English reader. An earlier work is that of J. A. Zunggo, *Historia generalis et specialis de ordine canonicorum regularium S. Augustini Prodromus* (Tiguri, 1742), 2 vols. One may profitably consult the articles in *DDS* and *DTC, Dictionnaire d'Histoire et de Géographie Ecclésiastiques*, ed. A. Baudrillart et al. (Paris: Letouzey et Ané), XII, 1953: 'Chanoines'. See esp. Ch. Boyer, 'Saint Augustin Législateur de la vie monastique,' dans *DDS* I (Paris, 1937), 1126-30.
26   I have quoted from the convenient summary of R. R. Post in *The Modern Devotion*, p. 340. It appears that the *lectio* and *oratio* continued in most houses throughout the fifteenth century: these constituted the core of the interior life of these communities.
27   It is striking that Gerlach Peters speaks of *scriptura* as the work of the hands and one finds this emphasis continued in ch. XIV of the *Vita domini Florentii* – De labore manuum eius pro commune bono: q. *Opera* of Thomas à Kempis. VII, 149 ff.
28   Associated with Windesheim but not incorporated in the congregation of Windesheim itself (Post, *Mod. Dev.* 657). See further the chapter on *Devotio Moderna* above.
29   Post 607.

30   According to Post, *Modern Devotion*, 518-9, the leaders of the chapter were alarmed, fearing a slackening of monastic observance. Yet the desired change was introduced, Post writes, and he adds: 'This may prove the seriousness of their intentions and their care for their monasteries, but it also shows that their idea cannot be considered as the only right one. *Variis modis bene fit* might also hold good here' (p. 519).
31   See Allen *OE*. I. 74, and see discussion below of books available at Steyn.
32   *Contemporaries of Erasmus*, I, 303.
33   Lucien Febvre, *Religious Unbelief in the Sixteenth Century*, pp. 310-11.
34   See Brian Stock, *Implications of Literacy* (Princeton: Princeton University Press, 1980). It is only a very slight extension of this most fertile term to think of Erasmus' monastery letters as constituting a vital bond for the textual community of humanism during those years.
35   M. Platt, Unpublished paper, 'Tradition and the Soul.' See also my paper on 'Erasmus in England: *Translatio studii* and the *studia humanitatis*,' in *Classical and Modern Literatures* (1987).
36   The following observations are based on Hyma, pp. 165 ff.
37   Busch, *Chronicon*, 313 (q. Post, *Modern Devotion*, 307-8).
38   Hyma, p. 147.
39   See Martin Reiss, 'Die Zitate antiker Autoren in der Imitatio des Thomas von Kempen,' *Thomas von Kempen* (Kempen, 1971), 63-77.
40   Q. Hyma, p. 148.
41   On the attacks on Valla, see J. Vahlen, 'Lorenzo Valla,' in *Almanach der kaiserlichen Akademie der Wissenschaften*, Vierzehnter Jahrgang (Wien, 1864), 181-225 (at pp. 213 ff.); and G. Voigt, *Die Wiederbelebung des klassischen Altertums oder das erste Jahrhundert des Humanismus*, 2 Aufl. (Berlin, 1880-1), I, 476 ff.

Q. by L. Pastor, *The History of the Popes from the Close of the Middle Ages*, ed. F. I. Antrobus (St. Louis, Mo., 1902), I, 51.
42   On the printing-press as an instrument of change, see Elisabeth L. Eisenstein, *The Printing Press as an Agent of Change: Communications and Cultural Transformations in early-modern Europe*, 2 vols. (Cambridge: Cambridge University Press, 1979), on which see my qualifying review in *ELN*.

By way of more detailed introduction to spiritual dimensions, see *The Pursuit of Holiness: Studies in Medieval and Reformation Thought*, X, ed. Charles Trinkaus and Heiko Oberman (Leiden: Brill, 1974).
43   The often-misquoted dictum of Lord Acton is: 'Power tends to corrupt, and absolute power corrupts absolutely,' and it was uttered with the Renaissance popes in mind – see my study of Acton's Inaugural Lecture on the Study of History, in *The Dissenting Tradition*, ed. Robert Coles (Athens, Ohio: University of Ohio Press, 1975), pp. 262-9.
44   For a summary picture of this 'small army' of clerics, see my 'Canon Law in England on the Eve of the Reformation,' *Med. Stud.*, XXV (1963), 125-47.
45   In my article on canon law cited in the preceding note, I have tried to stress the total penetration of the canon law into the life of the times. For the Western, as distinguished from the Eastern, Church, canon law was indissolubly fused with its theology: it was not only a valid, it was for them the vital legal system, the absence of which was unthinkable before 1520.
46   See J. LeClercq, *The Desire for Learning and the Love of God*; and B. Smalley, *The Study of the Bible in the Middle Ages*. Here the extraordinary work of the School of St. Victor and certain other monasteries can be seen in perspective.
47   The degree to which the Papal bull enjoining episcopal support for the sending of promising young religious to universities, with a view to the better education of parish clergy – the Bull *Cum ex eo* – has been studied by Leonard E. Boyle for England in the 14th and 15th centuries, but it does not seem to have been investigated for the Low Countries at the end of the Middle Ages. Cf. *Med. Stud.*, 24 (1962), 263-302.
48   On *Everyman/Everlickj*, see L. V. Ryan. For a conspectus of medieval literature, see John H. Fisher, ed., *The Medieval Literature of Western Europe, A Review of Research* ... (New York: The Modern Language Assn. of America, 1966).
49   There is a rich gathering of evidence concerning the complexity of belief in L. Febvre, *Religion and unbelief in the Sixteenth Century* – although one need not accept all of Febvre's conclusions.

For the twentieth-century reader the perceptive lines of Wallace Stevens have great relevance at this point: 'We live in a constellation/ Of patches and of pitches,/ Not in a single world...' ('July Mountain').

50   On the ordination of Erasmus by David of Bourgogne, Bishop of Utrecht, see Allen I, 588 (based upon *LB* X, 1573A), and II, 304 (with its comment upon the contradictory statement in the Letter to Grunnius of 1516). The date is not questioned in the recent speculation by A. J. van der Van in *Rotterdams Jaarboekje* (1970) that Erasmus was ordained by another bishop- 'sub' not 'a' David.

51   Q. from Pastor, *Popes*, I, 345 (citing Voigt, I, 435 & ff.). In 1491, John Fisher was ordained priest at 22 (17 Dec. 1491),

52   It is likely that David would have kept up some contacts with Cambrai after his translation to Utrecht, and in the light of Erasmus' entering the service of Hendrik van Bergen, Bishop of Cambrai, so soon after ordination, such contacts are important.

53   See Allen *OE*, Ep. 603; S. B. J. Zilverberg, *David van Bourgondie, bisschop van Terwaan en van Utrecht* (Groningen-Djakarta, 1951); H. Pirenne, *Histoire de Belgique des origines à nos jours* (Bruxelles: La Renaissance du Livre, 1948), 509 & *passim*; and *Contemporaries of Erasmus: A Biographical Register*... ed., P. Bietenholz *et al.,* (Toronto: Univ. of Toronto Press. 1985-7),I, 226-7.

54   *Ecclesiastes, LB* V. 808. In Ep. 645 (which is a commendatory letter to Gerard Geldenhouwer of Nijmegen) Erasmus comments on the installation − Lat. *inauguratio*, but surely installation is preferable to the *CWE* term inauguration (*CWE* 5 : 94/3) [see Niermeijer, s.v. *inaugurare*: consecrate] − of Philip of Burgundy Erasmus wrote: '... being himself a man of learning, he strove with all his might to see that ignorant, unlearned persons should not intrude into the sheepfold of the clergy, as we see they still do.'

55   See Allen *OE*, I, 43; *BR* I, 226.

56   See *BR* I, 226.

57   Erasmus' network of friends and acquaintances in Holland remains a complex story.

On 3 December 1529, in his *Epistola contra Pseudevangelicos*, Erasmus referred to David ('que illi in dignitatem successit, memoriam refricat'): *LB* X. 1573A.

58   I note the argument of Hirten in the introduction to his translation of *De contemptu mundi* (1967) that the work was possibly for William Herman, a pupil of Alexander Hegius, for Herman had been a good friend of Erasmus at Steyn. But if we give weight to the indication that Erasmus was in fact writing to a relative − as the *nepos* of the preface clearly indicates − then a more likely candidate is Servatius Rogerius of Rotterdam, who was not only a friend of Erasmus at Steyn but most likely a cousin as well. See Hirten, p. xii; and Hyma, *Youth*, p. 172. See also van Leijenhorst in *BR* I, 184-5 on Hermans. On the *De contemptu mundi* see further the introduction by Sem Dresden in *ASD*.

59   One can scarcely give too much consideration to the acceleration of change between 1490 and 1520: 'prospects of incalculable change,' indeed.

60   Cf. Hirten, p. xli, for a brief indication of the coming together of these three movements in one sharply drawn focal point; the contexts and traditions are much more fully discussed by Gilson in *Reason and Revelation in the Middle Ages* (1938), pp. 88-92, and, still more fully, in his *The Unity of Philosophical Experience* (1937), ch. iv. Especially in his chapters xiv and xv, R. R. Post deals with the complex relations between humanism and reformation in *The Modern Devotion*.

Dom Jean Leclercq has emphasized monastic traditions of learning in his book *The Desire for Learning and the Love of God*.

61   J.-C. Margolin has studied the question of the relationship of Erasmus to Petrarch, and he has well concluded that: 'Sans doute pourra-t-on interposer entre le texte de Pétrarque et celui d'Erasme tous les traités médiévaux qui portent le même titre et dont le contenu est semblable. Mais, en laissant de côté la question de savoir si le jeune Erasme, au couvent de Steyn, avait lu, parmi la masse d'ouvrages qu'il dévorait avec tant d'ardeur, le *Secretum* de Pétrarque, il semble bien qu'un même accent caractérise ces deux textes' (pp. 187-8). This entire essay is a splendid examination of the question of the relationship of the two humanists, both of whom 'ont représenté un moment exceptionnel dans l'histoire de la culture occidentale...' 'Pétrarque et Erasme,' dans '*Petrarca 1304-1375. Beiträge zur Werk und Wirkung,*' hrs. Fritz Schalk (Frankfurt: Vittorio Klostermann, 1975), 184-97. There is the larger question of the relations of Erasmus with Italy and with Italians, on which see: P. de Nolhac, *Erasme en Italie* (Paris), 1898), and A. Renaudet, *Erasme et l'Italie* (Genéve, 1954),

as well as the more recent studies of P.O. Kristeller, 'Erasmus from an Italian Perspective,' *Ren. Q.*, XXIII (1970), 1-14; E. Garin, 'Erasmo e l'umanesimo italiano,' *BHR* XXXIII (1971), 7-17; and L.-E. Halkin, 'Erasme en Italie,' in *Colloquia Erasmiana Turonensia* (Paris: Vrin, 1972), 37-53.

Innocent's *De contemptu mundi* (*PL* 217, 701-46) was printed several times before 1480 (as early as 1470: Hain 10209) and was certainly accessible to Erasmus. Petrarch's *Secretum* was published, prob. at Strasburg, c. 1473 (Hain 12800). Thomas à Kempis also wrote a *De contemptu mundi*.

62 On the reading aloud of the *Imitation of Christ* – a practise which has continued in Roman Catholic religious communities well into the twentieth century – see the summary-statement of Gottfried Georg Krodel in *EB*: 'It has been said that the *Imitation of Christ* has had a wider religious influence than any book except the Bible; if the statement is limited to Christendom, it is probably true.'

63 Thus Hirten, p. vii, citing Gilson, *Reason and Revelation*, 88-92.

64 The phrase is evocative: to religious it would suggest the waters of wisdom – and there is indeed the metaphor of the forsaken fountain in the Book of Baruch (see p. 87) – and there are numerous *loci* in both the *OT* and the *NT* for this scriptual *topos*. In later literature a spring or brook was often a part of the topos of the *locus amoenus*: see Curtius, *European Literature and the Latin Middle Ages* (Princeton, 1953), 195 ff.

65 1540 *Opera*, v. 1052 (translation from Paynell, xvi, 158).

66 For a brief introduction to the spiritual life of Thomas More, see R. J. Schoeck, 'Thommaso Moro,' in *Bibliotheca Sanctorum* (Rome, 1969), XII, 608-14, and 'On The Spiritual Life of Thomas More,' *Thought*, 52 (1977), 323-7.

Many passages in Paynell's early Tudor translation of the *De contemptu mundi* of Erasmus sound remarkably like Thomas More, but this is to introduce yet another variable into the comparison: how much was Paynell influenced by More as well as by Erasmus?

67 Cf. Hyma, *Youth*, p. 179. See Hirten's discussion of the addition of the preface, like chapter xii, to the publication in 1521 (p. xiv).

68 Hyma, ibid., 180-1. One of Hyma's arguments is that Erasmus quoted more than seventy times from the classics, as against but five from the Bible (p. 179): 'These texts from the Bible were frequently quoted in sermons, so they do not prove that he was familiar with the Scriptures.' But this is ridiculous: first, not all of the allusions to the Bible have been identified – it is much easier to spot classical quotations that carry a kind of flag in Renaissance texts, and in Erasmus' letters that are now being so carefully annotated in the *CWE*, there are numerous Biblical and patristic allusions that are not identified in the commentary. Second, Erasmus is presumably writing to one who has not yet adopted the monastic life, and he may have felt that references to the classics were more likely to be persuasive.

Another argument made by Hyma (p. 180) is that 'not a single letter written by him at Steyn reveals real love of God or Christ': but what are preserved are largely literary letters, and during Erasmus' lifetime only two letters written at Steyn were published. These are letters written to and from friends with whom Erasmus shared a love for the reading of the classics: they manifest that textual community. Erasmus either did not write or did not choose to preserve letters which manifest that other textual community in which he also shared: the love of the Bible (which continued all his life) and the love of the Church Fathers (to the editing of whom he devoted a large part of his career as a scholar).

It is nonsense to say of Erasmus that he was not, and had never been, a true monk who 'loved Christ with all his heart and mind and soul' (Hyma, p. 180). For him the interpretation of Scriptures was a lifelong devotion, and his love of Christ shines directly in his prayers.

69 See the brief discussion in *CWE* 1:4, and D. F. S. Thomson, 'Erasmus as Poet in the Context of Northern Humanism,' *De Gulden Passer*, 47 (1969), 192 ff. for the argument for literary imitation. Hyma presses the biographical element and argues that Servatius and Erasmus may have been cousins (*Youth*, 56 and 72); but the difficulty with this argument is that Pieter seems to have been unaware of such a relationship (cf. Ep. 3:36 ff.), and one would have to believe either that Pieter had never known his cousin or that Servatius and Erasmus were related (through Gerard Helius, not through the first husband of Margareta), but Pieter and Servatius were not. It seems more probable that Servatius and Erasmus were not so related. The conventionality of the early letters is discussed in Part III below.

70 The celebration of friendship is an old theme in the *studia humanitatis* (and of course among

Christian writers), and Renaissance humanists were fond of the letters of Cicero, Seneca, and others. The familiar letters of Petrarch were prime texts in the humanistic traditions of friendship, and this high valuation is continued in the letters of Ficino and others at the end of the fifteenth century. Erasmus and his circle of friends valued friendship itself very highly and they would have treasured the familiar letters of earlier humanists: there is no need to insist too rigorously on distinctions between the conventions of friendship and the conventions of letters among friends.

71 See *LB* VIII, 557-8. Van Leijenhorst in *BR* I, 189-90.
72 The poems are numbers 12 and 13 in Reedijk, and the *Oratio* is printed in LB VIII 551-60 (cf. also Ep. 28).
73 Luc Verheijen, *La Règle de Saint Augustin*, I (Paris: Etudes Augustiniennes, 1967), p. 441.
74 Thus Verheijen, loc. cit., II, 25: 'Erasme, et les deux auteurs anglais qui le suivent, ne peuvent pas s'imaginer que des hommes, conscient de leur dignité, se soumettent librement à une telle constrainte.' This significant observation compels us to ask again just how strict the constraints at Steyn were for Erasmus, and also to consider Erasmus' strictures in the light of the Rule.
75 There was little among the canons of that exactitude of St. Thomas de Villeneuve which spoke (early in the 16th c.) of 'l'exact intelligence de la Bible [qui] était la règle sure pour découvrir ces erreurs' (cf. *D de S* IV 992).
76 Some scholars feel that Post has been too rigorous in bringing forward all of the negative evidence and not considering non-archival evidence sufficiently. However, the recent studies of James K. Farge have helped to *préciser* the non-intellectual traditions of Erasmus' confrères at the Faculty of Theology of Paris: see my forthcoming study of this question in *Erasmus Yearbook*.
77 See Allen, *OE* I, 242 ff (Eps. 106-11) for the letters which record and continue the seminal discussions between Colet and Erasmus in the autumn of 1499.
78 See note 46 above, and *The Cambridge History of The Bible*.
79 May not one of the causes for Erasmus' turning away from his monastery and from monasticism generally have been his keen disappointment that they were not achieving the high goals which he had known all too well?
80 As one rightly expects, the works of Augustine occupied a privileged place in their libraries, sustained and enriched with exemplary care ('un soin exemplaire') from the 13th century onwards (*DofS* 994). Too much emphasis therefore can be put upon a secondary account of Erasmus' pleasure in finding a copy of Augustine in the abbey of Parc, which was Premonstratensian.
81 Gilles wrote at one point, on a disputed doctrinal point which he rejected, that not to follow St. Augustine is dangerous (quem non sequi est valde periculosum [999]). (References in brackets are to the *DAS*.)
82 See *CWE* 1:63.
83 Allen *OE* I, 150.
84 Post, *Modern Devotion*, p. 658.
85 I have discussed this relationship in 'Agricola and Erasmus,' forthcoming (1988) in *The Proceedings of the Rudolph Agricola Conference*, Groningen 1985, ed. F. Akkerman, and printed above in a somewhat expanded version.
86 Post, *Modern Devotion*, p. 670.
87 The metaphor of the fountain (see p. 64) is by no means exclusively classical, for the Book of Baruch, in its Exhortatio ad sapientiam (III, 4 − IV. 4) works from the core concept *Dereliquisti fontem sapientiae*.
88 Other themes later taken up and more fully developed by Erasmus include the extension of Epicurus read in an almost spiritual sense), 'whose authorite I wyll not yet forgo' (142) and the role of the Holy Ghost.

B. The Early Letters of Erasmus: Problems of Interpretation

It is like learning to write. To acquire this art, one must practice much, however disagreeable or difficult it may be, however impossible it may seem. Practicing earnestly and often, one learns to write, acquires the art.

MEISTER ECKHART, *The Talks of Instruction*

A letter by a humanist transcends the ordinary message, especially when it is edited by the humanist himself. It purports to be well-written and fit to be published; it is the successor of a classical genre endowed with a specific set of rules, defined by the illustrations examples [sic] of Cicero's and Plinius' letters. The accuracy of the names, details, date, the authenticity itself – as we understand it today – of a particular letter can sometimes be brought into question. This literary conception of the art of letterwriting explains why Lipsius does not only emend his own letters ... but also the texts of his correspondents with a view to a possible publication ...

A. GERLO, *Justi Lipsi Epistolas* (Brussels, 1978)

We have already turned to some of the early letters of Erasmus for information and illumination, and we have seen some of the problems of interpretation. It is time that those problems be taken up and discussed in some fullness. A remarkable figure in so many ways, Erasmus was the author of about 1600 letters, which form the heart of an extraordinary correspondence of more than three thousand letters from the broadest possible spectrum of European thought and letters of the late fifteenth- and early sixteenth-centuries!

The rich body of his letters is both a very rich resource indeed – almost an *embarras de richesse* – at the same time that individual letters and groups of letters demand special reading and sophisticated interpretation. One of the first groups will also illustrate what I call the silences of Erasmus. He tells us a great deal about some aspects of his life or career, and even in a few rare moments about his inner life; but he is totally silent, or even misleading, about some other aspects.[2] To illustrate: letters from his monastery years at Steyn (roughly, 1487 to 1492 or 1493, when he was in his twenties), were kept and a number of them published; but we have no letters for that crucial period just before he entered the religious life, or again just before he was ordained a priest. We would like to know much more than we do about his intentions or motives, but he has drawn a curtain across that part of his life, for whatever reasons. Similarly, there is a gap of about two years in the life-record of Erasmus from about 1509 to about 1511. To be more precise: from late 1509 (and the Epistle 216A from Daniele Scevola, discovered only in 1938 by Kristeller),[3] to Epistle 217 from Paolo Bombace, dated (we think) Bologna, March 1511, there is an hiatus and no actual evidence. One scholar, J. K. Sowards, has attempted to explain that Erasmus was in London and did not need to write letters, and he puts forward the tempting but unsupported hypothesis that Erasmus' letters during this period were filled with unfavourable comments on Julius II which he felt it advisable to suppress.[4] But, quite simply, we do not know, and there seems to be the inescapable conclusion that Erasmus did not want us to know, where he was and what he was doing for that period.

To sum up Erasmus' epistolary-editorial practice: he began to preserve copies of his letters only after he reached middle age, and in 1505 he announced his attention to publish a volume of his own epistles – being then about 38. Letters began to be published in 1515, and in 1516 and 1517 Maartens at Louvain published selections without Erasmus' permission – by then the manuscript circulation must have been considerable. The first major collection, with 63 new letters, appeared in Basel in 1518, and a much larger one of 333 letters was published by Froben in 1519 under the title of *Farrago nova epistolarum Erasmi*. For this last collection Erasmus added some dates (the years) from memory, but they are demonstrably mostly wrong. Erasmus was always unreliable with dates, and as was the case with so many of his contemporaries he generally dated his own letters only by day and month, with an indication of place, but not the year (*CWE* 1 : xix-xx).

As if all of this were not troublesome enough, Erasmus, we are now quite sure, at certain times manipulated or even deliberately falsified his chronology. Koch has discussed that problem in his monograph on the problems of chronology.

The major question now is, how do we interpret the letters that we have, and in the form and order that we have them? There are extant more than 3000 letters, of which some 1600 were written by Erasmus; but only about 15% of these were written before mid-1514, when he was about 47. We have no more than 16 letters, I judge, written by or to Erasmus before he was twenty-one; yet these early letters all seem to have been preserved by Erasmus himself, even though he may not have controlled their circulation. Large though it is, his total correspondence is by its nature fragmentary and it unevenly represents different periods of his life; and while the letters of this early period before 1500 are of extraordinary interest to his biographers, they are only a small part of a larger whole and they are more conventional than most of the later letters. How indeed shall we interpret them, and how can they validly be used for biographical evidence?

Erasmus himself comments at several points about his own letters, and we might well take up our study with one of these comments. I have already mentioned the early collections of his letters; and in his prefatory letter to the *Epistolae ad Diversos* (which was published at Basel by Froben in August 1521 and contained 617 letters, of which 171 were new), Erasmus addressed his friend Rhenanus – and that Beatus later became Erasmus' literary executor establishes a degree of credibility that we can attach to the letter in question. Erasmus admits that he had revised some of his letters and explains why he was reluctant to publish any of them:

> Though as a young man [Erasmus wrote] and also at a riper age, I have written a great number of letters, I scarcely wrote any with a view to publi-

cation. I practised my style, I beguiled my leisure; I made merry with my acquaintance, I indulged my humour, in fine, did scarcely anything in this way but amuse myself, expecting nothing less than that my friends would copy out or preserve such trifling compositions.

(*CWE* 1 : xx-xxi — Ep. 1206)

Now the last part of this can be dismissed as a characteristic ploy or stance of humanists: *I had a few idle moments, and I dashed off this insignificant trifle* — there are countless examples of humanistic versions of what rhetoricians call the modesty or humility topos, and which can be seen as an elegant rhetorical expression of *sprezzatura*. But there is a part of this quoted passage that calls for further analysis, and that is the part in which Erasmus tells Rhenanus (and us, his later readers) that he practised his style. Does this mean that he may not have been sincere? I think not, and indeed it may well be argued that the conventions he was so assiduously mastering were precisely the means by which he could achieve sincerity in expressing himself — with irony or mockery at times, to be sure, or in whatever mode he chose. But the point is that convention may liberate, and convention does not preclude sincerity.[5] There are further questions, of course. One is in large part historical, and it is that of the complex influences of traditional letters, of which classical epistolography formed only a part. Within the classical tradition Erasmus in the 1480s and 1490s seems to have been most attracted to the 'Römischen Freundschaftsbriefen' of Cicero and Pliny, as modified in the early humanistic correspondence of Petrarch and Coluccio Salutati.[6] A second question involves Erasmus' concept of the epistolary genre in the years before his own *De conscribendis epistolas* and especially during the monastery and Paris years. For there was a considerable amount of epistolary theory as well as the practice that provided models in the work of Filelfo, Perotti, Nigri, Valla, Poliziano, and others.

But now to the question of how far these early letters can be used for biographical evidence. Given that the humanists at the end of the fifteenth century were reading their Filelfo and others and were practising the different kinds and uses of the epistle — thus we find in Filelfo such topics familiar in the early letters of Erasmus as *consilium approbat, excusatoria epistola, hortatur amicum, accusat silentiam,* etc. — we must begin with the recognition that Erasmus was in fact practising his prose style in the writing of these early letters and that he made use of available models. A careful reader must recognize the conventionality of a letter that begins, 'My dear Servatius, I am more surprised every day at your silence' (Ep. 15), for this *is* conventional, as is much that follows; but not, I think, the final sentences that are couched in simple prose and make a clear and direct request. The totality of the letter, therefore, cannot be disregarded as merely conventional — and even if it were, would not the revelation that Erasmus was playing such a rhetorical game of conventions with a close friend tell us much?[7]

To pursue the larger point: the biographer who has identified apparent conventionality must then play the literary critic and endeavor to establish where the original notes have been struck. This process should move the interpreter of the letters more surely towards a careful and responsible use of the letters as evidence.

One respect which is striking in these early letters is Erasmus' skill in quoting from classical literature from Epistle 1 forwards; there is little of this in Filelfo's letters. If the Bishop of Cambrai in fact had selected Erasmus as his Latin secretary in 1492 on the strength of his Latin style, is it not possible that he had seen some of Erasmus' early letters in manuscript and that he, schooled for six years in Italy, had recognized the talent of the young Erasmus? A further observation: the degree of personal reference — both of the writer and of the addressee — is far greater in the epistles of Erasmus, and this looks forward to the development of that superbly casual and intimate style of the later Erasmus and, I am prepared to argue, marks a significant contribution by Erasmus to the development of the Renaissance epistle, in which only Petrarch and (to a lesser extent) Ficino share the top honors in this important genre. In short, I accept the letters of Erasmus as necessary and uniquely valuable evidence for the early years (and *a fortiori* for the middle and later years); but in making use of the letters for biographical or critical interpretation I shall want to examine the context, to consider the relationship between writer and addressee, and to try to establish the tone of each letter. Then we can make use of each letter individually, for by its rhetorical nature it must be so considered.

Erasmus was always enormously concerned with style, and at first glance this concern might seem obsessive. But to speak of the style of Erasmus is not simply to identify qualities of lucidity, suppleness, sparkle and wit, allusiveness, and the control of endless nuances and gradations of tone — important though these are, and fascinating as they are to perceive. For Erasmus, ultimately, language expresses the essence of human reality, and in this I would compare him with the twentieth-century poet Seamus Heaney, who may well be the best of living English poets and in whose work *lingua* is perhaps the central reality of man as man: the physical tongue and its marvellous workings, the power of speech, the language enjoyed and enriched. Language for Erasmus is the source of good order, civility, and understanding in human culture and society; through the Word — *logos* in Greek, *sermo* in Latin — truth and salvation, he believed, came into the world through the divine word-incarnation; but through the bad use of language (and all that is involved in that) have come also lying, violence, and the destruction of civil order. Thus language becomes an essential part of the teleology of Erasmian thought: language not only expresses order, but it becomes, in its proper functioning, a means to retrieve a sense of order and to strive towards higher goals. In this sense Erasmus would agree with the modern philosopher Whitehead that 'style is the intellectual morality of mind.' In an intellectual biography of Erasmus, therefore, the reader must never lose his sense of the central importance of style for Erasmus.

There is also a high sense of play: in a 1498 letter to a former student, Erasmus spends the first page in playfully exercising the rhetoric of invective, making use of the convention of insulting names that is modelled on Plautus as in *Asinaria* 297-8 (but Filelfo gave a separate category to invective, and he drew upon a rich tradition in fifteenth-century Milanese literature).[8] To his poor former student whom Erasmus was writing reproachfully for having failed to write:

> I shall call you rascal, butcher, gallowsbird, glutton, wretch, scandal, abomination, monster, nightmare, dung, dungheap, plague, ruin, disgrace, slanderer, wastrel, jailer (or rather jail itself), whipping block, kiss-the-rod, and any still more insulting terms I can invent; these, I repeat, are the names I shall use to humiliate you. So you will be forced to write a reply, even while you fume...
>
> Ep. 70, 13 February 1498 (*CWE* 1:145/24-9)

'Hac pagella lusum est satis, alteram seriis dabimus': Erasmus turns from the joking to serious matters, and he makes this clear with 'the second page will be devoted to serious matters.'

One excerpts from Erasmus at risk, for one must always look to the full context of the sentence, paragraph, and even letter, for from the biographical point of view much depends upon Erasmus' relationship with the recipient and from the historical point of view much depends upon the context. Thus Erasmus' 1494 letter to his old friend Willem Hermans, on the eve of leaving for Paris, was written at a time of civil war, but Erasmus evokes this sense of disorder and danger in only one sentence, 'The world is full of bitterness and uproar and no matter where I look I can see only gloomy and savage sights: "On all sides grief abounds," and "death in many a shape"' – but the last two phrases are echoes from Hermans' own ode 3 on civil war in Holland, his *Silva odarum (CWE* 1: 79 144 ff.).

From late summer 1495, when he arrived in Paris, to the summer of 1499, when he left for England, Epistles 43 to 102, we have 59 letters by and to Erasmus: a treasure when compared with only 42 letters for the 28 years before 1495, or before leaving for Paris in the summer of 1495. The range of correspondents widens and they include not only the dedicatory letter to Gaguin already mentioned but the letter to Adolph of Burgundy, heer van Veere, which was entitled

'Epistola exhortatoria ad capessendam virtutem ad generossissimum puerum Adolphum, principem Veriensem,' nearly four printed pages; Adolph was then about ten and was living with his widowed mother, Anna van Borssele, who had been kind to Erasmus; and his father, Philip of Burgundy, had held high office, which led to Adolph's career as admiral of Flanders and member of the council of Charles V. In 1513 Adolph married Anna, daughter of Jan van Bergen, the bishop of Cambrai's brother: yet another connection of Erasmus with the influential van Bergen family. I dwell at some length on this identification of Adolph of Burgundy, for it illustrates the widening circles of acquaintance with personnages of the Burgundian court (though I do not here attempt to speak of the connections of the Bishop of Cambrai with these lords and ladies of the Burgundian world). These individuals must identified, and the bulk of that work of identification is now being done by the three volumes of *Contemporaries of Erasmus* (BR), all three volumes of which have now been published; but even here, one must try to go further: one stumbles by accident on the fact that Erasmus' Bishop of Cambrai, who in a sense plucked him from the monastery, had studied six years in Italy, a fact neglected in the *Contemporaries* entry and virtually all contemporary scholarship on Hendrik van Bergen. In Italy Hendrik van Bergen, the bishop, had been praised for his eloquence in Italian as well as Latin, and this skill is surely relevant to the selection of Erasmus, however it was done.

To return to the point that we have 59 letters by and to Erasmus during the period from 1495 to 1499. In these letters we can see Erasmus growing in confidence, control, and a sense of easy mastery which he communicates unmistakably to his reader. For when he arrived in Paris, having been released from the service of the Bishop of Cambrai in order to pursue theological studies at the University of Paris, he was in his 28th year (if we take the year 1467 as the year of his birth, as now seems most probable).

What did he have to show for years of patient but frustrating study?[9] He had completed one early work, the *De contemptu mundi* (actually completed before Paris), and he had carried with him from Steyn an early version of the *Antibarbari*, which expresses vigorously enough strong ideas and feelings about the ennemies of humanism, as well as the nucleus of his later and more fully developed concept of good letters (*bonae literae*): but the *Antibarbari* was not yet honed to its final form and polish, and in fact it was not published until 1518, and then only in a rather different form. Erasmus had also composed an abridgment of Valla's *Elegantiae* — that most widely accepted manual of Latin style, which was a remarkable assignment for a young religious, given Valla's general reputation for being irreligious — but we cannot be sure whether the bulk of this work was actually done in the monastery at Steyn; in any case, Valla continued to be a dominant influence upon Erasmus, for as early as 1489 he wrote, 'again, in the niceties of style I rely on Lorenzo Valla above all' (Ep. 20, *CWE* 1:31: 99-100); he referred to the *Elegantiae* several times in his letters before

1499, as well as to the *Dialectica*, and to his own paraphrases. Valla was central to Erasmus' striving for good Latin style, and there was evidently a number of letters already circulating and contributing to his reputation as a stylist.

Epistolography, to conclude, was important to Erasmus for a number of reasons, and for the rest of his life the letter would remain, along with the dialogue, a favourite genre.[10] But epistolography was a part of rhetoric, and during Erasmus' Paris years a dominant concern — perhaps, all in all, *the* dominant — was rhetoric. For rhetoric was the central concern of Quattrocento humanists and their rallying-cry against what was felt to be the encroachment and arrogance of late Scholastic dialectic and logic. Rhetoric was a continuing devotion of Erasmus; and he studied, practiced and developed his rhetorical skills that he was to draw upon in a hundred ways in later years. He manifested those skills in an ever-widening range of literary and educational works until he was celebrated — or condemned by his critics — as the master-rhetorican of his age; and most of those works had their roots, or their seeds were being sown, during the Paris years when he tutored students and created for them improved textbooks for learning advanced Latin grammar and rhetoric and for improving their styles. The writing of letters to students, to friends, and to others must be seen as a vital part of Erasmus' humanistic program.[11]

On Interpretation — An End-Note

The preceding provisional discussion of problems of interpretation in the early letters needs both to be continued and also to be extended to other works of Erasmus. For at every step of the way in studying Erasmus' development we are concerned with hermeneutical questions: with his interpretations of classical as well as Scriptural writings (in his commentaries, prefaces, and letters) and with our own interpretation of Erasmus' writings.

I find E. D. Hirsch's *Validity in Interpretation* (1967) invaluable for its theoretical yet soundly practical approach to questions of interpretation, and for its general sense of the centrality of text in the functions of criticism. Yet I myself have a stronger sense of the integrity of the text, as I have tried to indicate in *Intertextuality and Renaissance Texts*.

But for that very large area of Scriptural texts and their interpretation which a study of Erasmus must involve, I follow the theory of Emilio Betti in *Teoria Generale della Interpretazione* (1955) to the conclusion that by virtue of their special weighting of authority Scriptural, like legal, texts belong to a category of writing different from literary texts and, consequently, that the hermeneutics appropriate for their interpretation are different from those appropriate for literary texts. But that is a problem which must be discussed elsewhere, as I hope to do in two critical essays to be completed later in 1988.

See further: Josef Bleicher, *Contemporary Hermeneutics: Hermeneutics as method, philosophy and critique* (London: Routledge & Kegan Paul, 1980); and Erika Rummel, 'God and Solecism: Erasmus as a Literary Critic of the Bible,' *Erasmus of Rotterdam Society Yearbook Seven* (1987), 54-72.

1 This chapter was originally offered at a Colloquium in the Herzog August Bibliothek (September 1986) in a much enlarged form.
For an introduction to and overview of Erasmian correspondence, see the introduction of W. K. Ferguson *CWE* 1.
2 I have not attempted to address the notion of self-portrayal in the letters of Erasmus: for that, see A. Gerlo, 'Erasmus von Rotterdam: Sein Selbstporträt in seinen Briefen,' in *Der Brief im Zeitalter der Renaissance*, hrsg. F. J. Worstbrock, Acta Humaniora, 1983, pp. 7-24. But, *pace* Gerlo, I do not see the correspondence as *ein Tagebuch*, though I agree that the letters are 'von unschätzbarem Wert' and 'ohnegleichen.' Rather than a journal, strictly speaking, I think it likely that Erasmus did keep and use a commonplace book.
3 Were it not for this letter from Scevole, our zone of silence would date from the previous letter (Ep. 216) of 30 June 1509, making the silence even longer.
4 J. K. Sowards, 'The Two Lost Years of Erasmus' *Stud. Ren.*, ix (1962), cap. 163-4, and 'Augustinian Erasmus', n. 4.
5 The question of sincerity is one that has occupied a number of twentieth-century critics: see most notably Lionel Trilling, *Sincerity and Authenticity* (Cambridge, Mass.: Harvard Univ. Press. 1972).
6 Cf. Peter L. Schmidt, 'Die Rezeption des Römischen Freundschaftsbriefes,' in *Der Brief im Zeitalter der Renaissance*, pp. 25-9.
7 See the most interesting contribution by Helene Harth to the volume of studies on *Der Brief im Zeitalter der Renaissance*: 'Poggio Bracciolini und die Brieftheorie des 15. Jahrhunderts – zur Gattungsform des humanistischen Briefs,' pp. 81-99.
There is a marked difference in tone between Ep. 56 to Christian Northoff (1497), which is largely serious, exhortatory, moral, and Ep. 70 a few months later to the same person, which begins with a playful catalogue of insulting names – and then turns serious. The difference in tone is significant, and Erasmus is far too skillful to play the game of the second letter with a correspondent who is more distant.
8 According to Aguzzi-Barbagli in *BR*, from 1485 to 1520 the letters of Filelfo appeared in at least 29 editions; but the *editio princeps* was 1473, certainly early enough to be known by Erasmus (and there was a Pafraet edition at Deventer in about 1488, already noted). The *Epistolarium* of Francesco Filelfo's son Giovanni Mario was printed in Paris 1482 and in Milan 1484; this we are certain that Erasmus knew (though we do not know how early), for in Ep. 117 and in the *De Conscribendi epistolis* (*ASD* 1-2, 265) Erasmus called it 'muddled and disorderly ... defective in both scholarship and suitability to the purpose in hand.'
9 One must speak to the significance of the letters between Erasmus and Gaguin, for Gaguin was an older scholar with whom Erasmus was yet able to exercise his wit, as in requesting the loan of a book from Gaguin's library: 'My request is that you should instruct this Macrobius to forsake your learned library and come to me; for you will not miss him, where he is but one among such a wealth of excellent authors, while he will bring the utmost delight to me in my poverty' (Ep. 121, Paris [March 1500], *CWE* 1: 248: 6-9).
We are missing the first letter from Erasmus to Gaguin, to which Gaguin replied in Ep. 43 (probably Sept. 1495), reproving Erasmus for writing in too flowery a style (*CWE* 1: 83-4). The effect of this advice upon Erasmus was salutary: doubtless his realization of the soundness of Gaguin's advice was what compelled him not to republish those first letters to Gaguin. Erasmus learned; he did not need many such reproofs in his mastering of style.
10 Erasmus' treatise on letter-writing, *De Conscribendis epistolas*, will be discussed elsewhere. Reprinted with great frequency during the sixteenth century, it was one of Erasmus' most widely read books.
11 See notes 20 and 21 in 'Erasmus and Agricola' above on the force of rhetoric.

PART IV

LIMINALITY – INTO ANOTHER WORLD

Erasmus' leaving the monastery fairly soon after ordination – but we cannot be certain of the dating – must be seen as a profound change for the young Augustinian canon. Thus I have focused first upon the question of Erasmus in the service of the bishop of Cambrai and have posed a number of questions, some still unanswered, in this part.

Liminality is not a term familiar enough to be in the *O.E.D.* or second edition (1985) of the *American Heritage Dictionary*, though it is in *Webster's Third International Dictionary*, where one finds a psychologically-oriented definition and a citation of Lindner on the *limen* (or threshold) of awareness (given below). It is a term recently made popular by anthropologists like Clifford Geertz. But the French analogue *liminaire* – also derived from the Latin *liminaris* (from *limen* or threshold, French *seuil*) – has been in use since the 16th century for that which is placed at the beginning of a book (the *seuil* in the sense also of beginning, or entrance), as with Scarron. In modern French literature the word has signified the beginning, as with Bloy, 'après une série liminaire de petits paysages' (*La Femme pauvre*, I, xvi); or André Maurois, 'lorsque'une journée finale répondra à la journée liminaire' (*Etudes littéraires*, Jules Romains, iv). As the psychologists have employed the term to signify that which is at the threshold, in the sense usually of barely perceptible, anthropologists at times have called attention to that experience which is at the threshold between two states of awareness.

This extended philological digression is to establish the terms *liminal* and *liminality*, which I wish to employ in order to develop the notable progressions of Erasmus from one stage to another, from one *paysage*, one landscape of the mind, to another. For Erasmus had a great capacity to respond to liminality and to exploit the threshold condition and potentialities of certain stages of his life.

Too many Erasmians have viewed Erasmus' entrance into the service of the bishop of Cambrai merely as an escape from the monastery. It may have been that, to be sure; but even if it were, it was not only that, an escape. Service with such a bishop – one at the inner circles of Burgundian politics – functioned in Erasmus' development, I urge, in at least three ways.

First, the service was liminal in the psychological sense suggested by the quotation from Lindner: it did make urgent the appetites and needs which were for Erasmus still smoldering below the limen, or threshold, of awareness. The drive to become a poet and a humanist became stronger, and the need to go to a university indeed became more urgent. (Cf. R.M. Lindner: make urgent the appetites and needs which are smoldering below the limen of awareness.)

Second, the bishop's service itself was *liminaire*: it was a *début* into another world other than the monastic, and it was an abrupt change from a provincial Dutch milieu into a sophisticated and courtly Burgundian one. Further, Erasmus encountered a number of humanists, poets, artists, and musicians at that most cultivated of European courts, and we can perceive the stirrings of that experience in his poetry of this period as well as in his letters and the revised *Antibarbari*.

Third, to return to the modern psychological employment of the term *liminal*, this period of service – perhaps only two years, but more likely three – was a threshold experience in the sense that it was the point at which a stimulus is of sufficient intensity to produce an effect: Erasmus was rapidly becoming the humanist writer that he had yearned to be during the adolescent years in 's-Hertogenbosch and his maturing years at Steyn.

A final point: as much as his stepping into the Burgundian world of the bishop's court (A, below) was one liminal experience, Erasmus' entering upon theological studies at the University of Paris (B, below) would be another.

A. A Bishop's Secretary (1492-1495)*

Even genius needs opportunity, and the chance of becoming a bishop's secretary was such an opportunity. It enabled Erasmus to leave the monastery that had become increasingly frustrating for him, and it plunged him into the milieu of the most splendid court of Europe, thereby providing many personal contacts which served him all his life, introducing him to the finest art and music of his age and, not least, affording him direct experience of the world of politics. To be a bishop's secretary was one thing, but to be this bishop's secretary was something quite special.

We know little about the steps which led to the appointment of Erasmus as secretary to the bishop of Cambrai; but much is known about the bishop himself and about the office of secretary at that time, and from that knowledge we can thus infer something of the nature of that appointment and discuss its importance for Erasmus. About 1492 or 1493 Erasmus came – we do not yet know how – to the attention of Hendrik van Bergen, bishop of Cambrai! Early writings of Erasmus perhaps were shown to the bishop; or the bishop of Utrecht may have recommended this young canon to his fellow-bishop – but we do not know. Usually in Erasmian studies the focus of this event has been placed upon its working to enable Erasmus to leave the monastery at Steyn; but some attention needs to be given as well to the importance and character of this Burgundian bishop, for he was at that time the leading ecclesiastic at the rich and powerful court of Philip at Brussels.[2]

Hendrik van Bergen (1449-1502) was a son of Jan I of Bergen and a member of a family of considerable standing and influence. One brother, Jan II (1452-1532), became a knight of the Golden Fleece in 1481 – that highest of the chivalric orders of which the membership was reserved to royalty and the most privileged of other individuals – and later this Jan was made first cham-

---

* Note: In a compressed form this paper was originally given at the Erasmus conference in Rotterdam (1985) and will appear in that earlier form in the proceedings of the conference.

berlain to Maximilian I in 1485 and to Philip the Handsome in 1493. (These two brothers are pictured together, see *CWE* 1:100.) Another brother, a natural son of the first Jan I of Bergen named Dismas, became master of requests to Margaret of Austria, a very high legal office, leading in 1517 to his becoming a member of the privy council of the future Charles V. Yet another brother Antoon (1455-1532) was a Benedictine abbot, and like Hendrik a patron of Erasmus; and it was apparently at the suggestion of Erasmus that Thomas More visited Antoon in 1517. This family then was clearly one that moved at the highest echelons of power and influence in the Bergundian world, and Erasmus learned much about court life and made a number of acquaintanceships and several friendships which were important in later years: this helps to explain his access to so many nobles and aristocrats. In 1499 Erasmus wrote to Adolph of Burgundy of his own experience at royal courts: 'I know by experience that royal courts contain those who neither hesitate to believe, nor blush to say, that Christ's teaching is no matter that need concern noblemen but should be left to priests and monks' (*CWE* 1, 185).

Hendrik van Bergen had studied at Louvain and Orléans (then a great center for legal studies), and he had received the doctorate of laws before his appointment as canon of Liège in 1473. After becoming abbot of St. Denis-en-Broqueroie near Mons in 1477, he was named Bishop of Cambrai in 1480.[3] Cambrai was then an unusually large diocese comprising about a thousand parishes, covering an area in what is now northern France and southern Belgium – Brussels was in this diocese until well after Erasmus' time. The renowned Pierre d'Ailly (1350-1420) had been a bishop of Cambrai, and he had left the diocese acclaimed for the religious formation of its clergy. But unlike d'Ailly, Erasmus' bishop was a lawyer, not a theologian. In the bull naming Hendrik to the bishopric, Sixtus IV praised his knowledge of letters, the purity of his life, his integrity, and other virtues; in the nature of such a document of nomination, some of this was the conventional rhetoric of praise. Yet he seems to have been an exemplary bishop for his age, and his portrait suggests an aura of piety.

As well as having ecclesiastic responsibilities Hendrik van Bergen was the head of the council of Philip the Good; and in April 1493, while Erasmus was his secretary, Hendrik was named chancellor of the Burgundian Order of the Golden Fleece.[4] The first five Grand Masters of the Order ('La Toison d'Or') were Philip the Good, Charles the Bold, Emperor Maximilian, Philip I of Spain, and Emperor Charles V; and a number of other European monarchs became members of this most prestigious order. A manuscript now in the Bibliothèque Royale, Brussels (an Armorial of 1537) is a magnificent testimonial to the splendor of the Order. For among the numerous monarchs, the English kings Edward IV, Henry VII and Henry VIII were all elected knights of the Order. In 1477 with the marriage of Marie de Bourgondie to the Archduke Maximilian, the Order passed into the House of Hapsburg. Chapters of the Order were held in different places – Valencienne in 1473, Brussels in 1500, Gant in 1559, e.g. – but I do not know where chapters were held in the 1490s, while Erasmus was secretary to Hendrik. As chancellor of the Order of the Golden Fleece, Hendrik would likely have travelled once a year for a chapter; and it is probable that Erasmus would have journeyed with him. For we know that Erasmus accompanied the bishop from one residence to another: from Bergen to Brussels, Mechlin and the country home at Halsteren (near Bergen). Preserved Smith has commented, 'Erasmus must have caught some glimpse of the gorgeous and polished Burgundian court'; but surely it was more than a glimpse. Hendrik's place of importance as the highest ecclesiastic at the court and in the council of Philip the Good commands our attention, for the secretary to such a bishop was expected to handle a varied official – and at times personal – correspondence, and there were likely other duties and functions to fulfill. While Erasmus in his letters tells us that he was very busy, the exact nature of his duties is not known – beyond our assumption that his principal responsibility was for Latin correspondence and perhaps orations. Paul O. Kristeller has reminded us that 'many Italian scholars entered the service of foreign princes or dignitaries, as tutors or secretaries, as librarians, as court poets or court historians. The list is long and distinguished...'[5] Yet, despite Erasmus' onerous duties, occasionally there were opportunities to visit monastic libraries, and at least once in the spring in 1494 at Halsteren there was some leisure to work on the *Antibarbari*, as he wrote Cornelis Gerard.

For the ambitious young, options must be kept open. Erasmus would increasingly have become aware that his credentials fell short of the reach of his ambition; for outside the monastery degrees were necessary in the professional and ecclesiastical world – at least as much as today. Finally, it is to be stressed that the Renaissance secretary – whether to a city or prince or prelate – was an important office, and increasingly it was one held by a humanist. The list of Renaissance secretaries is long and distinguished, and a number of Erasmus' friends were secretaries (like Pieter Gilles) or performed secretarial functions (as did Thomas More). A secretary's office also generated contacts and patronage, and these were for Erasmus perhaps even more important in the long run than the experience of writing letters and performing tasks for others.

That Hendrik van Bergen was a prelate of status and influence is now evident; but his connections with the Burgundian Court need further study.[6] Perhaps some clues are to be found in the extant administrative archives; some quite different evidence to the significant connections between Hendrik's archepiscopal court and the religious houses of the Netherlands, and between his court and the royal court, may yet be found in further studies of the provenance, patronage, and fortunes of such works as the breviaries and books of hours of the period, as well as other manuscripts, books and commissioned art. What can be argued is that we can no longer rest content with simply characterizing Hendrik van

Bergen as an influential prelate, and we must recognized that there were aspects of the life and activities of his court which would have been significant in the development of a young and ambitious cleric who was struggling to find his place in the sun. Not only was Hendrik an important prelate in the Church (who had ambitions for a cardinal's hat) and of importance in the culture of the Low Countries; he seems also to have been a good bishop, and there were what appear to be genuine expressions of universal regret and his death in October 1502. Erasmus composed three Latin epitaphs on the death of his bishop: the one published in a book of Jacob Anthoniszoon, the other two in Erasmus' own *Epigrammata* of 1507 — as well as a Greek epitaph, now lost.[7] To his friend Willem Hermans Erasmus complained in a letter of 27 September 1503 that he had been sent only six florins for his epitaphs: 'So as to keep up in death the character he had in life,' Erasmus added with some irony.

Thus the Erasmus who would more than twenty years later express his regrets that his friend Thomas More's going into the royal service of Henry VIII, in the year 1517, had taken him from good letters,[8] knew whereof he spoke. Yet he would also have understood the challenge of such service, even the allure of power and influence; and perhaps More himself was self-reflexive enough to have made his friend and co-humanist Erasmus at least in part the model for his Hythloday in Book I of the *Utopia* (completed the year before his own official entrance into the royal service). Certainly all of the conventional humanist arguments for and against such service are skillfully put forward in the dialogue between More, Pieter Gillis and Hythloday.[9]

However, at least occasionally Erasmus was able to take advantage of a degree of freedom from his routine duties to visit religious houses. On one occasion he visited a monastery of which the Bishop of Cambrai was a benefactor, the Augustinian priory of Groenendael in the forest of Zonia near Brussels, and he there discovered manuscripts of Augustine, which he took to his cubicle. One of the monks wrote later that 'they were all amazed and amused that a cleric should prefer one of those large codices to other things, and they could not understand what he found in the saint to delight him so.'[10] This early interest in Augustine continued throughout his life and culminated in the fine Augustine edition of 1530.

Another notable event of this period was Erasmus' making the acquaintance of Jacob Batt, who had been schoolteacher at Bergen and who, in attempting to introduce humanistic studies, had been harassed by the other teachers committed to the older ways and texts of scholasticism. Their actions led to Batt's having to resign from teaching, and he became the secretary to the city. Erasmus' own feelings against the 'barbarians' (those who opposed the new humanism and good letters) were stirred up again, and he set about reworking his earlier tract called *Antibarbari*, which he now recast into a dialogue with Batt as the leading speaker.[11] The opening scene was set in a garden, as was conventional in fifteenth-century Italian humanist dialogues; and yet it seems likely that it was also to a considerable extent drawn from life, as Erasmus consistently did in such works. 'In such case,' Allen comments, 'we may suppose that it was in fact the garden of the country house at Halsteren...' In this early work of Erasmus — not the earliest, for that was the *De Contemptu Mundi* — we note as significant the preponderance of laity as participants, a considerable use of classical myth, and elements of the Platonic or open dialogue at the same time that the rhetorical mode is also Ciceronian. More than being simply eclectic, the *Antibarbari* is a work that moves towards a fresh concept of dialogue[12] in a way that anticipates Erasmus' later explorations of the 'resources of kind.'[13]

The *Antibarbari*, though largely unread today except by Erasmian scholars, is valuable for throwing light upon an early stage of Erasmus' thought. It contains much of the values and principles of his more mature work. We can now mark three versions that indicate stages in the development of Erasmus within a relatively short period of time. The first state of work was apparently a speech (strongly influenced by Valla's *Elegantiae*, which, as we have seen, Erasmus studied, used as a model, and worked into an abridgment in the years before joining in the bishop) put into the mouth of his childhood friend Cornelis Gerard; and this is writing which can be dated about 1487-99, when he was about twenty. This early version appears to have been largely an attack on idleness and ignorance as well as a defence of humanism; it is the *De Contemptu Mundi* theme (in part) fused with an early excitement for good letters. The second stage of the work is marked by a change into dialogue form; and at this state Erasmus projected three more books: a refutation of the claims of eloquence, followed by a refutation of that position, and a defence of poetry. Reworked thus about 1494-95, Book I alone is what we now have, and it is a defence of the study of the classics through a dialogue among Erasmus and his friends: William Hermans, also a monk from Steyn; Jacob Batt, the humanist-secretary of Bergen; Willem Conrad, the burgomaster of Bergen; and the doctor Jodocus. They all discuss reasons for the resistance to the new study of the classics and the decline of true learning (the stars, Christianity, the aging of the world, and most of all bad teachers). It is clear, as Margaret Mann Phillips observes, that Erasmus 'is the link which binds these people together': and this early work portrays for us the first of a number of Erasmian circles which he was able to create and inspire in Paris, Louvain, England and Basle.

An attack against the opponents of good letters, Erasmus' little book is also an attempt to embody and show forth the spirit of the humanism he was defending: 'the brilliant beginning, with its insistence of friendship, the humorous backchat and shared enthusiasm for a cultural ideal, the beauty and calm of the surroundings, all lend themselves to the creation of what he had in mind, the actual and living flavour of the classics. It is a picture of civilization...'[14]

In a way, then, the *Antibarbari* is to be seen as the passport which would admit

Erasmus into the circles of thought and letters in Paris and elsewhere – for he showed the work to Robert Gaguin at once when he arrived in Paris in September 1495 – and it is also valuable for us by virtue of the light it throws on the essential consistency of Erasmus' values at the same time that there was a pronounced deepening of thought from 1488 to 1495. 'Consistent does not mean that one should always use the same language, but that one should always have the same objectives,' Erasmus later wrote.

That one of Erasmus' earliest works – which, to be sure, has come down to us in a form modified some years later – should have been recast into a dialogue is notable, for the dialogue was one of the two favorite genres of Quattrocento humanism: with Petrarch especially and continuing to the dialogues of Valla and many others. The mode of dialogue remained dominant with Erasmus throughout his career (a development to be discussed in the chapter on the *Colloquies*). More immediately, Agricola and Hegius (as seen above, Part II) had both written dialogues, and we can mark this early work of Erasmus as superior in the dialogue form to the work of his teacher Hegius. In the 1490s to write a dialogue was in itself to take a stand against scholasticism, with its favorite forms of disputation and *Quodlibets* (*disputationes quodlibetales*, or 'free' as distinguished from disputations with announced topics). The elements noted in the *Antibarbari* – the locus of a garden, the use of classical myth, the preponderance of laity, and the attempt at Platonic discussion – all mark the humanist effort towards the new, if not the innovational, in the Renaissance dialogue, and this effort so anticipates Thomas More's lay-oriented dialogue of 1516 that one wonders indeed if More had read the earlier dialogue of Erasmus.

Erasmus' support of Batt at a time of his troubles with the conservatives in the school at Bergen seems to have helped deepen that acquaintance into a friendship, with Batt becoming one of Erasmus' closest friends for the next decade. In discussing the *Enchiridion* later we shall note that it was while he was working on this book in February 1499 and again in 1501 that Erasmus visited Batt at the castle of Tournehem, where Batt was then living as tutor to the son of Anna van Borssele.[15] Himself a citizen of a village near Bergen, Jacob Batt had studied in the faculty of arts at Paris, and it was he who introduced Erasmus to Anna van Borssele and her circle, and in turn Erasmus who introduced Batt to Willem Hermans and William Blount, Lord Mountjoy. Among friends, all possessions are in common: including friends, as Erasmus wrote in the first, and one of the warmest of his *Adages* (I.i.1). About the same age as Erasmus (having been born about 1466) Batt died early, before 2 July 1502, as we learn from Ep. 170; and for some reason Erasmus suggested in Ep. 172 that it was by poison. Batt gave Erasmus financial help himself, and he was instrumental in securing Anna van Borssele as a patroness. After Batt's early death Erasmus wrote two epitaphs for him.

Anna van Borssele (c. 1471 – 8 December 1518) merits attention, and her figure — rendered by Michiel IJssewyn in a wooden statue now in the Stichting De Schotse Huizen, Veere (see *Contemporaries,* I) — must have commanded respect. She was an heiress in her own right, and her marriages carried her to still higher place in the Burgundian world. The daughter and heiress of Wolfar VI van Borssele and Charlotte de Bourbon, she married first Philip of Burgundy, a son of Anthony of Burgundy ('le grand Batard'). Upon the death of Anna's father the very young couple became lord and lady of Veere, and they had four children, of whom Adolph succeeded his mother. Apparently through the influence of Jacob Batt (by that time tutor of Adolph) Erasmus was invited to the castle of Tournehem at about the time that Anna's husband Philip died on 4 July 1498; she remarried in 1502. The son Adolph (1489 — 7 December 1540) grew up in the castle of Tournehem on the borders of France and Burgundy, where he was educated by his mother and tutored by Jacob Batt. For him Erasmus wrote an *Oratio de virtute* and some prayers (Eps. 93, 145, 181, 497, 1927). Adolph's physician was Reyner Snoy, another friend of Erasmus. In 1515 Adolph was admitted into the Order of The Golden Fleece: a mark of his high birth, to be sure, but also a mark of his having earned a place in the courtly world. Anna van Borssele was not the only widow whom Erasmus knew, but much of what he later wrote concerning Christian widows would seem to have been inspired by this strong woman.

From Brussels most likely, and (we infer) at some date in late 1494, Erasmus finally wrote his old friend Willem Hermans, who had been complaining about Erasmus's silence. The latter part of this letter suggests that late 1494 was a period of disappointment for Erasmus — perhaps even depression[16] — no doubt darkened by the bishop's decision to abandon his proposed trip to Rome, but perhaps also colored by his frustrations in his studies and in his writing. The letter to Hermans speaks of the Muses who were once 'my only love' (echoing his own *Carmen bucolicum*), but this portion of the letter may be at least in part the conventional *topos* or commonplace of the young poet lamenting the passing of time and his failure to achieve recognition as a poet.

In this biographically important letter to Hermans, and in other letters of the years 1493 and 1494, we have as well a sense of Erasmus' widening circle of friends, especially in Epistle 35 from Hermans to Batt: a letter from one friend of Erasmus to another reinforcing that ideal of *Adage* 1, that the friend of one is friend of all — 'anyone whom Erasmus loves, I must inevitably love also.' But for the period from 1490 to 1493 there is a gap in Erasmus' correspondence, the first of several. In this period we would want to know much more about Erasmus' ordination to the priesthood by the bishop of Utrecht in 1492, and about the steps that led to Hendrik's offer of a Latin secretaryship to Erasmus. It has been suggested that Erasmus himself applied for the post, but no evidence is known that suppports this notion; nor can we do more than speculate that perhaps the bishop of Utrecht had suggested Erasmus to the bishop of Cambrai, for the two had other connections. What we do know derives from the prefatory letter from Beatus Rhenanus to Charles V in the prefatory material to the *Opera Omnia* of 1540, where we read that,

> Hendryk van Bergen, bishop of Cambrai, having heard of the fame of Erasmus already ordained, called the young man to himself. For he saw from his elegantly written letters that Erasmus was a person of good character, who possessed some ability in learning and eloquence.

Inasmuch as Erasmus' first published letter to Robert Gaguin was not printed until 1495 — and assuming that Erasmus' early letters to Pieter Winckel, an unnamed nun, Pieter Gerard, Servatius Rogers, Cornelis Gerard, and other intimate letters (which are largely the early personal letters that have come down to us) would not have been shown to the bishop — we must conclude that there were other and perhaps more public and literary letters, perhaps like Epistle 32 to Jacob Canter, which were circulated (or called to the attention of the bishop). It has been previously suggested that perhaps David, bishop of Utrecht had recommended his promising young priest, whom he had ordained recently and who was in the monastery at Steyn, to his colleague the bishop of Cambrai. If this line of interpretation holds water, then the letters of Erasmus must be read with a view to the care with which Erasmus composed those letters and to the probability that after a certain date many of them were written as, or came to be, quasi-public documents. Our interpretation of the letters as biographical evidence must be weighed with this consideration, much as we have now learned to read the *Familiar Letters* of Petrarch![7]

After permission was granted Erasmus to leave for Paris, relations with his patron-bishop became less warm, and there was clearly a cooling-off after Erasmus left the Collège de Montaigu in 1496, after only one year of theological study. But other elements may have been involved, and it must be noted that the master of the Collège, John Standonck (a Fleming), had a number of close connections with the Low Countries: we do not know how Erasmus' departure from the Collège de Montaigu may have been represented to others.

What did Erasmus have to show for years of patient but doubtless frustrating study, and for all his ambitions, when in 1495 he left the Low Countries for Paris?

He had completed one early work, the *De Contemptu Mundi*, in many ways a quite conventional work, yet one that reveals Erasmus' personality and his latent philosophy, and especially his early feelings about the monastic life and religion. I have argued that the work is not a mere exercise, whether literary or religious, but expressive of his own feelings at the time concerning monasticism and the religious vocation. But because it was first printed only some thirty or thirty-five years after composition, when the key chapter XII was added with its open criticism of the abuses of monasticism, one must use the work guardedly for biographical evidence.

Erasmus carried with him an early version of the *Antibarbari*; but it was not yet honed to its final form and polish, and in fact it was not published until 1518. Erasmus had also composed an abridgment of Valla's *Elegantiae*, a remarkable piece of work for a young religious; but both at 's-Hertogenbosch and at Steyn Erasmus seems to have had something of the freedom of studies that was accorded to Thomas Merton at Gethsemane by an equally understanding prior.

By 1495 Erasmus had written a goodly number of letters in which he strove for a distinctive Latin style, modelled on Valla and certain others. But it is a mistake to call them 'mere exercises,' however embarrassing the expression of emotions may be to some twentieth-century readers. Those letters, we can agree with Allen and Huizinga, were sincere effusions, and they express early (perhaps sentimental) friendships which were important to Erasmus precisely because he had not yet lost his feeling about the stigma of illegitimacy and because he craved friendship as a replacement for the family he never really had. To his friend Servatius, Erasmus declared: 'My mind is such that I think nothing can rank higher than friendship in this life, nothing should be desired more ardently, nothing should be treasured more jealously' (Ep. 13). In nothing was Erasmus more consistent than in his capacity for friendship.

Leaving behind him the fatherland in which he had lived his years of growing to manhood – and even Cambrai was close to the border of France with Burgundy – Erasmus was completing one *rite de passage* and embarking upon another. In Paris he would enter into the federation of Dutch students with others from the north, the German Nation![8] To be sure, his feelings about being Dutch were mixed: at times he expressed great pride in his native country, but at other times he was ironically apologetic. We find that mixture still in the twentieth century in such Dutch writers as Huizinga, among others.

Not only was he Dutch, he was illegitimate. It has often been declared that Erasmus felt the stain of illegitimacy most keenly; and it may well be that the opportunity of removing that stain through becoming a priest – which for him as the illegitimate child of a cleric was possible, according to canon law, only by first becoming a member of one of certain religious orders – had been one of the motives for joining the Augustinian canons (a point discussed earlier). It is a probability, but we cannot be certain. Erasmus remained a priest and still canonically bound to his priestly vows. Dispensation from the monastic vows – from communal meals (which increasingly disturbed his delicate digestion), monastic dress, and other aspects of the prescribed religious life – had not laicized Erasmus, canonically speaking, and he remained a faithful priest all of his life.

In 1495 he was an aspiring poet, known as yet to only a small circle of friends. We are all poets until we are 25 – so T.S. Eliot has pronounced – and it is clear that Erasmus thought himself a poet; we must take seriously his early poems, although they have been too much neglected. At the heart of a portrait of Erasmus at 26 or 28 must be his growing humanism; he was becoming increasingly aware of the world of classical scholarship in Italy and of the exciting potential of *Philosophia Christi* (philosophy of Christ, discussed in Part II). Awakened to Greek by Hegius and inspired by the example of Agricola while still a schoolboy (ibid.), he clearly studied much on his own, and that tells us the force of his motivation. His music-teacher Obrecht, for one, would have brought back some news of Italian developments from Ferrara, and there was the double shock of the death of Politian and Pico in 1494: Pico at 31, and Politian at 40. Likely those events mattered more to the young Erasmus than the news of Columbus' discovery of the New World. Clearly, the all-important discovery for Erasmus was his coming upon Valla at an early age, and through Valla Erasmus became passionately devoted to the end of achieving a pure and elegant Latin – he would have applauded Whitehead's dictum that style is the ultimate morality of mind[18] – and he never ceased striving to understand the classics that he was reading with ever greater philological learning and enjoyment.[20]

Erasmus was an intellectual. Although devoted to his friends, he was passionately interested in ideas and committed all his life to the study of good letters, which for him had always a moral dimension. Erasmus was very much an intellectual of his age, perhaps the intellectual *par excellence*. But he was no ivory-towered academic, for his service with the bishop of Cambrai had plunged him into the demands and experiences of a huge diocese and introduced him to the culture and politics of the most splendid court of Europe. It would not have been surprising if Erasmus had remained in the bishop's service and sought ecclesiastical advancement with the perquisites and privileges that came with it. But being Erasmus he did not. Instead he was more than ever determined to go to university and to earn a theology, for that was (he thought) the union-card that he needed and wanted.

And so to Paris.

---

1 On the date of Erasmus' entree into the bishop's service, and whether it lasted more than one year: Allen asks whether Erasmus spent not more than one year with the bishop, but we must leave open the possibility, at least, that his service might have been as long as three years – documentary evidence is lacking at both *termini*, and later references are contradictory. About two years, given such lack of firm evidence, seems to be a reasonable estimate; i.e., from late 1492 or early 1493 to mid-1495. Erasmus stayed with the bishop until departing for Paris, where we know of his arrival by September 1495. See Allen's notes to Ep. 33, which he dates questioningly 1493, after Erasmus' departure to join the bishop of Cambrai, and to Ep. 43, which he dates questioningly September 1495, after Erasmus' arrival in Paris: *OE*, I, 128, 145, 587-590.
2 For fuller information on Hendrik himself and on his father and brothers, see *Contemporaries of Erasmus* (CWE, 1986), I, 132 ff. Moreau, *Histoire de l'Eglise*, IV, 68 ff., provides detail on the church history of the period.
3 On the jurisdiction of the metropolitan see of Cambrai, see Moreau, *Histoire*, IV, passim.

4   For a brief introduction to this order, see Smith, *Erasmus*, p. 19.
5   P.O. Kristeller, 'The European Diffusion of Italian Humanism,' rptd. in *Renaissance Thought II: Papers on Humanism and the Arts* (New York: Harper Torchbooks, 1965), p. 74.
   As yet the Renaissance secretary lacks his definitive historian, nor is there anything like a complete roster of humanists who served as secretaries. But one may cite a recent study on the manual of one Renaissance secretary as a point of beginning: Beningno Sánchez-Eppler, 'The Pen That Wills the Voice that Wills: Secretaries and Letter-Writing in Antonio de Torquemada's *Manual de Escribientes*,' *Neophilologus* 70 (1986) 528-38; and also A. Gerlo on the genre of letters in R.R. Bolgar, ed., *Classical Influences on European Culture, A.D. 500-1500* (Cambridge: Cambridge U.P., 1971).
   Rhetoric too needs special emphasis, and Cantimori writes quite admirably, 'we shall include in this word a faith sincere, though still somewhat ingenuous and crude, in virtue, in passion, in dignity – ideals which are open to many different interpretations – in short, aesthetico-moral theology. The fact that public opinion and the able leaders of the Humanist and Renaissance period attached so much importance to elegance in speech, to the use of pure Latin and the Latinized periods of Italian, to a general but exalted knowledge of maxims, of examples of perfect princes and perfect republics, to the patriotic and religious ideal of the return to Roman civilization – all elements of "rhetoric" – shows us the political importance of such "rhetoric."' Delio Cantimori, 'Rhetoric and Politics in Italian Humanism,' *JWCI* 1 (1938) 86.
6   The contexts for further study of humanism and the socio-political milieu have been well laid out by J. IJsewijn, in 'The Coming of Humanism to the Low Countries,' *Itinerarium Italicum* ... *P.O. Kristeller*, ed. H.O. Oberman & T.A. Brady, Jr., Studies in Medieval and Reformation Thought, XIV (Leiden: Brill, 1975), 193-301. A recent study in another direction is that of René Hoyoux, 'L'organisation musicale à la Cour des ducs de Bourgogne,' dans: Jean-Marie Cauchies, ed., *Publication du Centre Européen d'Etudes bourguignonnes*, XIVe-XVe s. no. 25-1985 – Actes des Recontres de Fribourg 1984 (Bâle, 1985).
7   The four epitaphs are to be found in Reedijk, *Poems*, 64-6. Erasmus received a remuneration of only six livres 'pour avoir fait aulcuns epitaphes et un aulmonne,' as the accounts specify (*Contemporaries*, I, 133).
8   The letter to Thomas More is dated April 1518 from Louvain (Ep. 829) and remarks that while More would serve under an excellent king, 'but certainly you are lost to literature, and to us' (*CWE* V, 401).
9   See my discussion of this dialogue in ch. iv of *The Achievement of Thomas More*.
10 Q. from Bainton, *Erasmus of Christendom*, 31; cf. Allen *OE* I, 590, who notes that this was a monastery of which the bishop of Cambrai was a benefactor, to which should be added consideration of Erasmus' being an Augustinian canon.
11 See the Introduction by Craig R. Thompson to vol. 23 of the Works (*CWE* 23, 1978). *De Contemptu Mundi* 'concerning the contempt of the world' was a medieval work said to have been written by Bernard, which generated a long tradition of poems and other writings expressing a turning away from the world and towards a love of 'Jerusalem the Golden' (to borrow the title of a 19th-c. Anglican translation of a section of the original). For, largely monastic in its origins, the *de contemptu mundi* theme or *topos* was conventional, and the work of that title by Innocent III had great influence from the 13th c. into the Renaissance period.
   K.A. Meissinger has discussed the *Antibarbari* as a clue to Erasmus' intellectual development: see 'Erasmus entdeckt seine Situation: Gedanken über die *Antibarbari*,' *ARG* XXXVII (1940), 188-198.
12 There was a fresh interest in the dialogue from the time of Petrarch, and new concepts of dialogue were generated: see David Marsh, *The Quattrocento Dialogue – Classical Tradition and Humanist Innovation* (Cambridge, Mass.: Harvard Univ. Press, 1980).
13 'Kind' is an analogue for genre, and in her posthumous book of this title, Rosalie Colie brilliantly argues for the resources of the Renaissance in conceptualizing and achieving new or modified genres – *The Resources of Kind* (Berkeley: Univ. California Press, 1973).
14 M.M. Phillips, Introductory note to the *Antibarbarians*, in CWE 23, pp. 8, 14.
15 On Anna van Borssele, see *Contemporaries*, I, 173–4, and on Batt, ibid., 100-01.
16 From Ep. 37 we learn of Erasmus' seeking a retreat in the country from an outbreak of the plague during this period; at this time it was found at the bishop's country home at Halsteren, and

he spent what leisure he had in revising his *Antibarbari*. Ep. 39 (late in 1494, it would appear) suggests a period of depression to some scholars (as commented on by the Toronto editors, *CWE* 1, 75). But Erasmus' allusion to being 'deprived of any opportunity to study at all' seems to point, rather, as much to being busy as to being depressed.

17 On Renaissance letters very generally, see *Achievement*, 25-38; and for an introduction to the importance of Erasmus' correspondence for the historian, see W.K. Ferguson, introduction of *CWE* 1. I have briefly discussed the extent to which Petrarca's celebrated letter on the Ascent of Mont Ventoux (*Fam.* IV. 1) is a 'carefully designed piece of art' in *Intertextuality and Ren. Texts*, 47-50; and on this point see further Hans Baron, *From Petrarch to Leonardo Bruni* (Chicago: Univ. of Chicago Press, 1968), p. 18, and G. Billanovich, *Petrarca Litterato*, vol. I (Rome, 1947), p. 195.

We might further note that many of Erasmus' letters are in effect requests for patronage or money, and this troubles some readers. But in an age of foundations and government grants, who are we of the 20th century to sneer at the conventional letters of his age that call for aid to study and write?

18 Students in medieval and Renaissance universities were divided into loose student organizations or nations (usually four in each university), according to their country or region of origin. See further Pearl Kibre, *The Nations in the Mediaeval Universities* (Cambridge, Mass.: Mediaeval Academy of America, 1948).

19 On 'the ultimate morality of mind,' see A.N. Whitehead, *The Aims of Education* (1929).

20 T.S. Eliot might well have written Erasmus in mind, in asserting that 'the end of scholarship is understanding, and the end of understanding is enjoyment, which is gusto disciplined by taste,' (I quote from memory, from Eliot's 1942 W.P. Ker Memorial Lecture).

B. Erasmus' Theological Studies at Paris

Paris, mother of the sciences, like another Cariath Sopher, city of letters, shines clear; where, as it were in wisdom's special workshop ... those prudent in mystical eloquence ... fit and decorate the spouse of Christ with priceless jewels.

GREGORY IX, *Parens scientiarum*[1]

... constant garrison [the Faculty of Theology in 1497] in the city of God, strong in the faith and in piety, a mirror of truth, a hammer and avenger against falsehood and false teachers.

Roberti Gaguini epistolae et orationes

Before viewing the Faculty of Theology at Paris through the eyes of an enthusiastic humanist like Erasmus, we would do better to attempt an understanding of its role and achievement as it was perceived in Paris — which the first two epigraphs suggest — and thus be able to measure his later judgment of that Faculty against a reasonably objective sense of the Faculty's traditions and achievements around 1495 to 1500.

Erasmus and the Faculty of Theology before 1500

In the extant correspondence of Erasmus there is no specific discussion of the Theology Faculty before 1500. We may not generalize from such negative evidence, however, and in fact we can work from the implications and allusions in a number of contemporary letters to individuals in order to establish many connections and attitudes. The long letter to Robert Gaguin of Sept/Oct 1495 (Ep. 45) is striking in that it says nothing of scholastic theology at the University of Paris; and there are others that in like manner are written to university professors or deans but speak rather of humanistic interests. This does not necessarily indicate that Erasmus shared no other interests with these individuals; rather, that he is putting his best foot forward, and the letter to Gaguin celebrates both Gaguin and himself as humanists in a public letter. But a number of letters do call attention to Erasmus' purpose in being at Paris; thus, to Nicolas Werner (Ep. 48, Sept 1496) he reiterates his intention to seek the doctorate in theology; and to Hendrik van Bergen (Ep. 51 of Jan 1497) he speaks of being occupied with studies in theology. Yet to Jan Mombaer, another Augustinian canon of the Windesheim congregation near Zwolle, Erasmus writes a letter (Ep. 52, Feb 1497) that is full of humanistic allusion; and to Thomas Grey (in Ep. 64, Aug 1497) he speaks ironically of Scotism and the 'holy schrine of theology' and then, in a direct mode, of a 'few quasi-theologians of our own day' (*CWE* 1: 138/97-8). If tempted to draw a line at this point, after which the young Dutch student in theology is presented as becoming disillusioned, the reader finds Ep. 73 to Mombaer (April [1498?]) speaking of an enterprise (the reform of the abbey of Livrey, apparently) which 'pleases me inexpressibly' (*CWE* 1: 150/30-1).[2]

Then in Ep. 75 (c. April 1498) to Arnoldus Bostius – a Carmelite from Ghent who was a friend of Gaguin and other literary men to whom he was a source of encouragement (*CWE* 1: 109) – Erasmus wrote:

> I had previously made up my mind to withdraw to Italy this year, and to study theology for a few months at Bologna, taking my degree there, and to visit Rome in the jubilee year [1500]; after which I would return to my people and make my life among you. (*CWE* 1: 151/15-8)

On the face of it this letter indicates that Erasmus had decided to abandon his studies at Paris (and there is no evidence that he had consulted either the bishop of Utrecht or the bishop of Cambrai, or his prior).[3] Equally, the Rotterdammer is still firm in a religious – but not a monastic – vocation:

> I only ask to be given leisure to live a life entirely devoted to God alone, in lamentation for the sins of my rash youth, absorption in holy writ, and either reading or writing something continually. (*CWE* 1: 151/7-10)

'Sins of my rash youth' may sound lurid to a modern reader, but to a religious at that time such indiscreet or even inconsiderate sins[4] might be of a kind rather like the stolen fruit of Augustine's youth (in the *Confessions* II, vi). The working of 'reading or writing something' (*aliquid aut legere aut scribere*) calls to mind the words of Bede in the Preface to his *Ecclesiastical History* — that he always thought it fitting to learn or to teach or to write (*semper aut discere aut docere aut scribere dulce habui*) — but our Augustinian canon does not include teaching in his dream of the ideal religious life.

The Faculty of Theology at Paris c. 1495

At Paris there had been since the mid-thirteenth century a college for secular theologians [that is, clerics who were not members of the regular orders]: this college was the famous Sorbonne, founded *circa* 1257 and named after Robert de Sorbon (1201-1274), chaplain of St. Louis.[5] From such beginnings and through the steadily increasing role of the friars — Dominicans and Franciscans (who sent their most promising clerics to the universities in increasing numbers during the later decades of the thirteenth century[6]) — in the teaching of Scripture and theology, grew the Faculty of Theology at Paris, with which the name of the Sorbonne soon became synonymous.[7] To the extent that there was a 'unity impressed upon medieval learning by the medieval university' (as John E. Murdoch, with some excess of emphasis, had put it[8]) — in part because all who went to advanced studies in law, theology and medicine had received much the same experience in the faculty of arts — the Faculty of Theology at Paris provided leadership for the unification of theology in the early and high middle ages; but after Ockham (c. 1290-1349/40) generalizations about a putative unity in philosophy and theology manifestly no longer hold.[9] There were other faculties of theology in other Western European universities, to be sure; but for three centuries Paris was the dominant center for theology, and at the end of the fifteenth century students still came to Paris from all over Western Europe because of that aura of greatness. The founding of the University of Louvain in 1425 created a new institution for students from the Low Countries, but it did not seriously challenge the University of Paris — especially not in theology — until the turn of the century.

In the theoretical scheme of things, theology was regarded by Aquinas as the highest of the sciences, whose needs were served by the other sciences, and, more popularly, theology was called 'the Queen of the Sciences.'[10] Thus Erasmus called theology 'queen of all the sciences' (*CWE* 2:94) in the Preface to his edition of Valla's *Annotationes* in 1504, and then cunningly went on to argue for the cause of grammar.

Teaching

Throughout the whole period from the thirteenth to the fifteenth centuries, university teaching in theology centred upon the Bible, works of the Church Fathers, *The Book of Sentences* of Peter Lombard (c. 1095-1160), several compilations from the work of Thomas Aquinas, and certain other medieval works. It had long been said that medieval theology subordinated, or even ignored, study of the Bible; but (building upon the modern scholarship of Denifle and others) Powicke and Emden have corrected that view in their commentary in Rashdall's *Medieval Universities*:

> The amount of time which the students were expected to give to attendance on Biblical lectures demanded from the *cursor* and *biblicus*, and the vast commentaries of the theological master go to show [that the Bible was the basis of teaching in theology] ... (494-5)

Yet one must insist that the question is not simply whether late scholastic theologians studied the Bible and lectured upon it, but also *how* they studied the Bible. However, admirable the *Sentences* were as extracts, they could not substitute for the full text of the Bible; and the humanists consistently called for a return to the sources (*ad fontes*) and for reading the Scriptures in context![1]

Length of course in theology

After the usual three and one-half years of study in arts, there was almost always a trial regency (often in grammar) of a year and a half — the whole five-year sequence was called the *quinquennium*. By the end of the quinquennium the student was generally old enough to satisfy the statutory requirement that a master be at least twenty-one; but dispensations from this rule were common enough![2]

After receiving the M.A. as described, the student faced a further study of at least twelve and as long as fifteen years of additional study, teaching, disputations and examinations, and required residence in one of the theological colleges (of which the Sorbonne and the Collège de Navarre were two secular colleges — the others being houses of the regulars, chiefly Dominicans and Franciscans).

In the early thirteenth century some limiting of the length of study by means of the number of bursarships may be seen, and there is evidence that secular masters of theology were paid fees![3] Reasons for restrictions are not altogether clear; in 1452 new statutes reduced the length of the complete course, which was approximately as follows (with exceptions, as for mature students):

A. About five years of study to qualify for 'publicly giving private lectures';

B. About three years as bachelor;[14]
C. Eight years of theological study.

Thus, the age of thirty-five was the minimum age for receiving the doctorate.[15]

For four years, Rashdall accounts (474) the theological student attended lectures on the Bible and for two on the *Sentences* of Peter Lombard:

> At the end of his first six years of study, provided he had attained the age of twenty-six or twenty-seven, the student might appear before the faculty with his certificates (*cedulae* or *schedulae*) of due attendance on the prescribed lectures and supplicate for his first course (*pro primo cursu*). He was then examined by four doctors, and, if passed, would be formally admitted.[16]

Farge presents a somewhat different scheme; but the general outlines of the program are much the same, and conclusions therefore much alike. It was a long preparation, as Farge writes, and it was 'clearly a marathon test of intellectual acumen and professional skill.' But it was more.

> Its length, its nature, its disciplinary aspects, and other characteristics which we shall examine made it also into a kind of psychological conditioning and a socialization process which formed not only the mind but the whole person of the candidate.[17]

When we reflect upon the disciplinary nature of the process and upon the scholastic rigor of the discipline, it becomes easier to understand Erasmus' rebellion at the Collège de Montaigu. For not only was the living of a harshly spartan nature, but the academic program was doubly uncongenial to Erasmus. It is clear that it was alien to his growing humanistic interests, but it was also alien to the values of the Brethren of the Common Life and even those of the Augustinian community. For it was rare for one of the Brethren to be sent to the university, and it was not very common for an Augustinian canon. One has only to read the *Imitatio Christi* to realize how hostile scholasticism was to that mode of thinking and spirituality: 'I would rather practice compassion than be able to define it' − such an attitude would not go far in the halls of the Sorbonne.

Method of Instruction

As in the university at large (chapter 10), the following were in general practice: the lecture by the master and the disputations (of several kinds). In theology, Saturday was a customary day for the public lectures and disputations (held at the Sorbonne), and both of these were held in large classrooms or lecture-rooms which – like the library – were open to outsiders. Some of the disputations and quodlibets were attended by large numbers, and many of these were circulated in manuscript or printed form. Thus, Thomas More cites the disputations of Adrian VI in his Correspondence![18]

Some Contemporaries of Erasmus

It may be heuristic to compare Erasmus with some of his contemporaries who were teaching and studying theology at Paris, though for studies in greater depth I defer to James K. Farge's bio-bibliographical studies in *Biographical Register of Paris Doctors of Theology* 1500-1536 (1980) and his monograph study of the Faculty of Theology in his *Orthodoxy and Reform in France* (1983)![19] The first of these volumes presents 'the concrete reality' of 474 individual lives and careers; the second, a collective picture, a prosopography, of the Faculty of the old Sorbonne during the first decades of the sixteenth century.

How good were the scholastic doctors of theology? In 1525 a French lawyer described the Faculty at Paris as famous around the world;[20] and a modern scholar asks, How could it fail to believe in its competence, given its role?[21] The course of study was rigorous, as we have seen, and it was also disciplinary and confirmatory.

Many of those who received the doctorate – perhaps two out of five[22] – apparently left Paris for other posts and benefices; another quarter were relatively inactive – we must remember nearly half of the doctors were members of about ten religious orders, which might well have other duties in mind (and clerics were bound by vows of obedience). Thus we learn that in a period of three decades from 1500 to 1536, there were only seven Augustinian Canons who received the doctorate; there was never more than one a year.

The professional activity of the Paris doctorates in theology can be questioned, for only 101 theologians – 20% of the 474 – published at least one title (significantly fewer of these among the religious orders), and twelve authors were most prolific, publishing 271 titles or half of all the books – and of these, only one was an Augustinian Canon, who managed to publish three titles. Clearly, the track record of the Augustinian Canons at Paris would not have appealed to or attracted Erasmus, who in Ep. 75, as we have seen earlier in this chapter, expressed his resolve to write something.

If we judge from publication – and it is only one measure of scholarly activity (*pace* the quantifying measurements of many contemporary deans) – this form of activity among Paris doctors of theology was concentrated among the Dominicans (whose members produced 71% of the publications tabulated by Farge), and it was marked by affiliations with seven of the twenty-four colleges, with the Collège de Sorbonne accounting for 54.4% of the total number of titles.[23] By far the bulk of the published works were theological or devotional. Erasmus' community, the Augustinian Canons, was clearly not marked by its publications, which is not surprising: for, owing so much to the *Devotio Moderna* (see part II A), the Windesheim Congregation did not greatly value scholarly learning – and certainly not for its own sake – and it was not supportive of advanced studies and publications as the Dominicans were. In 1495-96 Erasmus could not have failed to be struck by this difference, though of course the data of Farge would not have been available to him, or anyone.

Two or three – at most, a small handful of – names dominate: Noel Béda, John Mair (or Major), Jacques Almain, Josse Clichtove, Guillaume Petit, and Nicolas le Clerc. 'After Noël Béda, Nicolas le Clerc was the most active doctor of theology on the faculty during the first half of the sixteenth century,' Farge writes;[24] and while we can signal Béda as an implacable foe of Erasmus in the years to come, we must recognize Le Clerc as a generous friend of humanists who 'opposed the attempts of the Faculty of Theology and the Parlement of Paris to move against Lefèvre d'Étaples and Erasmus.'[25]

Also a mature student like Erasmus, John Mair/Major (1467-1550) began his studies at Paris in 1491 or 1492 and received his M.A. in 1494. Among his teachers and mentors were Jan Standonck and Noel Béda, and possibly Thomas Bricot, who is to be seen as the leading figure in philosophical studies at Paris during the 1490s and the publication of whose work in 1495 is likely to have been read, doubtless most unfavorably, by Erasmus that year. Mair was a student of theology during the 1490s and received his licentiate and doctorate in 1506. While studying theology, Farge has noted, 'Mair also taught logic at the Collège de Montaigu.'[26] Although their paths must have crossed, Erasmus' led in one direction and Mair's in another: to extraordinarily popular teaching and prolific writing in logic. Erasmus was hostile to the formal logic vigorously taught and espoused by Mair, and Mair himself later wrote (c. 1528) that 'theologians had too long dealt with merely philosophical matters matters rather than with real theological concerns'[27] Yet Mair strongly influenced such diverse thinkers as Buchanan (and through him John Knox), Francisco da Vitoria (and through him Domingo da Soto), and Francesco Suárez (and through him Descartes).[28]

Noël Béda (c. 1470-1537)[29] was an inveterate critic of Erasmus for more than thirty years, and he wrote against Lefèvre and Clichtove as well. Béda almost certainly studied arts at the Collège de Montaigu and during the last decade of the century taught there: Erasmus doubtless knew Béda at Montaigu. At least as early as 1495 Béda was a member of the reform-minded group that formed around Standonck, and this group counterbalanced the humanist circle of Gaguin (ch. 13). Béda's zealous pursuit of orthodoxy at all cost was a part of his great activity – according to Farge he was an 'extremely active man' – and he was 'the best known doctor of theology at Paris of the period 1500-1536.[30]

Conclusion

Out of the intense atmosphere of the Faculty of Theology at Paris during the 1490s emerged many orthodox theologians, formed by that rigorous scholastic discipline to which Erasmus had to submit during the year 1495-96 and for some time afterwards; and they obviously pursued that kind of theology actively and in the main unquestioningly. Yet there were those who sought a middle position between scholasticism and humanism: like Nicolas le Clerc, who ironically experienced both imprisonment by the archbishop of Paris in 1534 and a return to authority as Dean of the faculty of Theology – in part simply by virtue of outliving his three previous deans. And there were a few like Guillaume Petit (c. 1470-1536): a Dominican who became confessor and librarian to Francis I, dispensed sums of money to humanists, and with Budé and Cop urged Francis to launch the trilingual college at Paris. There were friends of humanism at Court as well as its enemies among the Paris Faculty of Theology.

Measured against his Paris contemporaries in theology, Erasmus has to be seen more as moderate and flexible, yet significantly more interested in tradition, than those contemporaries.[31]

---

1   Gregory's allusion to Cariath Sopher as a city of letters was not then in the early 13th c. so obscure for clerics who read their Bibles, but it was a learned allusion; and for us today that allusion sustains a gently ironic reading. The reference is to a nearly-forgotten Canaanite royal city in S. Judaea, and the old name of Kariath Soper or city of the scribe later became Debir. But in Josua 15:15 and Judges 1:11 we find Cariath Sopher described as *civitas Litterarum*: city of letters.
   This medieval Bull of Gregory speaks of the city and the university as though they were one, and it speaks during the first century of the university; the reputation of the university, built upon the earlier achievement of the cathedral schools, spread rapidly. On Gregory (who studied at Paris), see *LexThK*, IV, 1186-7.
2   We may well echo the suggestion that Erasmus was attracted to Mombaer – who had just arrived in Paris in September 1496 to lead the reform of the monastery of St Severinus at Château-Landon (near Fontainebleau) – and that Mombaer was for Erasmus a model of the canon regular of St Augustine at a time when Erasmus was having such difficulty in accepting his vocation as an Augustinian canon, in conventional terms or modes. Yet such letters as Ep. 52 also indicates that Erasmus would not turn away from his humanistic studies, even in writing one such as Mombaer. To stress his devotional side, it may be added that Mombaer's widely read *Rosetum* appeared in 1494. (Mombaer also Mauburnus)
3   Erasmus continued to hope that he would be able to continue his studies in Italy: see Epp. 78, 82, 92, 95, 118, 124 and 139.
4   Erasmus had written *peccata aetatis inconsultae: inconsultae* = indiscreet or inconsiderate. One cannot read too heavy a moral indictment in this phrase.
5   But it must be understood that after the thirteenth century the Sorbonne was only one of about forty colleges, that it was not even the largest theological college (and indeed 'only about 20% of the graduate doctors of theology from 1500 to 1536 had any connection at all with the Sorbonne' [thus Farge, p. 4]); what it was, Samaran and others have tried to distinguish, was an endowed college for certain doctoral candidates, and the place where many theological lectures and disputations were held. But to the Faculty of Theology were reserved such functions as the granting of degrees, the administering of examinations, or deliberation on matters of faith – even though these activities may often have taken place within the Sorbonne *qua* building. For a fine emphasis on this distinction

(and much else concerning the doctors of theology) I am indebted to James K. Farge, *Orthodoxy and Reform in Early Reformation France* (Leiden: Brill, 1985).
6   Cf. Rashdall, *Universities*, I, 244 ff., and Penn R. Szittya, *The Antifraternal Tradition in Medieval Literature* (Princeton: Princeton University Press, 1986).
7   P. Glorieux, 'Robert de Sorbon,' in *NCE*; and *Les Origines du Collège de Sorbonne* (Notre Dame, Ind.: University of Notre Dame Press, 1959).
8   John E. Murdoch, 'From Social into Intellectual Factors: An Aspect of the Unitary Character of Late Medieval Learning,' in *The Cultural Context of Medieval Learning*, ed. J. E. Murdoch and Edith Dudley Sylla (Dordrecht, Holland: Reidel, 1973), p. 272.

I demur from Murdoch's generalization because it ignores the force of monastic elements in medieval learning, on which see Jean LeClercq, *Desire for Learning* – a force which had its impact upon many monks before their entrance into the university – as was the case with Erasmus.
9   It can now be seen as ironic that it was in his Commentaries upon that most traditional book, Lombard's *Sentences* (composed c. 1318 to 1324, but then rewritten), that William of Ockham was already challenging theological, as well as philosophical orthodoxy. See L. Baudry, *Guillaume d'Occam* (Paris: 1950); P. Vignaux, 'Occam (Originalité philosophique et théologique),' *DTC* XIV, col. 882; and *LexThK*, X, 1142-5.

But commentaries on Lombard's *Sentences* continued to be written well into the sixteenth century, one must note; a conspicuous example is the commentary of Eck: *In Primum Librum Sententiarum Annotatiunculae D. Iohanne Eckio Praelectore* – probably given in the late summer of 1542 at Ingolstadt: cf. ed. by Walter L. Moore, Jr. (Leiden: E. J. Brill, 1976). On Peter of Lombard, see *LexThK*, VIII, 367-69.
10   Allen I, 408-12. On the history and discipline of theology in the Middle Ages, see the brief discussion and useful bibliography in *LexThK*, X, 73-6.

Cf. Quid tibi grammatica studioso parta labore? / Quid confert logica, quae certat laudis amore? / Quid fert rhetorica vernante superba decore? ...) Q. from B. Hauréau, *Histoire de la philosophie scholastique* (Paris, 1872), I, 506.
11   It is for this reason that the lectures of John Colet upon 1 Corinthians were so revolutionary: they insisted upon a sense of context. It is precisely the dependence upon 'vast commentaries that humanistic theology inveighed against.'
12   Rashdall's account (474) follows the statutes which dated from the 14th c., whereas Farge's (12 ff.) follows the registers, which more nearly reflect the practices.
13   Rashdall, *Medieval Universities*, I, 471, and Gaines Post, *Speculum*, VII (1932), 197-8.

It is not clear whether Erasmus' dependence upon money earned by tutoring is related altogether to lack of support from the bishop of Cambrai or to his failure to receive bursarships – or whether support may have been withdrawn because he was not (as the modern jargon would phrase it) demonstrating satisfactory progress towards his degree.
14   The suggestion has been made that the Jesuit requirement of a three-year period of teaching before going on the final period leading to ordination is a continuation of this triennium required by the theology course in 15th-c. Paris.
15   Rashdall, *Med. Universities*, 472.
16   Ibid., pp. 474-9, 490-6.
17   Farge, *Orthodoxy*, 16.
18   *The Correspondence of Thomas More*, ed. E. F. Rogers (Princeton: Princeton University Press, 1947), and *Selected Letters* (New Haven: Yale Univ. Press, 1967), pp. 26-7.
19   Cited as *Paris Doctors of Theology* and *Orthodoxy and Reform*. It seems churlish to call attention to the fact that necessarily some Paris doctors of theology during Erasmus' early years of association with the Faculty of Paris fall through the crack between the *Contemporaries of Erasmus* (CWE) and Farge's *Paris Doctors*.
20   Q. Bocard: Farge, p. 1.
21   De la Tour, Farge, ibid. The system of cooptation contributed to making the professional faculty very much a closed society.
22   Farge, p. 34.
23   Ibid., 104.
24   Ibid., p. 249.

25 Ibid., p. 369.
26 Ibid., p. 305.
27 Ong, *Ramus*, p. 144.
28 Farge, *Paris Doctors of Theology* 307, citing E. Gilson, and J. Durkan, 'John Major – After 400 Years,' *Innes Review* 1 (1950) 135 ff.
29 Although Erasmus thought Béda was from Picardy, Farge wrote that 'he was probably born about 1470 at Mont St.-Michel' (*Paris Doctors*, p. 30 and *BR* I, 116). He received the license and doctorate in 1508, having succeeded Standonck as principal of Montaigu in 1504 – but that part of his career, and his attacks on Erasmus, must remain for treatment later.
30 Farge, p. 31.
31 Citing the adage 'Ne Bos Quidem Pereat' I have sketched that aspect of Erasmus in 'The Place of Erasmus Today' (See Part I above).

PART V

TRANSLATIO STUDII AND THE *STUDIA HUMANITATIS**

In the essay which constitutes this part, I have identified the concept of *translatio studii* — that is, the carrying of studies (culture, if you will) from one centre to another — and I have endeavoured to describe the significance of Erasmus' first trip to England in 1499 in the light of this concept.

There is a deeper purpose as well. The *studia humanitatis* is not an achieved programme which once conceived hardens into dogma and curricula: the term *translatio* calls our attention to the process. One contemporary example can serve and must suffice; I quote from R. P. Blackmur's adaptation of Catullus' poem 'Phasellus Ille':

> I do not need the bluster and the wail
> in this small boat, of perilous high seas
> nor the blown salt smarting in my teeth;
> if the tide lift and weigh me in his scale
> I know, and feel in me the knowledge freeze,
> how smooth the utter sea is, underneath.

Frozen knowledge (to follow the commentary of Denis Donoghue in his fine introduction to the *Poems of R. P. Blackmur*/Princeton Univ. Press, 1977) enacts a fear in us, for it is 'knowledge that has lost its bearing and its nerve before it has taken possession of its experience'. The process — of knowing, of thinking — is living: for it must be. And like the sea in Catullus and Blackmur, the classical tradition carries us.

We owe to Ernst Robert Curtius the concept of the long road that leads from Rome to the modern world, together with the realization that it is indeed a neglected road in places, and at some points, to our loss, the road is crumbling![1] The title is intended to provide a *point d'appui*, a means of approaching the work of Erasmus as a whole; that is, to focus on the role of the classics in his educational program, and, in turn, to consider the central place and vitality of that program in his concept of Christian humanism, and then, finally, to provide a way of evaluating his contribution to the development of European humanism. For we need to keep in mind Erasmian humanism as a major stage in the long road from Rome to the modern world. But all of this would be too much for a single essay, and thus I shall try to provide focus first of all by talking about Erasmus

---

* Reprinted from *Classical and Modern Literature* vol. 7 (1987) ... a special number on Erasmus. Reprinted by permission of CML, Inc.

in England (a very large topic in itself), and within that field of inquiry to examine the concept of *translatio studii* itself as a means for understanding Erasmus' work in England and his contribution to Tudor and later humanism.

Translatio studii is a term familiar to most medievalists through the exposition of Étienne Gilson in 'L'humanisme médiéval'.[2] From this point of view of medievalists there was a continuum in the movement of studies which began with the first transfer from Greece to Rome, and was (with differences, of course) repeated in the later transfer from Rome to Paris during the time of Charlemagne. During the twelfth century philosophers and theologians in Paris saw much of their work as operating within this continuum. I have summarized this concept rather quickly, obviously, for what I have summarily called the continuum is far more complex than that: in this bird's-eye view the revival of letters in the fourth century in provincial centers like Bordeaux is skipped, and justice is not done to the Carolingian Revival.[3] One might indeed ask when the transfer of studies from Greece to Rome was completed: for did it not continue at least through the age of Augustine, to be resumed — after interruptions and diversions — in the fourteenth century in fuller flood? And, in a similar vein, one must observe that the transfer from Rome to Paris was not simply the work of Alcuin and a few confrères during one or two generations; for the immense labors of the Benedictines and some other religious communities had already begun and would continue outside of Paris, but then be transplanted to Paris *per diversa*, in different ways and at different times. And yet, this large-scale overlay has validity, I think: the main transferal during the Middle Ages was obviously from Rome (with all that is implied by that identification) to Paris, where during the twelfth and early thirteenth centuries there was an exciting focusing, a bringing together, an immensely fertile reworking of what had already been received and what was just then being rediscovered. There was, when all is said and done, a renascence of the twelfth century, though perhaps it would be more helpful to refer to the twelfth-century phenomenon as *renascence*, using a generic term for rebirth, and to refer to the fifteenth- and sixteenth-century phenomenon as *Renaissance*, using for this purpose a term that delimits the time-period, which I would take to have validity in describing the cultural and intellectual movements from about 1350 to about 1600, with allowances for later chronologies in parts of Europe other than Italy. And, a final point in this preliminary but necessary definition of the concept of *translatio studii* and of locating it in the time-frame of Renaissance, the received medievalism of Erasmus, Agricola, Lefèvre d' Etaples, Reuchlin, and their contemporaries has been altogether too much ignored — in general[4] — by students of the Renaissance. It was a continuum, the *translatio studii*, and even though the Renaissance humanists from Petrarch to Scaliger were fond of ignoring or sneering at the Middle Ages — after all, it was they who invented the term 'Dark Ages' — they were nonetheless schooled by medieval masters and continued to use, characteristically without acknowledgment, medieval texts and techniques.

Humanism is another troublesome term, for increasingly since the Romantic period it has come to mean different things, from belief in the mere humanity of Christ to the quality of being human, and thus any system concerned with merely human interests – as well as with some of us still the original concept of devotion to literary culture. For it is not a Renaissance term (having been coined in 1808), and for clarity and precision therefore I have returned to the older term *studia humanitatis*, as celebrated particularly in Cicero and Quintilian, which may at times have been something of a slogan but nonetheless after the early fifteenth century was understood as embracing a well-defined cycle of subjects and authors that included always grammar, rhetoric, and poetry, as well as history and moral philosophy, and then later, in a widening circle, texts from jurisprudence and medicine.[5] While humanism per se was not a single philosophical system (as Kristeller has rightly insisted), there was at the core of Renaissance humanistic studies the favorite theme of the dignity of man, most famously celebrated by Pico della Mirandola in his *Oratio de hominis dignitate*, but to be found everywhere and nearly continuously from the fifteenth century into the seventeenth.[6] But humanism was more than a program: it was a spirit, a new enthusiasm for the classics, leading to the desire to comprehend the ancient world as a whole.

Because the Renaissance version of the *studia humanitatis* gave a new emphasis to the reading and teaching of classical Latin and Greek authors – the Greek far more than had been done after Boethius, and the Latin now in a fresher light by virtue of the reorientation of the Latin to the Greek – and because the humanists characteristically called for a return to the original texts, *ad fontes*, the contributions of the humanists of the late fifteenth and sixteenth centuries to classical scholarship were very great in the effort first to issue the *editiones principes* and then to comment upon them and offer textual emendations. This is familiar ground, and the landscape has been surveyed by Sabbadini, Kristeller, Curtius, Garin, Kenney, and others;[7] but I offer these observations as an *accessus*,[8] both for the sake of the material itself and for making possible an approach to the area of Erasmus and his classical studies.

Erasmus of Rotterdam died 450 years ago at the age of sixty-nine, if we take what is now the more likely date of 1467 for his birth. He came therefore in the middle of the development of the *studia humanitatis* during the Renaissance period, for when he came of age at the end of the fifteenth century Italian humanism was perhaps at its height, but a full century of the development of textual criticism and of the transferal from Latin into the vernaculars lay ahead.[9] By the time that Erasmus made his first trip to Italy in 1506 his techniques and values had pretty much been formed, and he cannot be counted as a direct product of Italian humanistic teaching. But he had already learned much indirectly. His father, we are now certain, was a scribe in Italy during the 1450s and probably through the 1460s as well: he heard the great Guarino; and he learned the skills for copying Greek as well as Latin manuscripts, one of his manuscripts being now in London and the other in Berlin.[10] While a schoolboy Erasmus was inspired by the great Rudolph Agricola, doubtless the first major humanist north of the Alps, and Agricola had taught the rudiments of Greek to Alexander Hegius, who was schoolmaster in Deventer during Erasmus' last year in school there.[11] It is still difficult to say how much of the emphases of the Brethren of the Common Life influenced Erasmus' thought and spirituality, for we now know through the researches of R. R. Post especially that the Brethren did not generally operate schools and that any influence was more through their pastoral work and through individual teachers. Yet Erasmus shares many of the fundamental values of the *Devotio moderna*: an anti-scholasticism that sometimes took shape as an anti-intellectualism and that always emphasized the practical as against the theoretical and speculative. Thus we find in the opening of the *Imitatio Christi* a specific cautioning against the excessive speculation of medieval scholastic theologians: 'Quid prodest ardua de Trinitate disputatio, si animi summissione careas, ideoque displiceas Trinitati? Enimvero non ardua dicta sanctum justumque reddunt hominem, sed studiosa vita Deo charum efficit. Equidem peccatorum poenitentiam sentire, quam ejusdem definitionem tenere malim.'[12]

In the writings of Thomas à Kempis and others there is a fondness for the moral teaching of such classical authors as Seneca, and this is an emphasis that begins with the *Imitatio Christi* itself. What Erasmus called his *philosophia Christi* – and the term itself was probably taken by Erasmus from Agricola – sums up a much larger body of thought, and in it one finds prismatically the nuances of the religious as well as the humanistic thought of Erasmus.[13] The phrase first appeared in Erasmus' *Enchiridion* of 1503, and it was echoed and expanded in the Preface to the New Testament twelve years later, a preface separately printed in the *Paraclesis* (1519); later it was mirrored in many letters. With Erasmus the phrase signified the teaching of Christ without the philosophical system of Aristotle and the elaborations of the scholastics; its was at core distinctively non-intellectual, but it was not anti-intellectual. Yet it was a philosophy, not an emotional appeal, and it locates the Erasmian ideal mid-way between mysticism and intellectualism; for Erasmus never thought that life was anything but difficult, complex, and manifold – yet potentially full of joy.[14]

Erasmus has often been called a Christian humanist, and this term, as I understand it, marks Erasmus as one who saw the humanistic ideal as the fusion of classical letters with the revelation of Christianity, in the following of Christ in this world. Humanism, to echo Lucien Febvre, had never been for Erasmus and his kind merely 'un jeu littéraire, ni une perfection formelle. C'est une lumière qui dissipe les ténèbres.'[15] I shall not attempt to speak of his work as an editor of classical and patristic authors and of his work on the Scriptures, nor of his great skill and success as a translator both of the classics and of Scriptures: these important matters are only now receiving the careful study they deserve.[16] Nor it there time to talk about his remarkable range of original writings, from the *Moriae encomium* to the *Colloquia*, to his many *Apologiae*, and to his tracts pleading for peace (*De sarcienda ecclesiae concordia* notably) and for purity in the Church (*De puritate ecclesiae*). But we must remark how much of his energy in his final years at Freiburg and Basel was devoted to completing the last of his great editions, the Augustine in 1530 and the Origen in the year of his death, as well as his last major work, his longest and yet least studied, *De ratione concionandi*, or the *Ecclesiastes*, on the art of preaching.[17] The range of Erasmus' writings is remarkable, and his achievement in grammatical and rhetorical studies especially is deep and profoundly influential.

Now let us turn to Erasmus in the light of the concept of *translatio studii*, and for this effort I shall concentrate on a single work, the *Adagia*. In an important way, the totality of Erasmus' literary and educational writings constitute a program for reading and teaching the classics, and Craig R. Thompson has written admirably on that program in his Introduction to volumes 23 and 24 of the *CWE*. One could talk at great length about the program, for increasingly we can see the individual works falling into a larger structure. Even in his very early work the *Antibarbari*, there was a great deal more than simply a writing *against*, though Erasmus was then and always against the barbarians: this work of the 1490s (though it was not published until 1518) is even more positive and creative than it is an attack. For it insists upon friendship (that Ciceronian and Petrarchan ideal which is so central to Renaissance humanism), and it stresses the beauty and calm of its surroundings; these elements, and the classical role of dialogue, and the warm appreciation for the living study of the classics, all contribute to rendering a memorable picture of a civilized way of life. Here then we find not only a literary sense of *studia humanitatis* but more importantly all of that Ciceronian resonance of *humanitas* – that quality which distinguishes civilized man from the savage, that is, ultimately civilization and culture – and there is the extension into further significations and connotations of *humanus* and *humanitas*. Though an early work, and one little read today, the *Antibarbari* is a significant work for establishing *ab initio* the values and the consistency of Erasmus' humanism.

Only a few years after writing the *Antibarbari* Erasmus published his first book, which grew into the handbook of the Renaissance because like the *Noctes Atticae* of Aulus Gellius it was so readable. The *Adagia* is one of the most remarkable works of the Renaissance period, and it is one of the superlative examples of the Erasmian growing book. It began in 1500 modestly enough as the *Collectanea adagiorum*, yet the type and format announced it as something new and an ambitious and exciting little book. Published in Paris, it was in Roman type – not the first, to be sure – but for a humanistic book to appear in Roman type, rather than Gothic, was still (in the words of E. P. Goldschmidt) 'the visible expression of a changed attitude of mind.'[18] It was small, containing only 76 leaves, 152 pages in all, and offering 818 proverbs, with some Greek; and it was the Greek — together with the proud claim that there was nothing included that was not ancient and remarkable — that made it a book of the new humanism. Later Erasmus expressed shame at the haste in producing it and at its scanty Greek; but there were Greek versions provided for 154 proverbs in this first edition, and that was new in the world of learning. In 1508 Erasmus brought out a totally new book, the *Adagiorum chiliades* (literally thousands of adages), published at Venice by Aldus Manutius: a beautiful book, handsomely printed; and this new version contained 3,260 paroemia, compared with the 838 in the final edition of the *Collectanea*. Now each proverb is given its life-history, with Erasmus showing the change from one author to another; the *Collectanea* now becomes an ancilla to classical literature, learning, and life. As Margaret Mann Phillips observes in her splendid study of the adages, which has taught us all how the adages grew and how to read them, 'the specific business of the *Adages* was to teach good scholarship,'[19] for Erasmus occasionally corrected his authorities. The adages were also a defense of good letters (*bonae litterae* had by then become a shorthand for the *studia humanitatis*), and in itself the *Adagia* created a model of Latin style. For in the very language that he employed, Erasmus developed a style that was essentially classical and full of the echoes of his reading; but it was 'classical as to vocabulary except when modern things needed modern words, but free and personal and alive.'[20] It needs also to be said that the adages were also Christian, for the Church Fathers are quoted throughout, and the adages are full of Erasmus' lifelong reading of the Bible; one finds the references collected in a valuable appendix by Phillips. Thus the work gives a sense of the continuum of *bonae litterae* and at the same time provides an exemplar of the *philosophia Christi*; there is a consistency of moral teaching in the adages.

Everywhere the *Adagia* was read, and it was published in well over a hundred editions, translations and abridgments by the end of the sixteenth century, in France, Italy, Germany, Switzerland, and the Low Countries. In a forthcoming book that grows out of a cataloguing of the holdings of the Herzog August Bibliothek of editions of the *Adagia*, there are also essays on provenance and reception.[21] We shall then be able to see more clearly how European a book it was, for authors from Rabelais to Shakespeare read it and plundered from it.

Few of Erasmus' works manifest so vividly the fusion of the classical and the Christian, with the aim of making the classics contemporary and of measuring the modern against the antique. None of his works is a more striking example of the growing book, for Erasmus continued to add adages from one major edition to the next (reaching the final number of 4,251 adages at his death). At times Erasmus made minor revisions within existing adages, down to the 1533 edition especially, which is filled with personal reminiscences of books, places, and people.

But this is doubtless familiar to readers of this journal, and thus I may have been carrying coals to Newcastle – or as Erasmus puts it in one of the adages (I.vii.lvii): 'In sylvam ligna ferre, in mare deferre aquam, ululas Athenas' (*LB* 2.284B).

Erasmus in England[22]

Erasmus sometimes wished that England were joined to the Continent by a bridge, for he 'hated the wild waves and the still wilder sailors': the passage then could be very rough in the small boats of the time, which often had to wait out bad weather and storms. Generally his trips were of some duration, and even included a long stint of teaching; but on one occasion he dashed to England to consult a manuscript of the New Testament, and on another he seems to have made the trip only to receive the papal dispensation in 1517.

But he made at least six trips to England, and it helps to list them, for the evidence must be extracted from letters and other references, and biographers often differ about the dates. The first trip was in 1499, and it lasted six months, from June to December. It was during this first visit that Erasmus became friends for life with Thomas More and John Colet and established a number of other important relationships. The second visit was from the early autumn of 1505 to June of 1506, and during this period Erasmus stayed at Cambridge, thanks to the friendship of Bishop John Fisher, Chancellor of the University; Queens' College, Cambridge, records his admission to candidacy for the doctorate in theology, but the degree was never awarded. The third visit, by far the longest, was from August 1509 to August 1514, and it is a period of active teaching of Greek and theology at Cambridge, producing long-term results in both fields. The fourth visit was in May 1515, made apparently primarily for research on one manuscript essential for his work on the New Testament that was published in 1516. The fifth visit was during the summer of 1516; and the sixth, and apparently his last, was another brief visit, in April 1517 to receive the papal dispensation from the papal nuncio. Erasmus, as we can see, spent a long time in England, mostly in London and Cambridge, but with visits to Oxford, Canterbury, and other places. These were immensely productive years for Erasmus; the *Moriae encomium*, the major work on the New Testament, the *Institutio principis christiani*, the translations of Lucian, and other works were written or completed during these periods of time in England, and the continuing revising of the *Adagia*, the *Enchiridion*, et al., went on. What I think is most striking is that it seems to have been during these first two visits of 1499 and 1505–1506 (or as a direct result of them) that Erasmus was able to find his direction for his lifework on the New Testament and his scope for his educational program. For this he was largely indebted to John Colet, but clearly Thomas More and John Fisher played significant roles as well. If he owed much to England and to English friends (among whom must be counted his Maecenas of more than thirty years, William Blount, Lord Mountjoy), what did he give? How did Erasmus contribute to a *translatio studii* in England?

Erasmus taught Greek, and he encouraged his friends to study Greek; thus we note the number of Englishmen who turned to the translation of such authors as Plutarch, Aristotle, and Plato. Of the friends of Erasmus, many were immensely influential themselves: John Colet, who founded St. Paul's School, whose classical curriculum, guided and even inspired by Erasmus, became a model for other schools in Tudor England; Thomas More, whose epigrams, translations from the Greek Anthology, were the strongest single influence upon the epigram in England, and who defended the study of Greek at Oxford and defended Erasmus against his attackers; John Fisher, whose influence at Cambridge was very great; and others, like the younger Richard Croke, who edited Ausonius and continued his Greek studies at Paris and then went on to Leipzig to teach Greek there. It is difficult to measure these different kinds of influence; one can study editions and translations, as E. J. Devereux has done,[23] but much of the Erasmus that was read in England was through editions imported from the Continent: scholars' books, like books of the imagination, are truly international. One can study the salons and their humanistic circles in Tudor England, as J. K. McConica has done,[24] but the record is fragmentary and such results must be incomplete. Over and over again one must be reminded that the Reformation and the Council of Trent both made the name of Erasmus suspect even at the same time that his influence continued strong among humanists, schoolteachers, and humanist writers; yet there was, to put it another way, always a *presence* of Erasmus throughout the sixteenth century and into the seventeenth which must be taken account of, even though it is impossible to quantify. There have been studies already, to be sure, but far more research is needed upon the whole spectrum of Erasmian influence, as in the areas of classical scholarship, where one notes the extent to which Erasmus' earlier commentaries were made use of by such scholars as Vinet and J. J. Scaliger, and also in the actual teaching of the classics in the schools and universities of Tudor and Stuart England and Scotland.

Not only did Erasmian ideals and techniques help to shape the curriculum of Colet's St. Paul's School, but textbooks that he wrote were used in England as on the Continent, and these in turn generated other textbooks. T. W. Baldwin's studies of the texts used in Tudor public schools provide a necessary foundation, but there too much else remains to be done.[25] Here let it be remarked and emphasized that Erasmus always stressed the greater importance of Greek and hoped that someday translations from Greek to Latin might not be necessary, if there were a raising of educational standards. He himself exemplified in so much of his work the passage or *translatio* from Greek to Roman − in fact, a *transitus hellenismi ad christianismum* (to use a late-thirteenth-century term[26]); and works like the *Adagia* contributed mightily to the revival of ancient learning (*renata humanitas*, to use another expression of the Renaissance humanists like Chrysoloras and Guarino, who had a vivid sense of beginning a new *paideia*[27]).

The commentaries of Erasmus were subsumed into the growing body of commentary in the ever-newer and more substantial editions of classical texts in the seventeenth century; the editions themselves had been surpassed rather quickly in the sixteenth century by classical scholars like Denis Lambin, Elie Vinet, Muret, Scaliger, and others. Indeed, it was Lambin who was among those who adopted the new pronunciation of Greek introduced by Erasmus and who with Ramus defended it − but Erasmus' new pronunciation of Greek is not an unmitigated blessing.[28] More than the wealth of these individual contributions to texts and commentaries, I want to call attention to and emphasize Erasmus' exciting projecting of the ancient world, not just as archaeology, though there is much of that in Erasmus' discussions of agriculture, marriage customs, games, coins and many more aspects of Greek and Roman life. Erasmus was brilliantly successful in recreating for his age the mental climate of the ancient world. More than any other of the sixteenth century it is he who generated an excitement in his readers everywhere for what D. J. Gordon has called 'the great lesson of Renaissance humanist scholarship: that the ancient world existed as an entity, a separate, distanced, autonomous cultural domain − not merely a compendium from which fragments could be taken over and transmogrified, with no sense of context, of historical and cultural distance,' and, still more, that 'the classical world, the most prized of ancient cultures, had to be got right because it was real and recoverable.'[29] In this effort Erasmus was more than a model of scholarship, important though that is; he communicated a spirit of learning and provided the inspiration for a century of intense study and publication.

But let me pause to indicate that Erasmus was not blindly in love with the past, and at a time when there were excesses of enthusiasm − ranging from Bembo's having newly printed books recopied by scribes to the writing of an immense tome on the archaeology of a single ancient coin − Erasmus, characteristically, was one who coolly called for moderation. In this he was consistent, and in 1528 by his middle-of-the-road *Ciceronianus* he called down arrows of controversy from the unqualified imitators of Cicero; but already in 1515 Erasmus had indicated that consistent attitude of moderation towards the past in one of his adages, *Cecidis et Buphoniorum* (IV.iv.xxix): 'Siquidem Cecides pervetustus quispiam Dithyramborum Poeta fuit, cujus scripta jam situm olebant, unde in jocum vulgarem abierunt. Quemadmodum jure ridentur hodie, qui immodica & intempestiva affectatione vetustatis, e Duodecim tabulis, ex Ennio, Lucilioque petunt sermonem, perinde quasi cum Evandri matre loquantur: nec ullum verbum elegans esse putant, nisi quod sit ab usu vulgi, & nostro seculo procul remotum.'[30] A voice of moderation I have called Erasmus, but his *Ciceronianus* hit the world of letters like a bombshell and engendered the violent and virulent enmity of confirmed devotees of the Ciceronian style like J..C. Scaliger and Étienne Dolet; and the controversies that ensued continued for the rest of the century.[31]

In the adage *Ne bos quidem pereat*, added to the *Adagia* in 1526 (IV.v.i), Erasmus felt free to criticize those who had climbed aboard the bandwagon of humanism and pretended to a knowledge of Greek that was far beyond them: 'Sunt enim in hoc ordine quidam intolerabili insolentia, qui simul atque tenuerint duodecim verba Latina & quinque Graeca, Demosthenes ac Cicerones sibi videntur, effutiunt ineptos libellos, nonnunquam & virulentos, liberales disciplinas omnes miro fastu adspernantur, & in harum professores scurriliter debacchantur' (*LB* 2.1052B). And at the end of this 1526 adage Erasmus returns to the original theme of the *essai*, that it is important to have good neighbors in the world of learning as in the life of men: 'Quid igitur superest, nisi ut linguae bonaeque litterae postliminio redeuntes ac velut a radice repullulantes, civiliter & comiter sese insinuent in sodalitatem earum disciplinarum, quae tot jam seculis regnant in Academiis, neque cujusquam studium incessant, sed omnium studia potius adjuvent' (*LB* 2.1053E).

After 1499, the date of his first visit, England changed greatly, and one must of course be careful of *post hoc, propter hoc* argumentation in arguing for the influence of Erasmus. But the breadth and depth of Erasmus' influence is manifest, as Baldwin, Schirmer, Caspari, Devereux, McConica, Thomson, and others have shown,[32] and this was an influence that operated in many ways and in many fields. What remains to be declared is, again, that there was the *presence* of Erasmus: the man, the figure of the cosmopolitan humanist, the one humanist known to all others. There were of course always the writings: endlessly diverse, innovative, serving as models for an age that was fascinated with the 'resources of kind.'[33] There was in addition the splendid and marvelously exciting development of prose style by Erasmus: exemplary in itself, as a manifestation of style as the ultimate morality of mind, and exemplary as model because the effort to master a high standard of Latin prose continued to be valued in English, Dutch, German and some other schools throughout the sixteenth and well into the seventeenth centuries (and in some places well beyond). Erasmus himself was proud of being a grammarian in the sense understood by such fellow-*grammatici* as Poliziano, and he more than once justified his carrying the name of grammarian, while recognizing that knowledge of grammar alone does not make a theologian but insisting that competence in grammar contributes to the study of theology and that the absence of it would obstruct the development of theological knowledge. Erasmus at times also prided himself on being a rhetorician (sometimes a *rhetor*, sometimes playfully a *rhetorculus*). Erasmus had an abiding concern with language, and in his writings we find a deep understanding of the role of language in human culture and in exploring such human language-oriented relationships as that *sermo-verbum* which reaches from the human to the divine. The force of that grammatical-rhetorical tradition runs deep in Tudor England – the teaching of Erasmus is the underpinning of the Tudor public schools – and it is still to be felt in the humanistic education of John Milton in the early seventeenth century and in his equally deep and immensely learned knowledge of grammar and love of language. May we observe that Milton was educated at Cambridge, where Erasmus had contributed so lastingly to the *translatio studii* a century earlier.

To be sure, humanism itself changed after the 1520s – not immediately, not in a single year and not markedly even in a single decade. But by mid-century one can see the Protestantizing of humanism, as was discussed at the commemoration of the 450th anniversary of the death of Sir Phillip Sidney in September 1986,[34] and equally clearly one can see the reshaping of humanism after the Council of Trent into something propaedeutic to the education of Catholic children and to propaganda in a Catholic sense: in a word, a tutioristic humanism.[35] The reading and application of Erasmian writings necessarily changed; one has only to look at the fact of his being on the *Index prohibitorum librorum* and still more to the reasons given, and then to the changes in his works that were effected to respond to the *Index*. Even where his influence had been as deep as anywhere else, in the making of schoolbooks, his name drops out pretty quickly, though not altogether, of course, and in this sphere his influence continues anonymously.[36] If one were to examine the *ratio* or *ordo* of the Protestant educators and the *Ratio studiorum* of the Jesuits, one could see what happened to the consistent and lucid program of Erasmus in the pre-Reformation years. The Erasmian belief in the layman is not there in the Roman Catholic outlook, and his belief in tradition has been transformed in that of the Reformers; and both seem to have lost much of Erasmus' faith in the goodness of man and the potentials of education.[37] As early as his first major work, the *Antibarbari,* Erasmus had expressed the belief that a man is not born, he is educated.

There remains, then, after all efforts of analysis and generalization, that mysterious and fascinating figure of Erasmus himself, whose enigmatic smile has been caught by Quentin Metsys, Dürer, and Holbein. Small wonder that some sixty efforts towards a definitive biography of Erasmus have been made since the sixteenth century, and that some of us are still trying to write the biography that will see Erasmus clearly and see him whole. If asked how I should characterize his personality, which after all dominates his writings and helps us to explain his taking of positions (or refraining from taking a position) in public affairs – sometimes acting vigorously through his counsel, letters, and other writings; and sometimes remaining silent (which may after all be a deliberate act, and which may well be an act of courage, as his friend Thomas More so strikingly manifested) – I should reply that at the core of Erasmus there is indeed a strong element of paradox, and therefore his characteristic mode is ironic. The Dutch scholar E. H. Waterbolk has caught this aspect admirably in writing that Erasmus is continually hyper-subjective by observing himself objectively; that he brings himself to the fore by eliminating himself; that he names himself by not naming himself; and that he exalts himself in self-ridicule and in his modesty he is proud.[38] Above all, as Waterbolk underscores, there is the play of an irony that is classically schooled and oriented, that comes from his own awareness of the distance between his private self and his public image, between his private deep-felt and consistent core of belief and the complexities of ambiguity in his published writings. Need we wonder that Rabelais was so overwhelmed by his courage as a fighter for the truth? In December 1532 Rabelais wrote Erasmus (whom he had never met) and addressed him in the highest of terms: 'Salve itaque etiam atque etiam, pater amantissimus, pater decusque patriae, literarum assertor $\alpha\lambda\epsilon\xi\iota\kappa\alpha\kappa o\varsigma$, veritatis propugnator invictissimus' (*EE* 2743.15–17). Need we marvel that Montaigne should have learned from Erasmus the fascination for and the skill in observing himself? And the Tudor and Stuart world of letters learned from Rabelais and Montaigne, as it learned from others on the continent who had studied their Erasmus.[39]

In England during the sixteenth and seventeenth centuries (and later, of course, as well), men and women discoverd their Erasmus both directly through his Latin works and indirectly through the many translations, abridgments and epitomes; and again by such writers as Rabelais and Montaigne Erasmus was transmitted in turn through translations and adaptations. The imaginations of such Englishmen as Chapman, Shakespeare, Donne, Burton, and many others responded to the spirit of Erasmus, however it reached them. What is applicable to England is of course applicable in differing ways and degrees to all of Europe and to Colonial America; and we who commemorated in the year 1986 the 450th anniversary of his death may well pause to reflect upon our Erasmian heritage. He knew the classical world remarkably, in extraordinary detail and with a never-failing wonder, and he succeeded in transmitting that detail and that wonder to his own age, and to ours. The *translatio studii* in which he played such a vital role can never be completed, and our exploration of the *studia humanitatis*, founded to such a remarkable extent upon the work of Erasmus, is an essential part of a continuum.[40] The crumbling Roman world has led to our age, and we must make sure that it does not stop there.

In a slightly different form this paper was presented to the Institut für Griechische und Lateinische Philologie, Universität Hamburg, in November 1986.
1   I refer with admiration and a strong sense of indebtedness to Curtius' *Europäische Literatur und lateinisches Mittelalter* (Bern: A. Francke, 1948), but I must observe that curiously Curtius

speaks only once directly about *translatio studii* (see note 26 below), though it is implicit throughout his work.

2   Étienne Gilson, 'Humanisme médiéval et Renaissance,' in *Les idées et les lettres*, 2d. ed. (Paris: J. Vrin, 1955), 171-196. To cite Gilson is not necessarily to endorse all of his theoretical position about the continuity and originality of humanism in the Middle Ages and the Renaissance. Yet the work of 12th- and 13th-century Paris scholars underlies much of the work of 15th- and 16th-century humanists in Italy and France. The notion of imitation is involved in this larger question, and I have addressed some aspects of the notion in ' "Lighting a Candle to the Place": On the Dimensions and Implications of *Imitatio* in the Renaissance,' *ItC* 4 (1983): 123-143.

3   For the Later Middle Ages and Renaissance there are the excellent summary-papers in the collection edited by August Buck, *Die Rezeption der Antike: Zum Problem der Kontinuität zwischen Mittelalter und Renaissance* (Hamburg: Hauswedell, 1981). More recently there is a volume of essays edited by Warren Treadgold, *Renaissances before the Renaissance: Cultural Revivals of Late Antiquity and the Middle Ages* (Stanford: Standord U Pr, 1984).

4   But see the following studies in Buck (above, note 3): Charles Béné, 'Les Pères de l' Eglise et la réception des auteurs classiques'; J. IJsewijn, 'Mittelalterliches Latein und Humanistenlatein'; and F. J. Worstbrock, 'Die Antikenrezeption in der mittelalterlichen und der humanistichen Ars Dictandi?

5   For Paul Oskar Kristeller's influential definition of humanism, see 'The Humanist Movement,' in *Renaissance Thought: The Classic, Scholastic, and Humanistic Strains* (New York: Har-Row Torch, 1961), 10, and more recently 'The Humanist Movement,' in *Renaissance Thought and Its Sources* (New York: Columbia U Pr, 1979), 21-32.

6   Kristeller writes: 'We cannot escape the impression that after the beginnings of Renaissance humanism, the emphasis on man and his dignity becomes more persistent, more exclusive, and ultimately more systematic than it had ever been during the preceding centuries and even during classical antiquity,' *Renaissance Thought and Its Sources*, 170.

7   See further: Eugenio Garin, *Der italienische Humanismus* (Bern: A. Francke, 1947); Curtius (above, note 1); Kristeller, *Renaissance Thought* (1961); Remigio Sabbadini, *Storia e critica di testi latini*, 2d. ed., (Padua: Editrice Antenore, 1971); E. J. Kenney, *The Classical Text: Aspects of Editing in the Age of the Printed Book* (Berkeley: U of Cal Pr, 1974); and R. J. Schoeck, 'The Humanistic Concept of the Text: Text, Context, and Tradition,' *PPMRC* 7 (1982): 13-31.

8   The convention of the *accessus* familiar to all Renaissance writers was medieval, and it has been surveyed by Edwin A. Quain in 'The Medieval Accessus ad Auctores,' *Traditio* 3 (1945): 215-264. Note especially the observation of Quain that 'it seems clear that in the twelfth century the tremendous growth of interest in the studies of Antiquity led to the extension of a practice that had been a tradition' (262).

9   For the development of textual theory during this period, see Kenney and Schoeck, cited in note 7 above.

10   Giuseppe Avarucci, 'Due codici scritti da "Gerardus Helye," padre di Erasmo,' *IMU* 26 (1983): 215-225; but see the remarks of J. IJsewijn in *WRM* 9 (1985): 127-129, concerning the dating of Erasmus' birth.

11   On Erasmus and Agricola, see my essay in the Proceedings of the Agricola Conference 1985, ed. F. Akkerman (Groningen, in press).

12   On Erasmus and the *Imitatio*, see Léon-E. Halkin, 'La piété d' Erasme,' *RHF* 79 (1984): 675.

13   On the development of the *philosophia Christi*, see O. Schottenloher, 'Erasmus, Johann Poppenruyter und die Entstehung des Enchiridion militis christiani,' *ARG* 45 (1954): 109-116, and the introduction of Raymond Himelick, *The Enchiridion of Erasmus* (Bloomington: Ind U Pr, 1963).

14   I mean not only the rhetorical playfulness of the *Moriae encomium* and other Lucianic writings, and not only the delight in words and his frequent coinings and punnings, but also his exuberance in living: many passages in *Adages* and the *Colloquia* are as full of a sense of felt life as Brueghel's paintings.

15   Thus Lucien Febvre, *Le problème de l'incroyance au XVIe siècle: La religion de Rabelais* (Paris: Editions Albin Michel, 1942), 285.

16   In her recent study of *Erasmus as a Translator of the Classics* (Toronto: U of Toronto Pr, 1985), Erika Rummel summarizes: 'Erasmus was able to popularize and revivify the classics because he

satisfied the intellectual curiosity and the literary taste of his contemporaries, because he produced a competent, fluent, and readable version of Greek texts' (133). It is also important to note that despite his success, Erasmus 'lamented the state of education that compelled him to provide translations' (136). Further, in his letters he gave voice to his satisfaction at being 'outstripped' by younger scholars: Rummel, 170, and *EE* 1146.22.

17 This work has recently been called 'a major monument in the long history and continuing influence of the classical tradition in western culture' and perhaps the major work in the history of sacred rhetoric, whose 'only rival is the *De doctrina christiana* of Augustine'; thus John W. O'Malley, 'Erasmus and the History of Sacred Rhetoric: The *Ecclesiastes* of 1535,' *Erasmus of Rotterdam Society Yearbook* 5 (1985): 29. See also James Michael Weiss, '*Ecclesiastes* and Erasmus: The Mirror and the Image," *ARG* 65 (1974): 83-108.

18 E. P. Goldschmidt, *The Printed Book of the Renaissance,* 2d. ed. (Amsterdam: Gérard Th. van Heusden, 1966), 26.

19 Margaret Mann Phillips, *The 'Adages' of Erasmus: A Study with Translations* (Cambridge: Cambridge U Pr. 1964), 78.

20 Ibid., 85.

21 This volume, under the editorship of Mathieu Knops, details the more than 50 copies of the *Adagia* in the Herzog August Bibliothek, and it is to appear in late 1988.

22 Among surveys of Erasmus in England see Horst Oppel in *Renatae Litterae: Studien zum Nachleben der Antike und zur europäischen Renaissance.* August Buck zum 60. Geburtstag..., ed. K. Heitmann and E. Schroeder (Frankfurt: Athenaeum, 1973), 157–169. D. F. S. Thomson and H. C. Porter, *Erasmus and Cambridge: The Cambridge Letters of Erasmus* (Toronto: U of Toronto Pr, 1963) and H. C. Porter, *Reformation and Reaction in Tudor Cambridge* (Cambridge: Cambridge U Pr, 1958) are essential for the study of Erasmus at Cambridge.

23 E. J. Devereux, *Renaissance English Translations of Erasmus: A Bibliography to 1700* (Toronto: U of Toronto Pr, 1983).

24 James Kelsy McConica, *English Humanists and Reformation Politics under Henry VIII and Edward VI* (Oxford: Clarendon Pr, 1965), on which see my review in *Moneana* 8 (1965): 103-108.

25 T. W. Baldwin, *William Shakespeare's Small Latine & Less Greeke,* 2 vols. (Urbana: U of Ill Pr, 1944). On education, see further Joan Simon, *Education and Society in Tudor England* (Cambridge: Cambridge U Pr, 1966); and for Erasmus' place in the 16th century Continental school-text, see *Le livre scolaire au temps d' Erasme et des humanistes,* ed. René Hoven and Jean Hoyeux, introd. Léon-E. Halkin (Liège: Université de Liège, 1969).

26 At the end of the thirteenth century, Thomas of Ireland spoke of the *translatio*: 'Studies were first transferred from Greece to Rome, then from Rome to Paris during Charlemagne's time, around the year 800.' (*De tribus sensibus S. Scripturae,* Ms. Paris Nat. 15966: see M.-D. Chenu, *Toward Understanding Saint Thomas* [Chicago: Henry Regnery, 1964], 24n.15). On this theme see Gilson (above, note 2) 132-185. Curtius speaks briefly to this point (above, note 1) 27: 'Die Existenzweise der Antike im Mittelalter ist zugleich Rezeption und Umwandlung.' See further Paul Joachimsen on humanism, 'Der Humanismus und die Entwicklung des deutsches Geist,' *DVLG* 8 (1930): 419-420. Budé echoed this phrase and its concept in *De transitu hellenismi ad christianismum* (Paris, 1535), newly edited by Maurice Lebel (Sherbrooke, Que.: Editions Paulines, 1973).

27 See William Harrison Woodward, *Vittorino da Feltre and Other Humanist Educators* (Cambridge: Cambridge U Pr, 1897), 25, and G. Saitta, *L'educazione dell'umanesimo in Italia* (Venice: La Nuova Italia, 1928).

28 See Emile V. Telle, 'Erasmus's *Ciceronianus*: A Comical Colloquy,' in *Essays on the Works of Erasmus,* ed. Richard L. DeMolen (New Haven: Yale U Pr, 1978), 211–220. 'Owing to the fame of the great humanist and his Latin style, the *Ciceronianus* did not fail to delight, dismay, disturb, or fluster those fellow scholars whose overwhelming preoccupation lay with the purity and efficacy of Latin' (211). The history of Renaissance commentaries has yet to be studied in full, but I have suggested some directions, using Ausonius as a case in point: see 'The Early Printing History of Ausonius,' forthcoming in the *Acta* of the International Association of Neo-Latin Studies Congress at Wolfenbüttel 1985, ed. Stella Revard et al. (announced for 1988 publication by MRTS, Binghamton, N.Y.). On the matter of the new pronunciation of Greek, see Engelbert Drerup, *Die Schu-*

laussprache des Griechischen von der Renaissance bis zur Gegenwart (Paderborn: F. Schöningh, 1930).
29 D. J. Gordon, *The Renaissance Imagination*, ed. Stephen Orgel (Berkeley: U of Cal Pr, 1975), 23.
30 *LB* 2.1031A. See note 28 above.
31 See the summary of Jozef IJsewijn in *Companion to Neo-Latin Studies* (Amsterdam: North-Holland, 1977), 241. The *Ciceronianus* has been translated and annotated by Betty I. Knott in vol. 28 of *CWE*.
32 See note 22 above, and also the following: R. Weiss, *Humanism in England during the Fifteenth Century*, 2d. ed. (Oxford: Blackwell, 1957); Walter Franz Schirmer, *Antike, Renaissance und Puritanismus*, 2d. ed. (Munich: M. Hüber, 1933); Franck L. Schoell, *E tudes sur l'humanisme continental en Angleterre à la fin de la Renaissance* (Paris: Champion, 1926); Karl Brunner, *England und die Antike* (Innsbruck: F. Rauch, 1947); Fritz Caspari, *Humanism and the Social Order in Tudor England* (Chicago: U of Chicago Pr, 1954). There is a broader sweep in Bruce Mansfield's *Phoenix of His Age: Interpretations of Erasmus c. 1550-1750* (Toronto: U of Toronto Pr, 1979); and in the three volumes of Erasmian bibliography edited by J.-C. Margolin (1963, 1969 and 1977) Erasmian scholarship since 1940 is covered most thoroughly.
33 Cf. Rosalie L. Colie, *The Resources of Kind: Genre-Theory in the Renaissance (Berkeley: U of Cal Pr, 1973)*, and now *Alastair Fowler, Kinds of Literature: An Introduction to the Theory of Genres and Modes* (Cambridge: Harvard U Pr, 1982).
34 Conference held at Leiden, September 1986, the proceedings of which are to be published.
35 Tutiorism is a theological, not a philological, term, and it is used to describe a policy of doing things for the moral safety of the individual (see *New Catholic Encyclopedia* [1967] for a fuller discusion). *Tutioristic humanism* is used here to identify that post-Tridentine use of humanism, but without allowing a total freedom of inquiry. It might seem to be – and it is intended to suggest the – oxymoronic.
36 See note 25 above, and as a parallel, Helen C. White's demonstration that Erasmus was often appropriated without credit: *The Tudor Books of Private Devotion* (Madison: U of Wis Pr, 1951).
37 Cf. Halkin (above, note 12) 690, who writes, 'L'homme en plénitude, c'est le chrétien transformé par la prière'; by prayer, and we add, by study.
38 E. H. Waterbolk, *Verspreide Opstellen* (Amsterdam: Bert Bakker, 1981), 33: 'Erasmus verschuilt zich liever achter ... Erasmus; hij objectiveert zich zelf bijzonder graag; bij voortduring is hij hypersubjectief door zich te objectiveren; hij schakelt zich in door zich uit te schakelen; hij noemt zich door zich niet te noemen; in zelf-spot verheft hij zich; in z'n bescheidenheid is hij trots.'
39 The work of M. A. Screech on Rabelais has brilliantly demonstrated the fullness of Erasmian elements in Rabelais: see especially his edition of the *Tiers livre* (Geneva: Droz, 1964), and still further *Ecstasy and the Praise of Folly* (London: Duckworth, 1980). Terence Cave has explored the implications of Erasmian *copia* in vernacular literature of the sixteenth century with equal brilliance in his recent study, *The Cornucopian Text: Problems of Writing in the French Renaissance* (Oxford: Clarendon Pr, 1979). The thrust of these studies for our deeper reading of the English literature which drew so heavily from French intermediaries has yet to be explored in like depth.
40 I realize, of course, that the assertion of a continuum is itself a statement of a critical (and even a political and theological) position. I subscribe to the position of Dorothee Sölle – that 'Kontinuitätsschwund und eingeplante Gedächtnislosigheit sind dem hedonistischen Konsumismus notwindig" – in her essay ' "Du sollst keine andere Jeans haben neben mir," ' *Stichworte zur "Geistigen Situation der Zeit,'* ed. Jürgen Habermas (Frankfurt: Suhrkamp, 1979), 550; and I am largely in accord with Hans-George Gadamer's stress on the authority of tradition, as against the critique of Habermas that this authority is due to a social base and to systems of labor and political domination: see J. Habermas, *Zur Logik der Sozialwissenschaften: Materialien* (Frankfurt: Suhrkamp, 1970), 283f. But this is too large a matter to discuss in this paper; however, I have commented very briefly upon the force of tradition for our reading of Erasmus in 'The Place of Erasmus Today,' *Transactions of the Royal Society of Canada*, 4th ser., 8 (1970): 287-298: see Part I above.

PART VI

THE MASTERING OF CRAFT: *THE PRAISE OF FOLLY**

In this part is presented a rhetorical reading of *The Praise of Folly* for two reasons. The first is because I had thought it most desirable to have an indication of the continuing thrust of rhetoric in the thought and writing of Erasmus after 1500. Much more needs to be said, of course, and one must begin with the foundational work of Jacques Chomorat on the grammar and rhetoric of Erasmus; but further studies are needed on the rhetorical strategies and techniques in the individual *Adagia* and *Colloquia*, as well, of course, as in other works.

For now, then, let this be an earnest of further study of Erasmian rhetoric: a very short paper on *The Praise of Folly* that calls attention to the rich complexity of that rhetoric in a work apparently conceived in 1509 during a return journey from Italy, published in 1511, but much revised in 1514. (It is thus a prime example of what I have called the movement from work to text in *Intertextuality and Renaissance Texts*, and it signals as well the Erasmian growing book.) This part provides only a brief view, but it is a necessary one.

By the time that *The Praise of Folly* was published in Paris by Gilles de Gourmont in 1511, Erasmus was in his forties: this work is for us therefore a major landmark in the growing and maturing of the mind and spirituality of Erasmus. One will want, next, to turn to other works – not only the later and fuller *Adages* but also the more developed letters, and others – in order to study the grand maturing of Erasmus. That will be the task, and the challenge, of a full-scale intellectual biography of Erasmus.

>   Hier ben ik dan, halfweg, na twintig jaar –
>   Twintig jaar grotendeels verspild, de jaren van *l'entre deux guerres* –
>   Probeer woorden te leren gebruiken, en elke poging
>   Is een totaal nieuw begin, en een verschillende soort mislukking   175
>   Omdat een mens alleen maar geleerd heeft woorden te beheersen
>   Voor wat hij niet meer heeft te zeggen, of voor een manier waarop
>   Hij niet langer geneigd is het te zeggen. En zo is elke poging
>   Een nieuw begin, een strooptocht in het onverwoorde
>   Met een schamele uitrusting die als maar verslechtert,   180
>   In de ordeloze boel van onnauwkeurige gevoelens,
>   Tuchteloze benden emotie. En wat dient te worden veroverd
>   Door kracht en onderwerping, is reeds ontdekt
>   Eens of tweemaal, of meermaals, door mensen die men niet kan hopen
>   Te evenaren – maar er is geen competitie –   185

---

* This paper was prepared for delivery at a conference April 1986 in Barnard College, New York, from which I was barred from attending because of weather conditions. But the paper is here given as it was to be offered, within the time-frame stipulated.

> Er is enkel de strijd om te heroveren wat verloren ging,
> Gevonden werd, en verloren, telkens opnieuw; en nu, in omstandigheden
> Die ongustig lijken. Maar wellicht is er winst noch verlies.
> Voor ons is er enkel het proberen. De rest is niet onze zaak.
>
> T. S. ELIOT, *Four Quartets*
> (Vertaald HERMAN SERVOTTE, 1983)

Erasmus' great classic of irony was played out on the stage of European thought and letters: 'poised' (as Clarence Miller puts it quite admirably) 'between the urbanity of the Italian Renaissance and the earnestness of Northern Humanism' (*Praise*, p. x). All human life contains irony, and the complex metaphoric extensions of the *theatrum mundi* topos has a long lineage in European literature (as Ernst Robert Curtius has outlined in *European Literature and the Latin Middle Ages*, pp. 138–44 – though he omits Erasmus in his survey: a serious breach of continuity, a breach now happily addressed by Professor Grassi in his discourse on Erasmus' idea of life as a spectacle). The ironic double vision is a perilous equilibrium, because a tipping of the scales too much in the wrong direction leads to despair and cynicism, and too much in the other direction leads to preaching or propagandizing. The key to the balance, I shall urge, is rhetoric: the humanistic rhetoric of Renaissance humanism. But first let us turn directly to the work itself – for to echo Erasmus, who was quoting from Pliny in his Letter to Dorp, 'Who, after all, can live every minute wisely?' – and Maristella Lorch has stipulated a 20-minute communication from each of us.

'Recently, as I was returning to England from Italy' – you will all recognize the rhetorical gambit in the opening sentence of the prefatory letter addressed to Thomas More and prefixed to the *Moriae Encomium* [Ep. 222, dated 9 June 1511], and that recognition is reinforced a few lines later, in the words of Erasmus: 'I decided to compose a trifling thing, *Moriae Encomium*. You will ask how some Pallas Athene came to put that idea into my head.' And Erasmus then gives his readers the explanation that the name of More is close in form to *Moria* (or Folly). Much of the remainder of this preface is then a justification of the mock encomium with an appeal to the authority of Homer, Virgil, Ovid, Synesius, Lucian, and Plutarch for the *genre* of the work. Thus, Erasmus feels able to declare further, 'Others will judge me; but unless my vanity altogether deceives me, I have written a Praise of Folly without being altogether foolish.'

One might think that enough rhetorical clues have been provided already in the letter to More. Yet *The Praise of Folly* troubled the contemporaries of Erasmus, and it was frequently and bitterly attacked – by Martin Dorp, Edward Lee, Alberto Pio, and others – and it led, more than any other work of Erasmus, to the image of him as a jester, one who was not serious and did not deserve to be taken seriously. These contemporaries ignored altogether the genre of the work, despite the preface, and they missed its irony, for they 'picked various sentences out of their context and labelled them blasphemous or heretical' (thus Miller, *Praise*, p. xii). In the end, the Sorbonne condemned *The Praise of Folly* in 1543, and it appeared on nearly every index of forbidden books during the sixteenth century. It is clear that all his contemporaries did not enjoy the pleasures of folly, unless theirs was a surreptitious pleasure in reading books banned by the Sorbonne.

But in our own century there are still misunderstandings of Erasmus himself and of his purpose in *The Praise of Folly*. There is not time to draw up the map of misreadings of Erasmus, which would be legion. To take only some representative historians – Philip Hughes, Roland Bainton, and E. H. Harbison, who come to the *Praise* from a variety of theological positions – the misreading of the *Praise* has contributed grievously to misunderstandings of Erasmus himself. Johann Huizinga can be taken as central and symptomatic. For attracted though the modern Dutchman was to his fellow-countryman, whom he praised for manifesting the lasting virtues of tolerance and urbanity traditional with the Dutch, Huizinga nonetheless thought that the classicism of Erasmus alienated him quite radically from traditional Catholicism and that 'the foundation of his spiritual life was no longer a unity to Erasmus ...' (*Erasmus* [1952] p. 112). I have great respect for the work of Huizinga, but his biography of Erasmus is flawed precisely because of his failure to grasp Erasmus' ironic double vision and in particular to control the rhetorical dimensions of *The Praise of Folly*. As for the substance of Huizinga's conclusion, we have begun to see how profoundly Christian Erasmus – like Rabelais – was in fact, and I hope elsewhere to demonstrate that the spirituality of Erasmus was one of the highpoints in the long history of Christian spirituality.

The more recent work of Mikhail Bakhtin on Rabelais has had a wide vogue, and in it Bakhtin described the *Moriae Encomium* as the most complete expression of medieval Latin humor in the Renaissance and 'one of the greatest creations of carnival laughter in world literature' (1968, p. 14). But some reaction is setting in, and in a new study by Richard M. Berrong Bakhtin's views are challenged and, largely refuted (*Rabelais and Bakhtin*, 1986). Some remarks on this point are necessary, even in so brief a discussion of the pleasures of folly. One can see that the role of popular culture has been exaggerated even for Rabelais, who is closer to that culture than Erasmus. In the work of Peter Burke on *Popular Culture in Early Modern Europe* (1978) there is a parallel effort to stress that popular culture which, to be sure, had been too little understood by nineteenth-century scholars. But there are serious methodological flaws in applying the work of Bakhtin or Burke too simplistically to that of Erasmus. First, popular culture was not uniform everywhere in Europe, and one must see that the culture of the Low Countries in the 1480s and 1490s, when Erasmus was coming of age, was far more urban than it was in many other parts of Europe – certainly by comparison with that of England, for example. Second, there are kinds of literature — differing in part by virtue of genre, in part because of differences of audience, and finally in part because of the individual writer — which must be located differently upon a spectrum that ranges from the popular to the courtly, or from the folk to the intellectual. Writing in Latin, Erasmus evidently did not have the primary intention of reaching the general populace; and working in Menippean satire, in the instance of *Moriae Encomium*, he was addressing an audience that he assumed was already familiar with Lucian and the other *auctoritates* cited in the prefatory letter to More.

I do not for one moment deny that there are some folk elements in this work, or in many other works of Erasmus. Certainly the Feast of Fools or Abbot of Misrule provided one kind of precedent for the privileging of a person who could parody the pomp and satirize the errors of the ecclesiastical establishment. But even that tradition was not very widely a folk-practice and rather was closely connected with a cathedral and its schools and special hierarchy, as a rule. We have been well reminded of the *sociétés joyeuses* in France, with performances that presented a roll-call of fools.* There were these and other conventions for the licensing of fools and the celebration of folly (see the Introduction by Clarence Miller to his translation of the *Praise of Folly*, xvii–xx, for a convenient summary).

Let us accept those precedents, but let us not over-emphasize them. *The Praise of Folly, tout court*, is so demanding of its readership as to be almost a coterie piece, though to be sure it became a celebrated piece which reached a wider audience than one suspects was originally intended — not unlike the widespread popularity of Umberto Eco's *The Name of the Rose*, which one finds on the coffee-tables of many who, it would seem evident, do not read the Latin quotations or go very far into the historical overtones of the narrative. Erasmus' Praise of Folly assumes a knowledge of a complex literary tradition, a close familiarity with the Pauline tradition of the paradox of the Christian who is a fool in the eyes of the world but wise in the sight of God, and finally, a sophisticated ironic sense that permits the reader to move from one paradox to the next with enjoyment and to arrive at the ultimate ironic double vision, culminating in the comprehension and shared experience of the Pauline ecstasy of which M. A. Screech has written so compellingly.

First of all, then, *The Praise of Folly* is a piece of rhetoric. It is after all a mock encomium, a *declamatio* put into the mouth of Folly herself: it is a praising of folly by the woman Folly. She breaks most of the prized rules of conventional rhetoric and at the end tells her readers that if they are waiting for an epilogue, 'you are crazy if you think I still have in mind what I have said, after pouring forth such a torrent of jumbled words' [138]. If historians have been in error

---

*Holbein's drawing in the 1515 edition visualizes Folly's praise in a sermonic mode.

in their interpretations of *The Praise of Folly* because of their failure to comprehend the irony of the work, literary critics and scholars have in the main failed to understand the importance of rhetoric in the work and – this is the ironic turn, technically speaking – the manipulations of rhetoric, including but not limited to the medieval school rhetorics that preceded Erasmus' own educational program which had a new rhetoric at its center.

Erasmus would have laughed, one might think, to read the efforts of moderns to pin down the structure of his *Moriae Encomium* as following minutely the structure of classical oration (thus, stressing Quintilian as model, Hoyt H. Hudson in his translation of 1941); or the later efforts of Walter Kaiser, Jacques Chomorat, Richard S. Sylvester and Clarence H. Miller to tie the structure into the teachings of Aphthonius and other late rhetoricians (see Appended Note). It is not enough, I urge, to call attention to the affinities with structures in classical rhetoric, or to the inconsistencies in Folly's arguments, or to the parodical elements of her own presentation; *The Praise of Folly* is also a satirizing of the rigidities of much rhetorical teaching and also a parodying of the pretentious folly of so many professional rhetoricans, who were not unlike their colleagues, the theologians, lawyers, et al. There is still great fruitfulness in pursuing the suggestive observations of Sylvester that call attention to the movements from genesis (detailing the powers and pleasures of Folly herself) and change, to the catalogue and the explosive quality of the ultimate folly of the fool in Christ. For there is a dynamics in the rhetoric-play and development of the work, and a vital part of that dynamics is the metaphorical stretching that enlarges to include the final metamorphosis that is possible from an embracing, an understanding, of the true as opposed to the pretentious or factitious. Rhetoric, I am arguing, becomes a means or path to wisdom: to echo and expand that splendidly resonant concept of Professor Grassi, we are here experiencing *rhetoric as wisdom*.

It is my thesis that not only must we understand such a concept for the role of rhetoric in *The Praise of Folly*, and for the structuring of the work by modes of rhetoric; we must understand the work and its kind of wisdom in order to comprehend the relationship of *The Praise of Folly* to the totality of the Erasmian program. For reinforcement we can turn to Erasmus' Letter to Martin Dorp (1514), a letter printed in 1515 at Antwerp and appearing again in Badius' edition of the *Moria* (Paris, 1524) and in most important editions of the *Moria* during the rest of Erasmus' lifetime (Miller, *Praise*, p. 139). Like the *parerga* of More's *Utopia*, this letter is effect becomes part of the text of *Moria*.

In the Letter to Dorp Erasmus wrote:

> In the 'Folly' I had no other aim than I had in my other writings, but my method was different. In the 'Enchiridion' I propounded the character of a Christian life in a straightforward way. In my little book 'On the Education of a Christian Prince' I suggest explicitly the subjects in which a prince

> ought to be well versed. In that work I write openly and clearly, but my purpose was exactly the same in 'The Panegyric of Philip the Duke of Burgundy' [1504], where I proceeded indirectly and under the guise of praise. And in the 'Folly', under the appearance of a joke, my purpose is just the same as in 'The Enchiridion'. I intended to admonish, not to sting; to help, not to hurt; to promote morality, not to hinder it.
>
> (*Praise*, 142–3)

And the next sentence reminds us of the final words of the *Praise of Folly* and anticipates the aesthetic of Rabelais –

> Even such a grave philosopher as Plato approves of drinking rather freely at parties because he thinks that the merriment generated by wine can dispel certain vices which could not be corrected by sermons.

(I am referring, of course, to the last sentence of the *Praise*: 'Therefore, farewell, clap your hands, live well, drink your fill, most illustrious initiates of Folly'.)

There is yet another dimension – another rhetorical thrust, if you will – in the *Praise of Folly* that has received little attention, and that is the rhetoric of intertextuality (for a general discussion of which I refer to my monograph on *Intertextuality and Renaissance Texts*). The Prefatory letter to More – who had not yet won acclaim for his *Utopia*, but who would have been identified as the co-translator with Erasmus of Lucian – is notable, and in that letter there are allusions not only to Homer, Suetonius, Catullus, Lucian, Gellius, Seneca, Horace, and Aristophanes, but also to Erasmus' own *Adages*, which had received a more nearly definitive form in the Aldine edition of 1508, which was an instant success. If the notables of the classical canon (which was significantly widening in the first decade of the sixteenth century) are also to be found scattered throughout the work proper, allusions to or quotations from the *Adagiorum Chiliades* abound on nearly every page.

Rhetorically, it seems to me, this underscores the general principles of the Erasmian program: that classical letters contain much of wisdom, and that classical wisdom is not alien to the Christian revelation. More subtly, it would seem, the frequent echoing of the adages reminds the sophisticated reader of the connections between the *Praise of Folly* and a key work in the Erasmian program; it is another way of stressing the point that the *Praise of Folly* is in its deeper themes a sharing of purpose with the *Enchiridion* and the rest of Erasmus' writings in the first decade of the sixteenth century. To be sure, just as Folly is capable of sleight-of-hand manipulations of the scholastic syllogism (cf. Miller, *Praise*, p. xx), so too she is capable of creative misquotation: thus she misapplies the proverb about those who display their good character by their deeds to those who boast about their deeds (p. 11); and she from time to time cites ideas or proverbs that are contradictory – the one from the *Adagiorum*, the other, apparently, from the storehouse of proverbial wisdom of the Middle Ages:

> But why even bother to give you my name, as if you could not tell at a

glance who I am, 'prima facie' as it were, or as if anyone who might claim I am Minerva or Sophia could not be refuted by one good look at me, even if I did not identify myself in speech, 'that truest mirror of the mind'. (p. 13)

And despite the fact that Folly herself gave the straightarm to any conventional peroration – and recalled the old saying that 'I hate a drinking-companion with a memory' (from Plutarch, Martial and Lucian by way of the *Adagiorum*) – I shall try to provide an epilogue. Erasmus never forgot what he tried to instruct Martin Dorp: 'pleasure attracts the reader, and once attracted keeps him reading. For in other respects, various men pursue various goals, but all alike are allured by pleasure, except for those who are so insensitive that they are completely impervious to the pleasures of literature' (p. 148). There are the pleasures of folly: we are amused by the follies of vanity of *philautia* (an Erasmian concept which underlies the *Tiers Livre* of Rabelais); and we can add to the Erasmian *folies de grandeur*, especially in the world of the universities, for we have administrators, those professional non-scholars who have come to dominate the academic world. It is one thing to be a Sorbonniste; it is another to be a dean or vice-chancellor of Sorbonnistes.

In a world so dominated by rhetoric – and we might well recall the aperçu of C. S. Lewis, that we are separated from that world by our modern neglect of the resources of rhetoric – it is little wonder that the axis about which the structure, the themes, and the techniques of *The Praise of Folly* turn should be so dominantly rhetorical. If Erasmus thought that rhetoric was the *sine qua non* for the perilous equilibrium of an ironic double vision, we ought not to neglect that essentiality in our own readings of *The Praise of Folly*, for it would be folly to neglect the pleasures of this text and to forego the path that leads from rhetoric to wisdom.

Bibliography

Quotations are drawn from the translation of Clarence H. Miller (New Haven, Conn.: Yale University Press, 1979).

Bainton, Roland H. *Erasmus of Christendom* (New York: Scribners, 1969).

Bakhtin, M. *L'Oeuvre de François Rabelais et la culture popularie* Paris: Gallimard, 1970.

Berrong, Richard M. *Rabelais and Bakhtin* (Lincoln, Nebr.: Univ. of Nebraska Press, 1986).

Chomorat, Jacques. 'L'Eloge de la Folie et Quintilien,' *Information Littéraire*, No. 2 (1972), 77-82.

Curtius, Ernst R. *European Literature and the Latin Middle Ages* (New York: Bollingen/Pantheon Books, 1953).

Grassi, Ernesto and Maristella Lorch, *Folly and Insanity in Renaissance Literature* (Binghamton, New York: MRTS, 1986), esp. ch. 2.

Hudson, Hoyt H., ed. *The Praise of Folly* (Princeton, N.J.: Princeton Univ. Press, 1941).

Kaiser, Walter. *Praisers of Folly* (Cambridge, Mass.: Harvard Univ. Press, 1963).

Miller, Clarence H. 'Some Medieval Elements and Structural Unity in Erasmus' *Praise of Folly*,' *Ren Q* 27 (1974), 499-511.
Schoeck, R. J. *Intertextuality and Renaissance Texts* (Bamberg: Kaiser Verlag, 1984).
Screech, M. A. *Ecstasy and the Praise of Folly* (London: Duckworth, 1980).
Sylvester, Richard S. 'The Problem of Unity in *The Praise of Folly*,' *English Literary Renaissance* 6 (1976), 125-39.

Towards the ironic structure of *The Praise of Folly*

Quintilian	Erasmus	Yale ed.	Aphthonius	Sylvester	metamorphosis/ metaphorical
Exordium (pp. 7-8)	Folly's greeting (Hudson ed., pp. 7-8)	9-11		genesis, powers, pleasures	
narration (8-9)	Folly will praise herself extemporaneously (pp. 8-9)	11-12	proomion	§1-16 (pp. 7-47)	Past: 'variety for its own sake, as the spice of life' (RSS 138 n.)
partition	Folly will not make a partition (pp. 9-12)	12-16	genos		
	Folly's birth (11-12)		anatrophē		
confirmation (11-124)	Folly companions (13)	17-138		§17-18: change (pp. 47-52)	
	The powers and pleasures of Folly (13-67)		praxeis	§19-34: catalogue (Ship of Fools) (pp. 52-104)	Present: false metamorphoses
	The followers of Folly (67-103)		synkrisis		
	The Christian Fool (107-124)		epilogos	§35-39: 'ultimate folly of fool in Christ' (RSS 138)	
Peroration	Folly will not deliver a peroration (125)	138	(see Kaiser)	Finale - §40 (p. 125)	Future: final metamorphosis, the true

Cf. R. S. Sylvester, 'The Problem of Unity in *The Praise of Folly*,' ELR 6 (1976), 125-39.

Cf. esp. Screech, *Ecstasy and the Praise of Folly*

PART VII

THE AFTERLIFE OF ERASMUS AND HIS WORKS

'Influence' is too purely literary, and too restricting a term. The impact of Erasmus upon his age can be seen in a dozen ways: in that remarkable letter from Rabelais in 1532, in the numerous translations and adaptations as well as the almost-innumerable editions, in his function as a model for schoolbooks and curricula in England and on the Continent – yes, and in the reactions to him by the Reformers and by the Council of Trent. Each individual work by Erasmus has its own *Nachleben*, and still further there is the cumulative and much larger afterlife of Erasmus himself.

The essays in this section look at the question of Erasmian influence and attempt a 'rhetoric of influence.'

A. That Influential Clerk Erasmus*

There is much to commend in the essay by Jan van Dorsten, 'The Famous Clerk Erasmus' (*DQR*, 1980/4, 296-305). For it argues well that we should examine shifts in words like 'Erasmian', that we should be careful not to apply twentieth-century concepts and ideals to the sixteenth century, and above all that we should investigate the question of Erasmus' 'afterlife' more closely.

Van Dorsten's challenging probing leads to the necessity for our analyzing current assumptions about fame and influence, and certainly one must at the outset distinguish between fame and influence (a question which he raises initially). Whereas the title of his essay is 'The Famous Clerk Eramus', he is really talking about influence. Involved in a distinguishing of fame from influence, and of weighing and evaluating the degree of influence, is the question of evidence. How do we measure what we call influence? Is it only by quantitative data such as the number of copies or editions? If this were so, then the most influential writers of the twentieth century would be such popular novelists as Simenon and Barbara Cartland; but I scarcely think that this can be seriously argued as a main criterion.

I should like to propose consideration of three classes of evidence in discussing

---

* From *DQR* – Dutch Quarterly Review of Anglo-American Letters, vol. 12 (1982/3), 183-90.

questions of literary and intellectual influence, and these I shall call primary, secondary and indirect. Primary would be the demonstrable direct influence through publication and ownership of books, and through the documentary materials governing what is actually taught in the curricula of schools and universities. At this point or stage we must apply value judgments in our evaluation: what is the quality of mind or the level of scholarship of the person owning the books, and how has he used those books? A most suggestive methodology is offered by two recent works of scholarship: Virginia F. Stern on Gabriel Harvey, and Louis A. Knafla on Harvey's contemporary, the lawyer and jurist Lord Ellesmere; for both studies demonstrate convincingly the importance of marginalia in analyzing a scholar's use of his books.[1] Primary evidence is vital evidence, of course, but it cannot be considered to be the only kind of evidence. There is next secondary evidence, the demonstrable use of a writer as a resource through the allusions, quotations and other borrowings of his contemporaries and successors. Secondary evidence can also enter into the use of literary models (as with individual borrowings and influences within the sonnet tradition, for example) and with such conventions as the soliloquy, the several conventions of the Revenge Tragedy, blank verse, and the like, though manifestly there is the further problem of multiple influences in such matters. Indirect influence is not just fame, though perhaps the two are more closely allied than we might at first glance assume – surely the question of Miltonic influence in the eighteenth- and nineteenth-century English poets is closely related to his continuing fame. But is it not possible for a writer to have an 'underground' influence even when there is little public fame – that is to say, little primary or secondary evidence for that influence? There are several kinds of reason for driving an influence underground: political, religious, and some others, and both the political and religious pressures were operative in late sixteenth-century England and Holland.[2] In speaking about 'Traditions de la tolérance et de la civilité' in a recent paper on Erasmus and Postel,[3] I called attention to the reasons why it might not have been expedient, safe or fashionable to cite Erasmus directly in developing and transmitting ideas about tolerance in the world of the Counter-Reformation.[4] Yet the lines of influence seem unmistakably strong in running from Erasmus to Postel to Bodin and then surfacing in that remarkable work of the closing years of the sixteenth century, his *Colloquium Heptaplomeres* in which – among other influences, to be sure – the influences of Postel and Erasmus are unmistakably strong: and this *Colloquium* of Bodin's was not published at the time, thus providing a striking example of my point about certain ideas being frequently not safe or expedient to publish. I shall return to the problem of evaluating the true influence of Erasmus in the sixteenth century after a closing examination of the rationale of Jan van Dorsten's argument.

Having praised the essay by Van Dorsten that is in question – for its raising so clearly fundamental questions about influence – and having provided at least a provisional terminology for a further consideration, I should like now to argue that it does not follow that we must accept his conclusions:

> first, that Erasmus was read by only a small number of people (p. 303), or
> second, that 'for many years the voice of Erasmus — ambiguous, discursive, contradictory — seemed to have little relevance' (p. 304).

Even if it were true that Erasmus was read by only a small number of people, this would not — indeed, when one considers the nature of evidence for influence, it could not — tell the full story of his influence. Immediately one thinks of contemporary parellels or analogies: we now know that in the twentieth century (a period of cheaper books) only a small number of those who were influenced by Freud ever actually read him, and a still smaller number read him in the original language.[5] Ideas and ideals circulate outside of books as well as by the experience of one reader at a time reading one particular copy of an individual book.

Let us now consider the printing argument. To be sure, the number of copies or editions printed in a given country is important primary evidence, for it tells us much about what was available at a given time. But it does not do even that totally: the number of copies available in the year, let us say, 1590, includes not only the number printed in that year but also some part of the total number printed *before* that year as well. Further, books circulated easily in the sixteenth century, and no study of the availability of a single author in book form can be limited to what was printed only in that country. Italian books were printed in England, for example, and the *oeuvre* of an underground printer like John Wolfe (1579-1601) will demonstrate this point, and it will reinforce what is known from the data of what was printed in Italy, as well as emphasize the importance of unauthorized or forbidden printing. Similarly, if one were to make judgments about the reading of English readers in the sixteenth century purely on the strength of what the English printers turned out, the conclusions would be grossly misleading; for England imported nearly all of its works in speculative theology, liturgy, roman and canon law, even including an author like Lyndewode whose concern was with law in England. The office-journal of an Oxford bookseller fortunately gives us a vivid sense of what was being bought in Oxford at a given period (early in the sixteenth century) and how much of that was imported — including Erasmus. Thus one cannot speak with finality about what books of Erasmus were bought and owned — much less what was read — in Holland in the sixteenth century without considering texts that were imported. One would have to show that the libraries of Dutch scholars of the sixteenth century did *not* have Erasmus for Professor van Dorsten's argument to have weight.[6]

The primary evidence is important, again, but we cannot yet speak as though we as yet possessed all of the data of primary evidence in making a conclusion about that much of the evidence and its import. I should like now to turn to what I have classed as secondary evidence.

Much of Erasmus was transmitted in the late sixteenth and early seventeenth centuries through translations and abridgments or adaptations, yet often even these did not acknowledge the original hand of Erasmus.[7] In the valuable catalogue of the 1969 Liège Exposition *Le Livre Scolaire au Temps d'Érasme et des Humanistes* the hand of Erasmus is to be seen in these schoolbooks even where his name is not mentioned. In her work on *Tudor Books of Private Devotion* Helen C. White has shown how in instance after instance there were Protestant translations of Erasmus that did not acknowledge him as source.[8] That this occurred in a disputatious and warring century should not surprise us, but for us in the twentieth century it should not bar us from seeing the totality of the secondary evidence. As well as translations and the like, there is the enormous force of Erasmian influence in writers like Rabelais and Montaigne, each of whom had great influence in sixteenth-century Holland. Terence Cave in his recent study of *The Cornucopia Text* (1979) has amply demonstrated some of the ways in which Rabelais was influenced by Erasmus; he concentrated on the central rhetorical concept of *copia*, and he has explored the ramifications and implications of that borrowing brilliantly; but there are still other ways in which Erasmus influenced Rabelais. My point is that secondary influence is often the more difficult to chart when it is the deeper and stronger, as was the case with the writer whom Rabelais called 'pater mi humanissime'. While we all recognize, I am sure, that the *essai* of Montaigne is in large debt to the *adagia* of Erasmus, we have not yet begun to appreciate the manifold kinds and degrees of Erasmian influence in Montaigne.[9] As with Rabelais, so with Montaigne: the sheer quantity, and the complex intertextualities, of the veiled allusions to and evocations of the *Adagia*, the *Colloquia*, the Biblical commentaries and other works of Erasmus is staggering, but we shall not know even its extent, much less its force, until Rabelais and Montaigne scholars with the close Erasmian readings of Cave and Screech have carried their works still further. Rabelais and Montaigne are not isolated examples, though each in turn established another circle – if that metaphor is adequate (*system* might better serve to suggest the complexity of operation of influences, or even *galaxy*). Much further work is needed on this question with respect to Melanchthon, Sturm and their influences both in England and on the Continent, and with such diverse English Erasmians as Ascham and others, as well as the circles in St. John's College, Cambridge, and Corpus Christi College, Oxford, to name two prominent colleges with humanistic foundations that owned much to the impact of Erasmus.

How far do we trace influence? One might justly ask whether there isn't a law of diminishing returns when one talks about the influence of Erasmus upon 'X', who in turn influences 'Y': and rightly ask, is the second an Erasmian influence? This question is too complex to be dealt with here, but I would suggest that the framing of the question in such terms suggests a linearity – or, better, a belief in the efficacy of linearity in intellectual relations – that rarely exists in real life. Intellectual and literary relations more often are circular, repetitive, cyclical, and at times even like a Möbius strip.[10]

There is much else having to do with Erasmian influence that we simply lack. In my judgment we still do not have a sound and magisterial statement about the influence of Erasmus in Biblical scholarship or in the general public's reading of Scripture during the sixteenth century. How widely, in fact, did his paraphrases and editions continue to circulate, and how much did they continue to be read? – and by whom? Let us not forget that Erasmus was also an indefatigable editor of patristic texts: for present purposes the vital question is not so much how good they were from twentieth-century standards of scholarship, as how much they were read and used, and in what ways they influenced succeeding generations of scholars. Rudolf Pfeiffer's last book, *History of Classical Scholarship: 1300-1850* (1976) is uneven, but his chapter on Erasmus quite usefully pulls together much that will launch us on the enterprise which the questions in this paragraph call for. The large folio volumes of Jerome, Cyprian, Hilary, Ambrose, Irenaeus, Augustine, and Chrysostom bulk large not only on the shelf but in the minds and scholarship of the sixteenth century. J. de Ghellinck has given us a searching, and favourable, assessment of Erasmus' edition of Augustine: we need companion evaluations of the other patristic editions![11]

Finally, let us not forget that Erasmus was in addition an editor of humanistic texts. He translated parts of Xenophon, Plutarch, Galen, Lucian, and Euripides – all authors of great importance in the humanistic program of the century (the canon of which Erasmus was so influential in shaping) – and the contribution of Erasmus' translations needs continuing study.[12] In a century of many and sometimes great translations, Erasmus' own contribution was not insignificant. Finally, Erasmus contributed to the humanistic canon by his editions of Terence, Suetonius, Pliny, Livy, Aristotle and Demosthenes; we have hardly begun to evaluate that achievement.

We can make and surely accept one final summary statement: it was Erasmus more than any other individual (though it must be recognized that he stood on the shoulders of his humanistic predecessors) who created the humanistic texts that taught the schoolboy of the sixteenth and seventeenth centuries. Both in the original forms written by Erasmus and in innumerable adaptations, revisions, abridgments and translations, *De Copia, De Ratione Studii, Ciceronianus, De Conscribendis epistolis, Compendium rhetorices, Declamationes,* and others, all had wide and widening circles of influence. In all of these works there was a coherent and rather distinctively Erasmian program of study (as Craig R. Thompson makes clear in his admirable introduction to volume 23 of the Collected Works of Erasmus, the *Literary and Educational Writings,* volume 24 of which presents modern English translations of *De Copia* and *De Ratione Studii*[13] — a program which provided techniques and a structure of learning, includes the techniques of reading and writing together with models of a supple humanistic Latin. Yet, like an umbrella shading and colouring all of these parts, there was the final achievement of Erasmus himself which was the exemplar and model of a sixteenth-century humanist who was addressing all of the problems of his age, an 'optimum exemplar' if you will, who inspired students and future readers, as well as contemporaries, with the concept of a Ciceronian belief in the common good and ideal commonwealth, combined with a simple Christianity (of which I have written in my essay on the Renaissance *respublica literarum* in the forthcoming *Sir Thomas Browne and the Republic of Letters*[14]). Ideals of the commonwealth, of the republic of letters, of peace and harmony, of good letters — these are not easily inspired nor quickly extinguished, and it is on this higher plane that we must look for the deeper and more lasting influence of Erasmus.

Yes, the fame of a writer is different and must be distinguished from his influence. A medieval and even a Renaissance writer might himself distinguish on the basis of influence being real, whereas fame is illusory. Perhaps. But I would maintain that the matter of the influence of Erasmus at the end of the sixteenth century is far from closed, and that we must bring in more evidence and perhaps have a larger and better instructed jury. At present I am not persuaded that we should think that Erasmus was read by only a small number of people, in England or in Holland, nor that his voice seemed to have little relevance![15].

R. J. SCHOECK

A Reply

My article was intended to provoke a response, and it is gratifying to see that one of the world's leading Erasmus scholars has taken the trouble to voice his unhappiness with my conclusions.

I argued that in the late sixteenth century Erasmus continued to be famous, but that there also appears to have been a reduced interest in his writings, both in England and in the Northern Netherlands, because his 'method' did not solve any of the day's problems. The response to my article emphasizes the fact that we lack an authoritative, informed study of Erasmus' influence in the late sixteenth century, and offers an attractive methodology to prove me wrong. As Schoeck puts it, 'we must bring in more evidence' because he is 'not persuaded'. But where is his evidence?

I never talked about bestsellers (Simenon) compared with less popular authors; I referred to a complete absence of publications. I myself mentioned the 'modern parallels' to 'great men' 'to whom one can occasionally refer without ever having read the books'; but surely Professor Schoeck does not wish us to believe that we become Freudians by invoking the Master's name without any familiarity with his ideas? And if (a particularly slippery witness like) Rabelais was influenced by Erasmus' concept of *copia*, does that make him an Erasmian?

I may have erred; if so, show us. Schoeck tells us that Erasmus was an unsafe author to quote 'in the world of the Counter-Reformation' – but I was not discussing that world. He reminds us that some books were forbidden – was Erasmus on the Elizabethan *Index*, or on William the Silent's? – and that John Wolfe printed clandestine Italian books in England – but did he also propagate the works of Erasmus? All three 'classes of evidence' proposed by Schoeck are legitimate and important. But without seeing them, I cannot change my conclusions.

JAN VAN DORSTEN

1 Virginia F. Stern, *Gabriel Harvey: A Study of His Life, Marginalia and Library*, Oxford, 1979 – cf. rev. R. J. Schoeck *ELN* 18 (1981) 295-8 – and Louis A. Knafla, *Law and Politics in Jacobean England: The Tracts of Lord Chancellor Ellesmere,* Cambridge, 1977.
2 For a striking argument on this point, see Edward E. Lowinsky, *Secret Chromatic Art in the Netherlands Motet,* New York, 1946.
3 'Erasme et Postel: Traditions de la tolérance et de la civilité', (see B following) published in a forthcoming volume of papers given at the Postel Congress, Avranches 1981, ed. by J. C. Margolin.
4 Only for the case of Erasmus in Spain has there been sufficient research for a firm generalization about his influence – see M. Bataillon, *Erasme et l'Espagne,* Paris, 1937, which demonstrates a profound Erasmian influence even in this country. It is perhaps time to prepare a synthetic statement of the influence of Erasmus everywhere in Europe throughout the sixteenth century.
5 See F. J. Hoffman, *Freudianism and the Literary Mind,* Baton Rouge, 1945 – an interesting methodology for the study of an -ism.
6 In a forthcoming note I shall show how prevalent copies of Erasmus were in the individual libraries of Oxford scholars during this period. There is little in the scholarship dealing with other countries to compare with the careful bibliographical research of Marcella T. and Paul F. Grendler in their discussion of the fate of Erasmus' works in Seicento Italy: see 'The Survival of Erasmus in Italian Libraries', *Erasmus in English* 8 (Toronto, 1976), 2-22.
7 The monograph by E. J. Devereux dealing with sixteenth-century English translations of Erasmus is now in press (University of Toronto Press, 1982).
8 Helen C. White, *Tudor Books of Private Devotion,* Madison, 1951 – my review of this work in *Modern Philology,* 49 (1952) 279-81 comments on certain problems in identifying underground and surreptitious editions.
9 See my forthcoming essay on 'The Erasmian Model: Humanism and the Vernacular Literatures'.
10 Concepts of linearity and multidimensionality are discussed in my essay on 'Mathematics and the Languages of Literary Criticism', *Journal of Aesthetics and Art Criticism,* 26 (1968) 367-76, and in place of a linear metaphor I have there suggested a notion from topology.
11 See J. de Ghellinck in *Miscellanea J. Gessler* I (1948) 530ff.
12 See J. H. Waszink in *Antike und Abendland* 17 (1971).
13 I have extended the discussion of the Erasmian program in my essay on 'Erasmian Spirituality:

The Languages of Religion', an address given at the University of Dallas (1981).
14 Now in press and to appear as a Special Number of *English Language Notes* (June 1982).
15 In the collection of essays published in English translation as *Dutch Civilisation in the Seventeenth Century* (London, 1968), J.H. Huizinga has given some weight to the 'voice of Erasmus' (p. 53 & *passim*), and there is of course recognition of that voice in his biography of Erasmus.

A footnote to 'That Influential Clerk Erasmus': it is clear from Jan van Dorsten's reply that I had not succeeded in persuading him before publication in 1983. Proof is scarcely possible in such a case, and one can hope only that a logical and coherent argument has been put forward. What is important is to establish a concensus concerning the need for a rhetoric of influence, and then to weigh the different kinds of evidence that converge at the probability that the influence of Erasmus continued unbroken from the 16th century on into the 17th. A minor, but significant, part of my thesis is that one must look for evidence not only within the Netherlands (and in Antwerp as well as Amsterdam and Leiden), but also outside; for printing and scholarship were both international enterprises during the Renaissance. Jan van Dorsten's tragically early death in 1985 ended our dialogue on this and other questions.

B. Erasme et Postel: les traditions de la civilité et de la tolérance*

On a beaucoup écrit sur la question de la tolérance au XVIe siècle, et je rappellerai notamment les deux volumes de Joseph Lecler sur la tolérance et la Réforme, et les quatre volumes de W.-K. Jordan sur le développement de la tolérance en Angleterre au siècle suivant[1]. La question de la tolérance − c'est-à-dire les diverses manières d'aborder le problème et la façon même de le poser − connaît un développement si profond et si complexe du XIIIe au XVIIe siècle qu'on ne saurait, en une seule conférence, en esquisser l'histoire. Je voudrais seulement proposer quelques réflexions sur la nature de la tolérance et sur ce qui la distingue du tolérantisme, pour examiner ensuite en quoi l'humanisme d'Erasme et de Budé constitue le fondement de l'extraordinaire tolérance de Guillaume Postel[2].

A la fin du XVIe siècle, Montaigne, qui me semble devoir beaucoup à Postel même s'il ne cite pas son nom (ce pourquoi il avait ses raisons, quelles qu'elles fussent), exprime son esprit même quand il écrit:

> Non parce que Socrates l'a dict, mais parce qu'en vérité c'est mon humeur, et à l'avanture non sans quelque excez, j'estime tous les hommes mes compatriotes et embrasse un Polonais comme un François, postposant cette lyaison nationale à l'universelle et commune[3].

La tolérance est généralement considérée comme plus individuelle que le toléran-

*This essay is reprinted from *Guillaume Postel, 1581-1981*. (Avranches; Guy Trédaniels Editions de la Maisnier 1982).

tisme; et ceux qui ont médité le sujet la tiennent pour plus profondément humaine que lui. Dans une importante contribution intitulée « Toleration in Early Modern Times », le Professeur Herbert Butterfield écrit:

> Toleration, like religious liberty, can perhaps best be regarded as a system, or a regime[4].

Cette affirmation est contestable: la tolérance est plus qu'un système ou un régime (qu'il soit politique ou religieux), même si la notion de tolérance englobe l'idée qu'un gouvernement accorde ou concède la permission de pratiquer d'autres religions que celles qui sont établies. Le Dictionnaire de l'Académie Française définit la tolérance comme la

> Permission qu'un gouvernement accorde de pratiquer, dans l'Etat, d'autres religions que celles qui y sont établies, reconnues par les lois, pratiquées par le plus grand nombre des citoyens.

Dans l'*Utopie* de Thomas More, si cette sorte de tolérance existe certes, et y constitue un système, c'est au nom d'un esprit de tolérance qui la fonde[5]. En effet, la tolérance comme pure permission est ce qu'on pourrait appeler une tolérance simplement formelle – pour utiliser la distinction posée par Gustav Minchling dans son *Toleranz und Wahrheit in der Religion* (1955); elle se réduit à une non-intervention; c'est en ce sens d'une liberté formelle que nous employons le mot aujourd'hui encore, quand nous parlons des privilèges ou de la liberté religieuse qui sont accordés dans certains pays. Mais il existe une sorte de tolérance plus profonde: celle qui admet une autre religion comme une possibilité même, sincère et authentique, de l'expérience du sacré; celle-ci est la tolérance positive.

Au Quattrocento, deux penseurs remarquables ont conçu cette sorte de tolérance: Nicolas de Cues et Marsile Ficin. Dans son *De Pace seu Concordantia*, Nicolas de Cues écrit qu'à travers la diversité et la variété des cultes on peut percevoir l'existence d'une unique religion:

> et cognoscent omnes quomodo non est nisi religio una in rituum varietate[6].

Marsile Ficin a, de même, déclaré qu'à travers l'histoire, c'est une religion commune qui s'exprime. Ces idées n'eurent le temps ni de se répandre largement, ni de se développer avant la Réforme: presque immédiatement après octobre 1517, la Réforme a conduit les adversaires, à l'intérieur même du Christianisme, à se considérer en ennemis; et les Turcs furent presque oubliés. Il vaut la peine de remarquer que les métaphores guerrières surgissent dans les polémiques presque immédiatement après que Martin Luther eut affiché ses thèse en 1517, et qu'elles se maintiendront pendant tout le siècle: trop souvent, du reste, ces images ont pris des significations qui n'étaient plus seulement métaphoriques. Les combattants furent à ce point aveuglés par les controverses et par la valeur absolue qu'ils attachaient à leur propre profession de foi, à leur propre « symbole », qu'il leur devint presque impossible de voir les autres comme des variantes d'une même religion. Au demeurant, avant le XXe siècle, peu d'hommes pouvaient atteindre à une telle tolérance œcuménique[7].

J'ai parlé de *tolérantisme*. Ce néologisme du XVIIIe siècle est défini par le Dictionnaire de l'Académie Française — que je suis une fois encore — comme « l'opinion de ceux qui étendent trop loin la tolérance théologique »; non sans ironie, le Dictionnaire cite ensuite cette formule: « La tolérance dégénère en tolérantisme. » *Tolérantisme*, comme aussi *tolérance*, a des connotations de condescendance, d'indulgence, voire d'indifférence. Quand la tolérance, de formelle, devient positive, elle implique nécessairement une disposition à accepter, dans leurs différences, les croyances, les usages, les habitudes. On peut donner une expression légale à la tolérance formelle; on ne peut jamais, par les lois, réaliser la tolérance positive, qui, elle, procède de la conscience et de la raison, et exige la bonne volonté. C'est de cette tolérance positive dans la pensée de Postel que je me propose de traiter.

Un des éléments de la tolérance positive est l'idée stoïcienne de l'homme comme animal raisonnable, et de tout individu, homme ou femme, comme membre d'une fraternité — idée que notre tradition occidentale n'a pas complètement perdue, même si elle n'en a pas toujours bien compris les racines. *Humanitas:* au fond de l'idée stoïcienne de l'homme, il y a l'idée d'*humanitas*. Au IVe siècle avant Jésus-Christ, est venue s'y ajouter l'idée d'une « sympathie » pour et avec son semblable. Parlant de ce nouveau sentiment de la dignité de l'homme, Bruno Snell a écrit dans son *Discovery of Mind* (je cite en anglais):

> ...a modicum of *humanitas* for which no particular talent is needed. The eternal absolutes which rule over us, especially justice and truth, unhappily often make us forget that the absolute which accedes to our understanding is not entirely absolute after all. On occasion they will even allow us to act as if we were the absolute embodied, to the great sorrow of our fellow-men. At that point, morality turns into dynamite, and the explosion increases in violence as more and more men come to believe that it is their duty to follow the absolute. Finally, when it is agreed that certain institutions have come to represent the absolute, the catastrophe becomes inevitable. Then is the time to remind oneself that each and every human being has his own share of dignity and of freedom. All we require is a little courtesy, a bit of tolerance, and *o sancte Erasme,* just a dash of your irony[8].

Si les origines de ces réflexions remontent loin dans l'histoire de l'humanité, on peut en saisir assez clairement le fondement dans ce que dit Plutarque — je cite encore Snell — sur

> the admired polity of Zeno, the founder of the Stoic school, [which] was directed to the single conclusion, that... we should count all men fellow-citizens, and be as one flock on a common pasture feeding together by a common law...

L'historien anglais Ernest Barker a admirablement récapitulé ces éléments de la tradition stoïcienne que j'ai voulu mettre en œuvre. Il écrit dans son livre intitulé *Traditions of Civility* (1948):

> In the Stoic theory of the *cosmopolis* the rational faculty of man was conceived as producing a common conception of law and order which possessed a universal validity, transcending alike the cities of the Greeks and the nations of the Gentiles: and according to Stoic thought — already anticipated in action by the policy of Alexander — this common conception included, as its three great notes, the three values of Liberty, Equality, and the brotherhood or Fraternity of all mankind. This common conception, and its three great notes, have formed a European set of ideas for over two thousand years[9].

Laissant de côté les développements ultérieurs de cette « conception commune », je voudrais insister sur l'idée essentielle d'*humanitas* et sur le grand idéal d'égalité qu'elle implique. La conception érasmienne de l'*humanitas*, soutenue par sa conception de la *civilitas*, appelle logiquement, comme une des ses parties, la tolérance. Pour Erasme, comme a dit Wallace K. Ferguson, la tolérance

> was an integral and perhaps largely unconscious part of his Christian humanism. To a greater or less degree, it was implicit in every book he wrote, from the *Enchiridion* to the *Praise of Folly*, from the *Adages* to the *Familiar Colloquies*..[10].

Précisons toutefois que le propos de Ferguson omet la quintessence de l'humanisme érasmien. Entendre *humanisme* comme la traduction ou l'équivalent moderne de *studia humanitatis,* c'est limiter le sens *d'humanitas*. Dans le latin classique, *humanitas* signifie la nature humaine ou l'humanité: en principe, les qualités ou même les souhaits du genre humain; ainsi la conduite humaine ou polie envers autrui, l'humanité au sens moderne de philanthropie, et aussi la bonté, la douceur et même la politesse. Cette signification classique est diversement modulée par les Pères de l'Eglise: Lactance oppose *humanitas* à *divinitas*; et l'on trouve d'autres occurrences de l'opposition de l'humain et du divin chez

Tertulien et ailleurs. Quant au sens cicéronien de bonté, il s'amplifie avec Ambroise et Cassien, qui emploient le mot dans un sens proche d'hospitalité. On note encore chez Augustin (et dans une lettre à un évêque) la formule honorifique: *humanitas tua*[11]. Ainsi, fort de ces connotations classiques et patristiques, Érasme peut employer *humanitas* pour désigner ce qui se rapporte à la nature humaine, à l'humanité du Christ lui-même, et encore pour ce qui, à nos yeux, inclut la civilité. *Alioque si more domesticos spectes,* écrit-il de ses compatriotes bataves, *ad benignitatem propensior*[12]. Les qualités qu'Érasme prisait le plus étaient la douceur, la bonté, la simplicité: vertus qu'on ne peut avoir sans *humanitas* et *civilitas*[13].

Le terme de *civilitas* est plus difficile à analyser et à définir brièvement. Au temps où Postel était à Paris, quelques humanistes anglais formaient un groupe; tous avaient fait leurs études en Italie; ils ont pris part au dialogue entre le Cardinal Pole et Thomas Lupset, rapporté par Thomas Starkey, dont le thème principal était le « very and true civil life, or what is called civility ». *Civilitas* empruntait aux traditions stoïciennes, que les jurisconsultes romains avaient recueillies, puis fondues dans leur notion de *ius naturale*, notion qui elle-même avait été assimilée par les Pères de l'Eglise et englobée dans leur théorie générale de la société, comme elle avait été transmise, non seulement par le droit canon romain (avec la foule des écrits de ses commentateurs), mais aussi par les nombreux ouvrages d'Augustin, de saint Thomas et de leurs successeurs, – ainsi que M. Reulos, spécialiste du droit, le montre dans sa conférence sur « l'humanisme juridique dans le *De orbis terrae concordia* ».

Parmi les manifestations de cette tradition complexe de l'humanisme avant Érasme, j'ai cité Nicolas de Cues et Marsile Ficin, auquel, à Florence, il faut joindre notamment Jean Pic de la Mirandole. Mais il faudrait mentionner aussi les autres centres de l'humanisme en France et en Italie, et, plus généralement, analyser les concepts *d'humanitas, de civilitas, d'aequitas* dans la perspective de l'ensemble de l'humanisme de la Renaissance, – travail qui reste à faire. Contentons-nous de nommer, parmi les contemporains d'Érasme, Thomas More – il s'agit ici de ses écrits humanistes, non de ses ouvrages polémiques –, Jérôme Busleiden et, naturellement, Guillaume Budé. Tous ont tenu une place dans la publication de *l'Utopie* de More[14]. C'est là une raison de considérer ici ce livre. De ce chef-d'œuvre bien connu de la Renaissance, on observera, au moins, que la tolérance est un trait dominant de la société utopienne et que le livre II note que c'est parce que les Utopiens sont disposés à admettre une grande variété de croyances religieuses (pourvu qu'il y ait une foi commune en l'immortalité de l'âme) qu'ils ont pu recevoir le christianisme lui-même.

Mais *l'utopie* n'est pas seulement un chef-d'œuvre de l'humanisme, c'est aussi un cas exemplaire d'intertextualité[15]. Il s'y trouve tout un tissu (en latin, *textura*) d'allusions et de références qu'on a commencé à débrouiller grâce à l'érudition du R. P. Edward Surtz dans son édition de Yale, et, plus récemment, à celle d'André Prévost dont l'édition française comporte un appareil critique élaboré[16]. Et, avant tout, plusieurs mains ont collaboré à l'ouvrage: celle de More lui-même, et celles de Pierre Gilles, d'Érasme et de plusieurs autres humanistes des Pays-Bas. Mais, il faut, au sujet *d'humanitas* dans *l'Utopie*, s'arrêter à Busleiden et à Budé. Jérôme Busleiden était membre du Conseil de Charles-Quint; il fonda le Collège Trilingue de l'Université de Louvain, qui a sans doute suggéré à Budé l'idée de faire des démarches pour faire ouvrir en France un collège comparable. La lettre de Busleiden à Budé (qui précède le texte dans l'édition de 1516, mais le suit dans celle de 1518) appelle More: *doctissime et idem humanissime*: Busleiden y formule aussi l'idée de l'amour de la patrie, idée qui était également chère à More. Quant à Budé, il était, comme More et Busleiden, juriste et humaniste; et il se trouvait être conservateur de la bibliothèque royale quand il a suggéré à François Ier de créer le Collège des Lecteurs Royaux; ouvert en 1530, celui-ci prendra plus tard le nom de Collège de France. Dans sa lettre à Lupset, qui précède l'édition parisienne de *l'Utopie* (1517), Budé traite explicitement du droit naturel et du droit des gens (*ius gentium*)[17]. Il n'est pas douteux que le droit romain et son idée de l'individu n'avaient déjà cours à la veille de la Réforme; rappelons encore les recherches de Guido Kisch sur *Erasmus und die Jurisprudenz seiner Zeit*, qui établit non seulement qu'Érasme entretenait des relations avec l'école bâloise du droit, mais encore que sa pensée sera ensuite dominée par des concepts comme *summum ius summa iniuria*; de même, les idées du droit tiendront une grande place chez les humanistes français (comme l'ont montré, entre autres, Linton Stevens, E. Nardi, D.-R. Kelley)[18]. On voit aussi, dans toute la correspondance d'Erasme, de More, de Budé et d'autres, se développer l'idée de la République des Lettres[19]. Les citoyens de la République des Lettres mirent en circulation et répandirent ces idées de l'homme et de l'individu. Postel devait donc les connaître; Jean-Claude Margolin a montré comment Postel lecteur mobilise toutes les ressources de sa culture[20].

Que l'humanisme érasmien se soit diffusé n'est pas douteux; on peut toutefois s'interroger sur l'étendue et les formes de son influence. Plusieurs savants ont établi qu'il existait des courants érasmiens dans beaucoup de cours princières, ou séculières ou ecclésiastiques: qu'il suffise de rappeler l'action de Caesar et Julius Pflug à la Cour de Georges de Saxe, et de mentionner les recherches de Bataillon, de Flitner, de Stupperich, de Jedin et de Lecler[21]. S'il est vrai qu'à Regensburg, en 1541, les efforts de conciliation ont échoué − et Jedin a pu écrire qu'on avait alors tenté l'impossible[22] −, l'humanisme érasmien a continué à agir par d'autres voies: rappelons notamment les recherches de Marcel Bataillon sur Erasme en Espagne, et l'étude de McConica sur l'influence d'Érasme en Angleterre[23]. Toutefois, après 1541, l'atmosphère en Europe est profondément différente; à partir de 1545 siège le Concile de Trente; la Contre-Réforme est en marche. Dès lors, à compter de 1545, l'humanisme érasmien baisse pavillon; les décrets et les définitions du Concile de Trente durcissent les positions dogmatiques; les chances d'un rapprochement diminuent, et la possibilité même d'un dialogue recule. La tolérance n'est plus du tout ce qu'elle avait été ou donné l'espoir d'être dans la Florence du Quattrocento.

Pendant que siège le Concile, Calvin laisse percer son manque de tolérance dans la *Declaratio orthodoxae fidei* (1554); et, la même année, Castellion, dans le *De haereticis,* souligne que la tolérance jusque-là prônée par Calvin est maintenant refusée par lui aux athées et aux rationalistes extrémistes. L'année de sa mort, en 1563, Castellion publiera l'intéressant *De arte dubitandi et confitendi, ignorandi et sciendi,* où il essaie, comme Nicolas de Cues, Érasme et Postel, de trouver un terrain commun de discussion et des voies vers un accord; comme Postel, il fait dériver la liberté religieuse de la faculté de la raison. Quant à Michel Servet, qui fut exécuté aux portes de Genève en octobre 1553, il ne fut pas la simple victime de la tyrannie de Calvin, son adversaire religieux: l'opinion à la fois protestante et catholique encouragea son exécution[24].

La *via media* érasmienne, qui déjà dans les années 1517-1520 était chose malaisée, s'avéra une route de plus en plus hérissée d'écueils à mesure que le siècle avançait. Il n'est donc pas étonnant que ceux qui s'étaient déclarés érasmiens aient appris ensuite à agir plus prudemment.

Considérons maintenant Postel lui-même. On soulignera l'influence qu'exercèrent sur sa formation intellectuelle Érasme et Budé à la fois. S'appuyant sur *l'Histoire de Sainte-Barbe* de Quicherat, le pr Bouwsma a indiqué l'ouverture que, semblablement, le collège de Sainte-Barbe manifesta à l'égard de la culture nouvelle:

> Thus Gelida had wanted his philosophy in Greek, classical studies received an honored place in the curriculum, and an effort had been begun to replace scholastic with classical Latin[25].

C'était là, me semble-t-il, une œuvre considérable, dont le projet demande qu'on face plus de place que ne l'a fait Bouwsma aux forces humanistes. Dans les débats universitaires sur la *ratio studiorum* — ils ont lieu partout, des années 1520 à 1540 —, c'est une grande victoire de l'érasmisme que d'avoir obtenu que la philosophie fût enseignée en grec et les études classiques à ce point remises en honneur.

Mais il faut aussi mettre en lumière l'influence de Guillaume Budé. Il était, comme on sait, l'ami de Postel au moins lors de la nomination de celui-ci comme lecteur au Collège des Lecteurs Royaux. Il est possible que Budé ait contribué à lui faire accorder cette fonction dans une institution dont la fondation devait beaucoup à l'action de Budé. En tout cas, Postel a rendu hommage à Budé dans l'épître liminaire du *De magistratibus Atheniensium liber* (Paris, 1541), étude de la constitution athénienne qui dut être fort prisée de l'humaniste juriste qu'était Guillaume Budé.

Lié aux milieux humanistes parisiens, Postel, de 1538 à 1542, donne des cours au Collège; il poursuit ses recherches sur l'hébreu (s'intéressant notamment aux origines juives de la langue et de la civilisation) et en arabe (on lui doit la première grammaire européenne de l'arabe classique). En 1542, une controverse le fait congédier; il travaille à son *De orbis terrae concordia*[26]. En 1544, il se rend à Rome pour entrer dans la Compagnie de Jésus, dont il est exclu en décembre suivant. C'est en 1544, à Bâle où les idéaux érasmiens demeurent très vivants, qu'il publie quatre livres de son grand ouvrage, le *De orbis terrae concordia*. Au centre du livre (1. II, chap. 10), il rassemble, sous le titre de *Persuasionum omnium canones communes,* les thèses principales d'un Christianisme simplifié sur lesquelles tous les hommes raisonnables devraient pouvoir tomber d'accord, – accord qui, conformément à l'esprit de Ficin et de Jean Pic, inclut tous les religions de l'humanité[27]. *Humanitas* est ici présupposée, et l'appel à la raison constitue le *sine qua non,* comme en général dans les écrits et dans la pensée de Postel.

A nouveau, dans son extraordinaire *Panthenosia* de 1547, Postel traite des vérités communes, valables pour toutes les confessions religieuses et pour tous les hommes de raison, vérités qui pourraint permettre un rapprochement de toutes les nations et de toutes les croyances. Dans les dernières pages du livre, Postel fait l'éloge de l'esprit d'entente, de la tolérance et de la charité, en invoquant trois raisons:

1. personne ne saurait anticiper le jugement de Dieu;
2. Dieu seul sait nos intentions (alors qu'elles nous échappent à nous-mêmes en raison de nos passions);
3. la paix religieuse demande un accord des hommes sur un certain nombre de questions essentielles (idée très érasmienne)[28].

Lecler, dans son remarquable ouvrage sur la tolérance, a souligné à quel point Postel agit ici en véritable humaniste; voici sa conclusion:

> En bon humaniste, Postel continue de poursuivre, au delà de l'union des chrétiens, celle des hommes de toute race et de toute religion. Ce passage n'en est pas moins d'un grand intérêt pour l'histoire de la tolérance du protestantisme en France. A cette date il classe Postel parmi les précurseurs, bien avant la génération des 'politiques' qui fera parler d'elle à partir de Charles IX[29].

Dans un livre publié en 1562, mais aujourd'hui perdu, Postel indiquera les raisons du nécessaire accord des protestants, dits Huguenots en France, et des catholiques, dits Romains ou Papistes. Et de 1563 jusqu'à sa mort, en 1581, détenu au monastère de Saint-Martin, il continuera à travailler à la réforme et à la réalisation de l'unité du monde sous le Christ, contribuant notamment à la Bible Polyglotte éditée par Plantin[30].

J'aimerais un instant noter la publication, en 1543, du grand ouvrage de Copernic, le *De revolutionibus Orbium cœlestium,* et rappeler que Copernic, canoniste, avait principalement étudié Gratien et sa *Concordia discordantium canonum*[31]. En droit canon comme ailleurs, le XVIe siècle s'intéressait essentiellement à harmoniser les théories et les faits – *conserve les données,* disent les astronomes –, comme à harmoniser les textes entre eux, pour parler comme les éditeurs. *Concordia,* comme *methodus,* est un maître-mot de l'époque[32]. Frances Yates a aussi montré l'importance que la Renaissances hermétique et cabbalistique attachait au thème ancien de l'harmonie du monde. L'harmonie est une des préoccupations principales de la pensée de Postel. Notons-le encore, au XVIe siècle, les analogies musicales et juridiques de *concordia* ne sont peut-être pas complètement oubliées.

Avant de conclure, il faut redire que c'est une thèse fondamentale de cette étude qu'il a existé une tradition du droit naturel (même si elle n'est pas toujours apparente et même si les circonstances et les urgences l'ont souvent déformée) – et une tradition qui va assez continûment d'Eschyle à l'époque moderne à travers le Moyen Age, qui trouve une brillante expression, à la fin du XVIe siècle, chez le théologien élisabéthain Richard Hooker, qui est répétée en écho dans l'Éclaircissement, qui s'énonce dans la Déclaration d'Indépendance des récents Etats-Unis, en 1776, comme dans diverses proclamations où s'exprime toute la philosophie de la Révolution Française[33]. Eschyle et Sophocle (et je pense surtout à des tragédies comme l'*Orestie* et *Antigone*) formulent la notion d'une justice éternelle et immuable, née de la nature de l'univers, c'est-à-dire de l'être de Dieu et de la raison de l'homme. En parlant d'une tradition du droit naturel, j'entends, comme le fait D'Entrève (qui est ici mon maître), une tradition qui implique, qui même exige, un sens du *semper bonum et aequum*[34]. C'est là, selon moi, une vue qui, même en matière de loi, est toujours nécessaire.

Le XVIe siècle fut le siècle de la Renaissance, de la Réforme, et de la réception du droit romain. Ces grands mouvements ont touché presque tous les hommes, consciemment ou non. Postel vivait au cœur des mouvements intellectuels de la Renaissance comme de ceux de la Réforme; on doit, de même, prendre en compte le rôle du droit romain dans la formation de sa pensée et chercher comment ses idées ont pu être fortifiées par lui. A ce sujet, Bouwsma s'arrête seulement aux critiques de Postel à l'égard des jurisconsultes romains incapables de se mettre d'accord; mais, dans une note importante, il mentionne la condition requise par Postel:

> lex una, assumptum unum, vox simplex, quae ipsa una veritate tantum niti potest[35].

Ce rapide regard sur le droit romain permet de mieux comprendre le combat de Postel pour la concorde et l'unité. Car c'est là un fondement de ses principes si fermement affirmés de tolérance et de civilité; toutes deux doivent aux traditions du droit.

En conclusion, bien que le temps n'ait pas permis de dessiner la carte complète du paysage, il est certain que la route principale qui conduit à la pensée de Postel en matière de tolérance et de civilité part d'Érasme (vers qui convergaient beaucoup de grands chemins comme beaucoup de sentiers détournés) et de Budé (qui, par ses recherches et par ses fonctions auprès du roi, fut un guide pour bien d'autres). Je me propose, l'an prochain, de poursuivre cette étude en direction de Bodin.

Il est trop facile de dire, comme l'a affirmé le Pr Butterfield dans l'article cité plus haut, que le mouvement dont Érasme fut le grand inspirateur a – pour citer Butterfield – « captured some famous men, at least for a time, but failed completely in the long run »[36]. A coup sûr, le programme érasmien de réforme se trouva pris en enfilade entre les Réformateurs et les défenseurs de la citadelle romaine; pour continuer la métaphore militaire, on pourrait dire que la position d'Érasme fut celle d'un pacifiste ou d'un arbitre soumis à un tir de barrage. Mais la bibliographie érasmienne est un fait incontournable: Érasme a continué à être imprimé et réimprimé à travers tout le XVIe et jusqu'au XVIIe; il a directement exercé une très forte influence intellectuelle et littéraire sur Rabelais (comme Terence Cave l'a récemment montré dans *The Cornucopia Text*[37]), sur Montaigne et sur d'autres, et, à travers eux, sur d'autres encore. Dans l'étude de la Bible, son influence s'est maintenue longtemps après qu'on ne le citait plus. Il est significatif de noter que, pendant la période élisabéthaine, on traduisait en anglais les prières d'Érasme en omettant de lui en faire hommage.[38] A ces preuves s'ajoute l'image l'Érasme comme premier citoyen de la République des Lettres: elle eut son importance au temps des guerres de religion, comme aussi son pacifisme et son sens critique. Non, Érasme et le mouvement qu'il inspira ne me semblent pas avoir échoué[39].

Il se peut que la tolérance ne soit, dans le vaste spectre de l'activité humaine, qu'une étroite bande; et bien des chercheurs ont pu écrire sur la Renaissance en se contentant de quelques phrases aimables sur le sujet de la tolérance aux XVIe siècle. Pourtant, sans cette étroite bande, Postel est inintelligible, de même qu'un certain nombre des plus grandes questions de la Réforme ne s'éclairent que pour autant que l'on cherche à voir comment cette bande se déplace dans le spectre. Pour poursuivre la métaphore, on pourrait dire que la tolérance ressemble à une surface de Möbius, qui se meut dans plus d'une dimension et doit être regardée de plus d'un point de vue.

Quant à la tolérance elle-même, je pense que, sans Érasme, sans Budé, sans Postel, sans Bodin, Mirabeau n'aurait pu dire:

> Je ne viens pas prêcher la tolérance: la liberté la plus illimitée de religion est, à mes yeux, un droit si sacré, que le mot tolérance, qui voudrait l'exprimer, me paraît, en quelque sorte, tyrannique lui-même, puisque l'autorité qui tolère pourrait ne pas tolérer[40].

Aujourd'hui, c'est grâce à Postel et à d'autres que nous pouvons tenir la liberté religieuse pour un droit naturel, un droit qu'une tolérance purement formelle viole d'une façon ou d'une autre et qui n'est pleinement reconnu que grâce à la tolérance positive.

1 Joseph Lecler, S. J., *Histoire de la Tolérance au Siècle de la Réforme,* 2 vol, Paris, Aubier, 1955; W.-K. Jordan, *The Development of Toleration in England, 1640-1660,* 4 vol., London, 1940; H.-A. Enno van Gelder, *The Two Reformations in the 16th Century,* (The Hague: Nijhoff, 1964).
2 Cf. Érasme: 'How happy should we be if we could lay aside dissensions and dwell with one heart and one mind in the house of the Lord!' cité et traduit par P.-S. Allen, *Erasmus,* Oxford, Clarendon Press, 1934, p. 96.
3 Montaigne, *Essais,* II, ix.
4 Herbert Butterfield, « Toleration in Early Modern Times », *Journal of History of Ideas,* 38 (1977), p. 573.
5 Cf. André Prévost, *L'Utopie de Thomas More,* Paris, Mame, 1978, *passim.*
6 Gustav Minchling, *Toleranz und Wahrheit in der Religion* (1955).
7 Nicolas de Cues, De *Pace sue Concordantia,* I, dans *De Pace Fidei,* éd. R. Klibansky et Hildebrandus Bascour, London, Warburg Inst., 1956, p. 7.
7 Cf. Butterfield, *art. cité.*
8 Bruno Snell, *Die Entdeckung des Geistes* (1947), trad. par T.-G. Rosenmeyer, *The Discovery of the Mind,* Cambridge, Mass.; Harvard University Press, 1953, pp. 262-263.
9 Ernest Barker, *Traditions of Civility* (1948; rééd. 1967), p. 10.
10 W.-K. Ferguson, « The Attitude of Érasmus Toward Toleration », dans ses *Renaissance Studies,* 1963, rééd 1970, p. 76.
11 Cf. A. Blaise, *Dictionnaire Latin-Français des Auteurs Chrétiens,* rev. par H. Chirat, Turnhout, Editions Brepols, 1954. Pour les sens divers de *humanitas,* voir E. von Jan, « Humanité », dans *Zeitschrift für französische Sprache und Literatur,* LV (1932), 1-66: J. Nierdermann, *Kultur,* Florence, 1941, pp. 29 sq. et 72 sq.
12 Érasme, *Opera* (Leiden, 1703-6) I, 920 F; IV, 627 C; IX 29 B-F.
13 J. Huizinga, *Erasmus* (Leyden, 1924), and *Dutch Civilisation in the Seventeenth Century...* (1968).
14 Peter Allen, « Utopia and European Humanism... » dans *Studies in the Renaissance,* 10 (1963), 91-107.
15 V. l'essai autour de l'intertextualité par R.-J. Schoeck, *Intertextuality and Renaissance Texts* (*Gratia,* Bamberg, 1984).
16 Edward Surtz, *Utopia, The complete Works of St. Thomas More,* vol. 4 (New Haven, Conn.: Yale University Press, 1965) et Prévost, cité en n. 5.
17 *Utopia,* ed. Surtz, p. 9.
18 *Pédagogue et juristes – Congrès du C.E.S.R. de Tours, 1960* (Paris: Vrin, 1963), notamment M. D. Maffei « Les débuts de l'activité de Budé, Alciat en Zasius », et R. Coing, « Développement de la réception du Droit Romain », Aussi: Donald R. Kelley, *Fundations of Modern Historical Scholarship* (New York: Columbia, 1970), et R. Schoeck, « Recent Scholarship in the History of Law », *Renaissance Quarterly,* xx (1967), 279-91.
19 V. Maffei, *ut supra,* et les introductions de W. K. Ferguson dans l'édition de Toronto, *Collected Writings of Erasmus, Correspondence vol. 1* et de Mme. M.-M. de La Garanderie.
20 J.-C. Margolin, « Sur quelques ouvrages de la bibiothèque de Postel annotés de sa main », dans ce volume.
21 Voir Bataillon, Huizinga, McConica, W.-K. Ferguson, et al.
22 H. Jedin, *Geschichte des Konzils von Trent,* Freiburg, 1948, I, 315.
23 Marcel Bataillon, *Érasme et l'Espagne,* Paris, Droz, 1973; J.-K. McConica, *English Humanists and Reformation Politics under Henry VIII and Edward VI,* Oxford, Clarendon Press, 1965.
24 Roland Bainton, *Hunted Heretic: The Life and Death of Michael Servetus,* Boston, 1953; B.

Becker, *Autour de Michel Servet et de Sebastien Castellion: Recueil,* Haarlem, 1953. Autour de l'*Apologia pro Serveto* par Postel, v. Bouwsma, p. 23.
25 Bouwsma, p. 4.
26 Bouwsma, pp. 8-12.
27 Bouwsma, pp. 233-4.
28 Bouwsma, pp. 195, 198.
29 Lecler, II, 34.
30 Bouwsma, p. 26.
31 G. Le Bras et al., éd., *Histoire du droit et des institutions de l'Eglise en Occident,* Paris, 1955, t. 7, *L'Age classique, 1140-1378; Sources et théorie du droit,* Paris, 1965, 51-129. Voir n. 34, *infra.*
32 N. W. Gilbert, *Renaissance Concepts of Method,* New York, Columbia University Press, 1960.
33 Barker, *Traditions,* ch. VIII, « Natural Law and the American Revolution », pp. 263 sq.
34 A. P. D'Entrèves, *Natural Law,* London, Hutchinson's, 1951; rptd. rev. ed.). Aussi: Guido Fasso, *Storia della filosofia del diritto,* vol. 1: *Antichità e Medioevo,* Bologna, 1966. Voir n. 31, *supra.*
35 Bouwsma, *Postel,* p. 100, n. 8.
36 Butterfield, « Toleration », p. 577.
37 Terence Cave, *The Cornucopian Text: Problems of Writing in the French Renaissance,* Oxford, Clarendon Press, 1979.
38 Helen C. White, *The Tudor Books of Private Devotion,* Madison, Wisc. University of Wisconsin Press, 1951.
39 Bouwsma a écrit « Postel's most significant use of *reason* was his persistent tendency to identify it with the methods of mathematics, and specifically with geometry », dans *Postel,* p. 123. Cf. R.-J. Schoeck, « Mathematics and the Languages of Literary Criticism », *Journal of Aesthetics and Art Criticism,* XXVI (1968), 367-76.
40 *Dictionnaire de l'Académie Française,* s.v. *Tolérance.*

CONCLUSION

Only the hand that erases can write
the true thing.

MEISTER ECKHART

Why do you seek rest?
You were only created to labor.

THOMAS À KEMPIS

The forms and tasks of life are many,
but holiness is one ...
Each one, however, according to his
own gifts and duties must steadfastly
advance along the way of a living faith,
which arouses hope and works through love,

Lumen Gentium

With a looking forward to Erasmus' mastery of rhetoric in *The Praise of Folly* we come to a marking in his growth and development: *Vägmäarken* is the title of Hammarskjöld's remarkable spiritual diary – guideposts, or markings. Such a work as *The Praise of Folly* is not only an achievement in its own right, it is a marking of an achievement which justified the course of action that Erasmus had taken in leaving the University of Paris and striking out as a pioneer. For he was a pioneer, not only in making his living through the publication of his works, but also in creating his own vocation as a cleric; he was an Augustinian canon, and remained one, but he had won permission to live his vocation on his own terms. And *The Praise of Folly* justified his vocation. Hammarskjöld declared, boldly and quite unconventionally, 'In our era, the road to holiness necessarily passes through the world of action.' *The Praise of Folly* along with his many other writings were Erasmus's world of action, and through them he gained the road to holiness.

Erasmus himself was not merely *peregrinus*,[1] though there is much of that in the itinerary of the early years – Holland, Brabant, Flanders, Paris, England, Louvain – and this habit of travel continues. Yet he had a strong sense of place: the pattern of Erasmus' middle years is not simply one of movement. Rather it is a questing for a place to stand, a place and a milieu where he might work his best.

His was a slow self-growth and maturing; but it involved three or more stages or levels within himself. There was first the mastering of vocation as a humanist[2]; as we have seen in the chapter on the letters and poetry, Erasmus achieved complete technical competence while still a teen-ager – a remarkable achievement. His achievement of a Latin style took longer, but prose usually does. Involved in this double stylistic achievement was a reading of and a lifelong ability to drawn upon the widest possible range of Greek and Latin authors. This reservoir of allusion and model remained with him even to his final years, and it is a key to the richness of the *Adages*, the *Colloquies*, the Letters, and nearly everything he wrote.

Second, there was the writing of individual works that manifest a remarkable expansion of vision and spirit. For there was nothing in previous literature to prepare us for the spirit of the *Adages*: that effervescent *joie de vivre*, that urbanity of style, that playfulness which is a part of Erasmus' ultimate morality of mind. And there is nothing to prepare us for the adventurous play of mind in *The Praise of Folly*, with its rhetorical thrust that is such a superb overreach of all of the traditional rhetoric.

Still more, we find an impressive and exciting vision of vocation in the world that is the more remarkable for its being germinated in a canon, that is to say, one whose spiritual formation as novice and monk was within a monastic community. And it is in his unique vocation that classical studies and Christian piety are so marvellously fused.

When we measure the Erasmus of 1509 – the conception of *The Praise of Folly*, the publication in 1508 earlier of the fully developed form of the *Adagia Chiliades* (as distinguished from the earlier, 1500, version in the *Collectanea*) – against the uncertain youth who had entered Steyn only twenty years earlier, we must be struck by an extraordinary growth in mind and spirituality.

He was thirty-three years of age before he published he first book. After that the *Enchiridion*, new editions and revisions poured forth in an increasing flood, and there were always new works, often as unpredictable as *The Praise of Folly* and the enlarged *Adagia* had been. When Erasmus reached his 50s there would then be the *Colloquia*.[3]

He never stopped growing — always working, yes, for that is obvious — but also growing. He was *Erasmus grandescens*.

1 Erasmus was perhaps at home in Anderlecht; he was certainly later at home in Basel, and it is doubtful that he would ever have left, if the violences of the Reformation had not driven him away.
2 We have questions concerning his mastering of humanistic vocation. Who were his models? To a considerable degree, Valla, as we have long known; and one can scarcely overestimate the impact and sustaining power of Valla for Erasmus during his monastery years and then the years with the bishop of Cambrai and at the University of Paris. But by 1509, one feels strongly, Erasmus was Joycean enough to construct his own model: he was his own model, measure, and guide. And this was a course of action which demanded vision, courage, and faith.
3 Craig R. Thompson has most ably presented the *Colloquies* as the fruition of a rhetorical enterprise, and so they are. They are a major marking in the history of western rhetoric, as, at the end of his career, his treatise on preaching will be another. Erasmus was — or at least became — *homo naturaliter rhetoricus*, and there are several instances where we find a delightful self-reflexivity about himself as *rhetor* or *rhetorculus*.

A SELECTIVE BIBLIOGRAPHY

The following bibliography includes works cited or alluded to, as well as those used in other ways, even if only indirectly. It does not include all works consulted.
I have not thought it necessary or desirable to follow the customary scholarly procedure of listing manuscript and primary sources separately; this procedure will be followed in the formal biography.

Acton, Lord. *Lectures of Modern History.* (London: Macmillan, 1906).
Allen, P. S. 'The Letters of Rudolph Agricola,' *EHR* 21 (1906), 302-17.
Arts Libéraux et Philosophie au Moyen Age – Actes du Quatrième Congrès International de Philosophie Médiévale. 1967 (Montréal: Institut d'Etudes Médiévales/Paris: Vrin, 1969).
Augustijn, Cornelis. *Erasmus* (Baarn: Ambo, 1986).
Aumann, Jordan. *Christian Spirituality in the Catholic Tradition.* London: Sheed & Ward, 1985).
Avarucci, Guiseppe. 'Due codici scritti de 'Gerardus Helye,' padre di Erasmo,' *Italia medioevale e umanistica*, xxxvi (1983), 215-25.
Axters, Stephanus. *Geschiedenis von de vroomheid in de Nederlanden* (Antwerpen: De Sikkel, 1956).

Bainton, Roland H. *Erasmus of Christendom* (New York: Scribner, 1969).
Bakhtin, Mikhail. *L'oeuvre de Francois Rabelais et la culture populaire...* (Paris: Gallimard, 1970).
Baldwin, T. W. *William Shakespeare's Small Latine & Less Greeke*, 2 vols. (Urbana: Univ. of Illinois Press, 1944).
Barker, Ernest. *Traditions of Civility*, (Cambridge: Cambridge Univ. Press. 1948).
Barnikol, Ernst. *Studien zur Geschichte der Brüder vom gemeinsamen Leben* (Tübingen: Mohr, 1917).
Baron, Hans. *The Crisis of The Early Italian Renaissance...,* 1 vol. ed. (Princeton: Princeton Univ. Press, 1966).
Baron, Hans. *From Petrarch to Leonardo Bruni: Studies in Humanistic and Political Literature* (Chicago: Univ. Chicago Press, 1968).
Bataillon, Marcel. *Erasme et l'Espagne* (Paris: E. Droz, 1973).
Béné, Charles. 'Les Pères de l'Eglise et la réception des auteurs classiques,' in *Die Rezeption der Antike*, ed. A. Buck (Hamburg: Hauswedell, 1981).
Bernardo, Aldo S., ed. *Francesco Petrarca – Citizen of the World* (Padova: Editrice Antenore; Albany: State University of New York Press, 1980).
Bernays, Jacob. *Joseph Justus Scaliger* (Berlin: Hertz, 1855).
Berrong, Richard M. *Rabelais and Bakhtin* (Lincoln, Nebr.: Univ. of Nebraska Press, 1986).

Betti, Erilio. *Teoria Generale della Interpretazione*, 2 vols. (Milan: Giuffrè, 1967).
Bietenholz, P. G. and T. B. Deutscher, eds. *Contemporaries of Erasmus: A Biographical Register of the Renaissance and Reformation*. 3 vols. (Toronto: Univ. of Toronto Press, 1985-1987).
Blackmur, R. P. *The Poems*. ed. Denis Donoghue (Princeton: Princeton Univ. Press, 1977).
Bolgar, R. R. *The Classical Heritage and Its Beneficiaries* (Cambridge: Cambridge Univ. Press, 1954).
Bolgar, R. R., ed. *Classical Influences on European Culture, A. D. 500-1500* (Cambridge: Cambridge Univ. Press, 1971).
Bolgar, R. R., ed. *Classical Influences on European Culture, A. D. 1500-1700* (Cambridge: Cambridge Univ. Press, 1976).
Bonnard, Fourier. *Histoire de l'abbaye royale des chanoines réguliers de St.-Victor de Paris*, 2 vols. (Paris, 1904-7).
Bouyer, Ch. 'Saint Augustin Législateur de la vie monastique,' *DDS* I (1937), 1126-30.
Bouyer, Louis. *Autour d'Erasme* (Paris: Edition du Cerf, 1955).
Boyle, Leonard E. 'Cum ex eo...', *MedStud* 24 (1962), 263-302.
Brooke, Christopher. *Monasteries of the World - The Rise and Development of the Monastic Tradition* (New York: Crescent Books, 1982) [first published in U. K. under the title of *The Monastic World* (1974)].
Brown, Peter. *Augustine of Hippo: A Biography* London: Faber & Faber, 1967.
Brunner, Karl. *England und die Antike* (Innsbruck: F. Rauch, 1947).
Buck, August, ed. *Die Rezeption der Antike: Zum Problem der Kontinuität zwischen Mittelalter und Renaissance* (Hamburg: Hauswedell, 1981).
Budé, G. *De transitu hellenismi ad christianismum* (Paris, 1535), ed. M. Lebel (Sherbrooke, Que.: Edition Paulines, 1973).
Burckhardt, Jacob. *Die Kultur der Renaissance in Italien* (Basel, 1860-trans. (1878), publ. London: Phaidon, 1944).
Burke, Peter. *Popular Culture in Early Modern Europe* (London: T. Smith, 1978).
Busch, J. *Chronicon Windeshemense und Liber de Reformatione monasteriorum*, ed. K. Grube, in: *Der Augustiner Propst, Johannes Busch* (Geschichtsquellen der Provinz Sachsen, vol. 19) (Halle 1886).

The Cambridge History of the Bible, ed. S. L. Greenslade, Cambridge: Cambridge Univ. Press, 1963).
Caspari, Fritz. *Humanism and the Social Order in Tudor England* (Chicago: Univ. of Chicago Press, 1954).
Cave, Terence. *The Cornucopia Text: Problems of Writing in the French Renaissance* (Oxford: Clarendon Press, 1979).
Chaytor, H. J. *From Script to Print* (Cambridge: W. Heffer, 1945).
Chenu, M.-D. *Toward Understanding Saint Thomas* (Chicago: Henry Regnery, 1964).
Chomorat, Jacques. 'L'Eloge de la Folie'et Quintilien,' *Information littéraire* 2 (1972), 77-82.
Chomorat, Jacques. *Grammaire et Rhétorique chez Erasme*. Les Classiques de l'Humanisme. Collection Publiée sous le Patronage de l'Association Guillaume Budé, X (Paris: Société d'Edition 'Les Belles Lettres', 1981), 2 vols.
Classen, C. J. unpublished paper given at the IANLS Congress (Wolfenbüttel, 1985).
Colie, Rosalie L. *The Resources of Kind: Genre-Theory in the Renaissance* (Berkeley: Univ. of California Press, 1973).
Combes, André A. *Essai sur la critique de Ruysbroeck par Gerson*. (Paris: Vrin 1945).

Congar, Yves. *Der Laie — Entwurf einer Theologie des Laientums* (Stuttgart: 1957). trans. as *Lay People in the Church* (London: Bloomsbury, 1957).
Constable, Giles. 'Petrarch and Monasticism,' in *Francesco Petrarca*, ed. Aldo S. Bernardo (Albany: State University of New York Press, 1980), 53-99.
Contemporaries of Erasmus: see Bietenholz.
Croll, M. W. *Style, Rhetoric and Rhythm* — Essays by Morris. W. Croll, ed. J. Max Patrick ... R. J. Schoeck (Princeton: Princeton Univ. Press, 1966).
Curtius, Ernst R. *Europäische Literatur und lateinisches Mittelalter* (Bern: Francke, 1948) - translated as *European Literature and the Latin Middle Ages* (New York: Pantheon, 1953).

Debongnie, Pierre. *Jean Mombaer de Bruxelles, abbé de Livry, ses écrits et ses réformes* (Louvain: Librairie universitaire, 1928).
Delehaye, H. *The Legends of the Saints,* ed. R. J. Schoeck (Notre Dame, Ind.: Univ. of Notre Dame Press, 1961).
DeLubac, Henri. *Exégèse Médiévale, Les Quatre Sans de l'Ecriture* (Paris, Aubier, 1959-64), 3 v. in 4.
DeMolen, Richard L., ed. *Erasmus of Rotterdam: A Quincentennial Symposium* (New York: Twayne, 1971).
DeMolen, Richard L. 'Erasmus' Commitment to the Canons Regular of St. Augustine.' *RenQ* xxvi (1973), 437-43.
DeMolen, Richard L., ed. *Essays on the Work of Erasmus* (New Haven: Yale Univ. Press, 1978).
Devereux, E. J. *Renaissance English Translations of Erasmus: A Bibliography to 1700* (Toronto: Univ. of Toronto Press, 1983).
Dickens A. G. and John M. Tonkin. *The Reformation in Historical Thought* (Cambridge, Mass.: Harvard Univ. Press, 1985).
Dickinson, John C. *The Origins of the Austin Canons and Their Introduction Into England* (London: S.P.C.K., 1950).
Dictionnaire d'archéologie chrétienne et de liturgie. ed. F. Cabrol and H. Leclercq (Paris, 1907 ff.) = *DACL*.
Dictionnaire d'histoire et de géographic ecclésiastique, ed. A. Baudrillart et al. (Paris, 1912 ff.) = *DHGE*.
Dictionnaire de spiritualité ascétique et mystique, doctrine et histoire, ed. Marcel Viller (Paris: Beauchesne, 1932 ff.) = *DSAM*.
Dictionnaire de théologie catholique, ed. A. Vacant et al. (Paris, 1930 ff.) = *DTC*.
Dols, J. M. E. *Bibliographie der moderne devotie* (Nijmegen: N. V. Centrale drukkerij, 1941).
Dorey, T. A., ed. *Erasmus* (London: Routledge & K. Paul, 1970).
Drerup, Engelbert. *Die Schulaussprache des Griechischen von der Renaissance bis zur Gegenwart* (Paderborn: F. Schöningh, 1930).

Eisenstein, Elisabeth L. *The Printing Press as an Agent of Change: Communications and Cultural Transformations in early-modern Europe.* 2 vols (Cambridge: Cambridge Univ. Press, 1979).
Eliot, T. S. *Four Quartets* (London: Faber & Faber, 1943).
Erasmus, Desiderius. *Desiderii Erasmi Roterodami Opera Omnia.* ed. Jean Leclerc (Leiden, 1703-1706) = *OO*.
Erasmus, Desiderius. *Opera Omnia Desiderii Erasmi Roterodami* (Amsterdam: North-Holland, 1969 -. In progress) = *ASD*.

Erasmus, Desiderius. *Erasmi Opuscula.* ed. W. K. Ferguson (The Hague: Martinus Nijhoff, 1933). = Erasmus, *Opuscula.*
Erasmus, Desiderius. *Opus Epistolarum Des. Erasmi Roterodami.* ed. P. S. Allen, H. M. Allen and H. W. Garrod (Oxford: Clarendon Press, 1906-1958) = *OE.*
Erasmus, Desiderius. *Poems of Desiderius Erasmus,* ed. Cornelius Reedijk (Leiden: Brill, 1956). = Erasmus, *Poems.*
Erasmus, Desiderius. *Collected Works of Erasmus* (Toronto: Univ. of Toronto Press, 1974 -. In progress) = *CWE.*
Erasmus. *Adages.* See M. M. Phillips.
Erasmus. *The Colloquies,* trans. Craig R. Thompson (Chicago: Univ. of Chicago Press, 1965).
Erasmus. *The Education of a Christian Prince.* trans. L. K. Born (New York: Columbia Univ. Press 1936).
Erasmus, Desiderius. *The Praise of Folly,* trans. Hoyt H. Hudson (Princeton, N. J., 1941), and trans. Clarence H. Miller (New Haven, Conn.: Yale Univ. Press, 1979).
Erasmus: J.-C. Margolin. *Douze années de bibliographie érasmienne (1950-1961)* (Paris: Vrin, 1963).
Erasmus: J.-C. Margolin. *Quatorze années de bibliographie érasmienne (1936-1949)* (Paris: Vrin, 1969).
Erasmus: J.-C. Margolin. *Neuf années de bibliographie érasmienne (1962-1970)* (Paris: Vrin and Toronto: Univ. of Toronto Press, 1977).
Etienne J. *Spiritualisme érasmien et théologiens louvanistes* (Louvain: Publications universitaires de Louvain, 1956).

Farge, James. *Biographical Register of Paris Doctors of Theology 1500-1536.* Subsidie Mediaevalia, 10 (Toronto: PIMS, 1980).
Farge, James. *Orthodoxy and Reform in Early Reformation France: The Faculty of Theology of Paris, 1500-1543* (Leiden: Brill 1985).
Febvre, Lucien. *Le problème de l'incroyance au XVIe siècle: La religion de Rabelais* (Paris: Editions Albin Michel, 1942) - trans. as *The Problem of Unbelief in the Sixteenth Century: the Religion of Rabelais* (Cambridge, Mass.: Harvard Univ. Press, 1982).
Febvre, L. and H.-J. Martin. *L'apparition du livre* (Paris, L'évolution de l'humanité, 1958).
Fisher, John H., ed. *The Medieval Literature of Western Europe, A Review of Research...* (New York: Modern Language Assn. of America, 1966).
Fowler, Alastair. *Kinds of Literature: An Introduction to the Theory of Genres and Modes* (Cambridge, Mass.: Harvard Univ. Press, 1982).

Garin, Eugenio. 'Erasmo e l'umanesimo italiana,' *BHR* 33 (1971), 7-17.
Garin, Eugenio. *Der italienische Humanismus* (Bern: A. Francke, 1947).
Gay, Peter. *The Bridge of Criticism: Dialogues among Lucian, Erasmus, and Voltaire on the Enlightenment...* (New York: Harper Torchbooks, 1970).
Geertz, Clifford. *Islam Observed: Religious Development in Morocco and Indonesia* (New Haven: Yale Univ. Press, 1968).
Gerlo, A. 'Erasmus von Rotterdam: Sein Selbstporträt in seinen Briefen,' in *Der Brief im Zeitalter der Renaissance.* ed. F. J. Worstbrock (Weinheim: Acta Humaniora, 1983), 7-24.
Gilmore, Myron P. *The World of Humanism* (New York: Harper Torchbooks, 1952).
Gilmore, Myron P. *Humanists and Jurists* (Cambridge, Mass.: Harvard Univ. Press, 1963).
Gilmore, Myron P. 'Erasmus': in *New Catholic Encyclopedia.*

Gilson, Etienne. *Die Mystik des Heiligen Bernhard von Clairvaus* (Wittlich, 1936, Engl. trans. London: Sheed & Ward, 1940).
Gilson, Etienne. *The Unity of Philosophical Experience* (New York: Scribner, 1937).
Gilson, Etienne. *Reason and Revelation in the Middle Ages* (New York: Scribner, 1938).
Gilson, Etienne. *History of Christian Philosophy in the Middle Ages* (New York and London: Sheed and Ward, 1955).
Gilson, Etienne. 'Humanisme médiéval et Ranaissance,' in *Les idées et les lettres*, 2nd ed. (Paris: Vrin, 1955), 171-196.
Goldschmidt, E. P. *Mediaeval texts and their first appearance in print.* (London: Bibliographical Society - Supplement, 16 - 1943).
Goldschmidt, E. P. *The Printed Book of the Renaissance.* 2nd ed. (Amsterdam: Gérard Th. van Heusden, 1966).
Gordon, D. J. *The Renaissance Imagination.* ed. Stephen Orgel (Berkeley: Univ. of California Press, 1975).
Grassi, Ernesto. *Verteidigung des individuellen Lebens* (Bern: A. Franck, 1946).
Grassi, Ernesto. *Rhetoric as Philosophy: The Humanist Tradition* (University Park, Pa.: Pennsylvania State Univ. Press, 1980).
Grassi, Ernesto & Maristella Lorch. *Folly and Insanity in Renaissance Literature* (Binghamton, N. Y.: MRTS, 1986).
Grendler, Paul F. 'The Survival of Erasmus in Italian Libraries,' *Erasmus in English* 8 (1976), 2-22.

Haas, Alois M. *Sermo Mysticus: Studien zu Theologie und Sprache der deutschen Mystik* (Freiburg/Schweiz: Universitäts-Verlag, 1979).
Habermas, Jürgen, *Zur Logik der Sozialwissenschaften: Materialien* (Frankfurt: Suhrkamp, 1970).
Hain, L. F. T. *Repertorium bibliographicum*, 4 vols. (Stuttgart & Paris, 1826-1938); rptd. 1903. Suppl. W. A. Copinger, 3 vols. London, 1895-1902).
Halkin, L.-E. 'Erasme en Italie,' in *Colloquia Erasmiana Turonensia* (Paris: Vrin, 1972), 37-53.
Halkin, L-E. 'La Devotio Moderna et l'humanisme,' *Réforme et humanisme*, Actes du IVe Colloque (Montpellier 1977), 103-112.
Halkin, L.-E. 'La piéte d'Erasme,' *Revue d'Histoire Ecclésiastique* lxxix (1984), 671-708.
Halkin, L.-E.: 'Bio-bibliographie de Léon-E. Halkin' par J.-P. Massaut et A. Willicot, *Bulletin de l'Institut Historique Belge de Rome.* Fasc. 55 – 56 (1985-1986), 3-32.
Hammarskjöld, Dag. *Markings.* trans. Leif Sjöberg and W. H. Auden (1964; New York: Ballantine 1983).
Handlin, Oscar. *Truth in History* Cambridge, Mass.: Harvard Univ. Press, 1979.
Harbison, E. H. *The Christian Scholar in the Age of The Reformation* (New York: Scribners, 1956).
Heath, Terence. 'Logical grammar, grammatical logic, and humanism in three German Universities,' *StudRen* 18 (1971), 9-64.
Himelick, Raymond. *The Enchiridion of Erasmus* (Bloomington: Indiana Univ. Press, 1963).
Hirsch, E. D., Jr. *Validity in Interpretation* (New Haven: Yale Univ. Press, 1967).
Hirsch, Rudolph. *Printing, Selling and Reading 1450-1500.* (Wiesbaden, 1967; rev. ed., 1974).
Hoven, René and Jean Hoyeux, eds. *Le livre scolaire au temps d'Erasme et des humanistes* (Liège: Université de Liège, 1969).
Howell, W. S. *Logic and Rhetoric in England 1500-1700* (Princeton: Princeton Univ. Press, 1956).

Hudson, Hoyt H., ed & trans. *The Praise of Folly* (Princeton: Princeton Univ. Press, 1941).
Huizinga, Johan. *Erasmus of Rotterdam* (New York: Scribners, 1924).
Huizinga, Johan. *Herfsttij der Middelleeuwen* (1924) - trans. by F. Hopman as *The waning of the Middle Ages* (London: E. Arnold, 1952).
Huizinga, Johan. *Dutch Civilisation in the Seventeenth Century* (London: Collins, 1968).
Hyma, Albert. *The Christian Renaissance, a History of the Devotio Moderna* (Grand Rapids, Mich.: The Reformed Press, 1924).

IJsewijn, Jozef. *Companion to Neo-Latin Studies* (Amsterdam: North-Holland, 1977).
IJsewijn, Jozef. 'Mittelalterliches Latein und Humanistenlatein,' in *Die Rezeption der Antike*, ed. A. Buck (Hamburg: Hauswedell, 1981).

Jayne, Sears. *John Colet and Marsilio Ficino* (Oxford: Oxford Univ. Press, 1963).
Joachimsen, Paul. 'Der Humanismus und die Entwicklung des deutschen Geistes,' *DVLG* 8 (1930), 419-20.

Kaiser, Walter. *Praisers of Folly: Erasmus, Rabelais, Shakespeare* (Cambridge, Mass.: Harvard Univ. Press, 1963).
Kenney, E. J. *The Classical Text: Aspects of Editing in the Age of the Printed Book* (Berkeley: Univ. of California Press, 1974).
Knafla, Louis A. *Law and Politics in Jacobean England: The Tracts of Lord Chancellor Ellesmere* (Cambridge: Cambridge Univ. Press, 1977).
Knowles, David. *The English mystics* (London: Burns & Oates, 1927).
Koch, A. C. F. *The Year of Erasmus' Birth...* (Utrecht: Heantjens, Dekker & Gumbert, 1969).
Kretzmann, N., et al., eds. *The Cambridge History of Later Medieval Philosophy... 1100-1600.* (Cambridge: Cambridge Univ. Press, 1982).
Kristeller, Paul O. *Renaissance Thought: The Classic, Scholastic, and Humanistic Strains* (New York: Har-Row Torch, 1961).
Kristeller, Paul O. *Iter Italicum.* (Leiden: Brill, 1963 ff.).
Kristeller, Paul O. *Eight Philosophers of the Italian Renaissance* (Stanford, Calif.: Stanford Univ. Press, 1964).
Kristeller, Paul O. *Renaissance Thought II: Papers on Humanism and the Arts* (New York: Harper & Row, 1965).
Kristeller, Paul O. 'Erasmus from an Italian Perspective,' *RenQ* 23 (1970), 1-14.
Kristeller, Paul O. *Renaissance Thought and Its Sources* (New York: Columbia Univ. Press, 1979).

Ladner, Gerhart B. *The Idea of Reform: Its Impact on Christian Thought and Action in the Age of the Fathers* (Cambridge, Mass.: Harvard Univ. Press, 1959).
Lausberg, H. *Handbuch der literarischen Rhetorik*. 2 vols. (München: Hüber, 1960).
LeClercq, Jean. *The Desire for Learning and the Love of God* (New York: Fordham Univ. Press, 1957).
Lexikon für Theologie und Kirche, ed. J. Höfer and K. Rahner, 10 vols. (Freiburg, 1957-1968), rptd. 1986 in 14 vols. = *LexThK*.
Lowinsky, Edward E. *Secret Chromatic Art in the Netherlands Motet* (New York: Columbia Univ. Press, 1946).
Lückr, Maria Alberta. *Meister Eckhard und die Devotio Moderna* (Leiden: E. J. Brill, 1950).

Mann, Nicholas. *Petrarca* (Oxford: Oxford Univ. Press, 1984).
Mansfield, Bruce. *Phoenix of His Age: Interpretations of Erasmus c. 1550-1750* (Toronto: Univ. of Toronto Press, 1979).
Margolin, *Bibliographie*: See Erasmus.
Margolin, J.-C. 'Pétrarque et Erasme,' dans *Petrarca 1304-1375. Beiträge zu Werk und Wirkung.* ed. Fritz Schalk (Frankfurt: Vittorio Klostermann, 1975), 184-97.
McConica, James K. *English Humanists and Reformation Politics under Henry VIII and Edward VI* (Oxford: Clarendon Press, 1965).
McDonnell, E. W. *The Beguines and Beghards in Medieval Culture* (New Brunswick, N. J.: Rutgers Univ. Press, 1954).
Mestwerdt, Paul. *Die Anfänge des Erasmus, Humanismus und Devotio Moderna* (Leipzig: R. Haupt, 1917).
Migne, J. P. see *Patrologiae Cursus Completus*.
Miller, Clarence H. 'Some Medieval Elements and Structural Unity in Erasmus' Praise of Folly,' *RenQ* 27 (1974), 499-511.
More, Thomas. *Selected Letters*, ed. Elizabeth F. Rogers (New Haven, Conn.: Yale Univ. Press, 1961).
More, Thomas. *The Complete Works of St. Thomas More, Responsio ad Lutherum*, ed. John M. Headley, 2 vols. (New Haven: Yale Univ. Press, 1969).

New Catholic Encyclopedia. 15 vols. New York: McGraw-Hill, 1967. = *NCE*.
Niermeyer, J. F. *Mediae Latinitatis Lexicon Minus* (Leiden: E. J. Brill, 1984).
Nolhac, P. de. *Erasme en Italie*, nouv. éd. (Paris: C. Klincksieck, 1898).

Oberman, Heiko. *The Harvest of Medieval Theology* (Cambridge, Mass.: Harvard Univ. Press, 1963).
Oberman, Heiko. *Masters of the Reformation* (Cambridge, Mass.: Harvard Univ. Press, 1981).
Oelrich, Karl Heinz. *Der späte Erasmus und die Reformation* (Münster: Aschendorff, 1961).
Olin, John C. *Christian Humanism and the Reformation - Desiderius Erasmus, Selected Writings*. (New York: Harper Torchbooks, 1965).
O'Malley, John W. 'Erasmus and the History of Sacred Rhetoric: The *Ecclesiastes* of 1535,' *Erasmus of Rotterdam Society Yearbook* 5 (1985), 1-29.

Patrologiae cursus completus, Series Latina, ed. J. P. Migne, 221 vols. (Paris, 1878-90) = *PL*.
Pattison, Mark. *Isaac Casaubon*. 2nd ed. (Oxford: Clarendon Press, 1892).
Pelikan, Jaroslav. *The Christian Tradition*. Vol. 4, *Reformation of Church and Dogma (1300-1700)*. (Chicago: Univ. of Chicago Press, 1984).
Phillips, Margaret Mann. *Erasmus and the Northern Renaissance*. (London: English Universities Press, 1949).
Phillips, Margaret Mann. 'La 'Philosophica Christi' reflétée dans les 'Adages' d'Erasme,' dans: *Courants Religieux et Humanisme à la fin du XVe et au début du XVIe siècle*, Colloque de Strasbourg 1957 (Paris: 1959), 53-71.
Phillips, Margaret Mann. *The 'Adages' of Erasmus: A Study with Translations* (Cambridge: Cambridge Univ. Press, 1964).
Pirenne, H. *Histoire de Belgique des origines à nos jours* (Bruxelles: La Renaissance du Livre, 1948).
Platt, M. 'Tradition and the Soul' (unpublished paper).

Porter, H. C. *Reformation and Reaction in Tudor Cambridge* (Cambridge: Cambridge Univ. Press, 1958).
Post, R. R. *The Modern Devotion: Confrontation with Reformation and Humanism* (Leiden: E. J. Brill, 1968).

Quain, Edwin A. 'The Mediaeval *Accessus ad Auctores,*' *Traditio* 3 (1945), 215-264.

Rashdall, Hastings. *Universities of Europe in the Middle Ages.* ed. F. M. Powicke and A. B. Emden, 3 vols. (Oxford: Oxford Univ. Press, 1936).
Reiss, Martin. 'Die Zitate antiker Autoren in der Imitatio des Thomas von Kempen,' in *Thomas von Kempen* (Kempen, 1971), 63-77.
Renaudet, Augustin. *Etudes Erasmiennes* (Paris: Droz, 1939).
Renaudet, Augustin. *Préreforme et Humanisme à Paris... 1494-1517*, 2 ed. (Paris: Librairie d'Argences, 1953).
Renaudet, Augustin. *Erasme et l'Italie* (Genève: E. Droz, 1954).
Robb, Nesca A. *Neoplatonism of the Italian Renaissance* (London: Allen & Unwin, 1935).
Robins, R. H. *Ancient and Medieval Grammatical Theory in Europe* (London: Bell, 1951).
Rummel, Erika. *Erasmus as a Translator of the Classics* (Toronto: Univ. of Toronto Press, 1985).

Sabbadini, Remigio. *Storia e critica di testi latini.* 2nd ed., (Padua: Editrice Antenore, 1971).
Saitta, G. *L'educazione dell'umanesimo in Italia* (Venice: La Nuova Italia, 1928).
Sandys, J. E. *History of Classifcal Scholarship*, 3 vols. (Cambridge: Cambridge Univ. Press, 1903-1908).
Schirmer, Walter. *Antike, Renaissance und Puritanismus.* 2nd ed. (Munich: M. Hüber, 1933).
Schmidt, Peter L. 'Die Rezeption des Römischen Freundschaftsbriefes,' in *Der Brief im Zeitalter der Renaissance*, ed. F. J. Worstbrock (Weinheim: Acta Humaniora, 1983), 25-9.
Schoeck, R. J. 'Canon Law in England on the Eve of the Reformation,' *MedStud*, 25 (1963), 125-47.
Schoeck, R. J. 'Mathematics and the Languages of Literary Criticism,' *Journal of Aesthetics and Art Criticism*, 26 (1968), 367-76.
Schoeck, R. J. 'Tommaso Moro,' in *Bibliotheca Sanctorum* (Rome 1969), XII, 608-14.
Schoeck, R. J. 'The Place of Erasmus Today,' *Transactions of the Royal Society of Canada*, 4th ser., 8 (1970), 287-298.
Schoeck, R. J. 'The Historian as Dissenter,' in *The Dissenting Tradition*, ed. C. Robert Coles (Athens, Ohio: Univ. of Ohio Press, 1975), 262-9.
Schoeck, R. J. 'On the Spiritual Life of Thomas More,' *Thought*, 52 (1977), 323-7.
Schoeck, R. J. 'Renaissance Guides to Renaissance Learning.' *Acta Conventus Neo-Latini Turonensis.* 3. Congrès International d'Etudes Néo-Latines, ed. J.-C. Margolin (Paris: Vrin, 1980). I. 239-62.
Schoeck, R. J. 'Erasme et Postel: Traditions de la civilité et de la tolérance,' *Guillaume Postel 1581-1981* (Avranches: Guy Trédaniel, 1982), 151-8.
Schoeck, R. J. 'The Humanistic Concept of the Text: Text, Context, and Tradition,' *PPMRC* 7 (1982), 13-31.
Schoeck, R. J. ed. *Sir Thomas Browne and the Republic of Letters* (English Language Notes; 19,4) (Boulder: Univ. of Colorado, 1982).

Schoeck, R. J. 'That Influential Clerk Erasmus,' *Dutch Quarterly Review of Anglo-American Letters*, 12 (1982/83) 183-90.
Schoeck, R. J. " 'Lighting a Candle to the Place': On the Dimensions and Implications of *Imitatio* in the Renaissance," *Italian Culture* 4 (1983), 123-143.
Schoeck, R. J. *Intertextuality and Renaissance Texts* (Bamberg: Kaiser, 1984).
Schoeck, R. J. 'Telling More from Erasms: An *Essai* in Renaissance Humanism,' *Moreana* XXIII, 91-2 (1986), 11-9.
Schoeck, R. J. 'Erasmus in England, 1499-1517: *Translatio Studii* and the *Studia Humanitatis*,' *Classical and Modern Literature*, 7 (1987), 269-83.
Schoeck, R. J. 'The Early printing History of Ausonius,' in *Acta* of the International Association for Neo-Latin Studies Congress at Wolfenbüttel 1985, ed. Stella Revard et al. (Binghamton, N. Y.: MRTS, 1988).
Schoeck, R. J. 'Agricola and Erasmus,' in *The Proceedings of the Rudolph Agricola Conference Groningen 1985*, ed. F. Akkerman (forthcoming).
Schoell, Franck L. *Etudes sur l'humanisme continental en Angleterre à la fin de la Renaissance* (Paris: Champion, 1926).
Schottenloher, O. 'Erasmus, Johann Poppenruyter und die Entstehung des Enchiridion militis christiana,' *ARG* 45 (1954), 109-116.
Screech, M. A. *Ecstasy and the Praise of Foly* (London: Duckworth, 1980).
Screech, M. A. ed. *Rabelais, Le tiers livre* (Geneva: Droz, 1964).
Shannon, A. C. 'Augustinians,' *NCE*.
Short-title Catalogue of Books Printed in England... 1475-1640 (London: Bibliographical Society, rptd. 1950).
Simon, Joan. *Education and Society in Tudor England* (Cambridge: Cambridge Univ. Press, 1966).
Smalley, Beryl. *The Study of the Bible in the Middle Ages*, 2nd ed. (New York: Philosophical Library, 1952).
Smith, Preserved. *Erasmus: A Study of His Life, Ideals and Place in History* (New York: Harper, 1923; rptd. Dover, 1962).
Sowards, J. K. 'The Two Lost Years of Erasmus,' *StudRen* 9 (1962), 161-86.
Spitz, Lewis W. *The Religious Renaissance of the German Humanists* (Cambridge, Mass.: Harvard Univ. Press, 1963).
Spoelhof, William. *Concepts of Religious Nonconformity and Religious Toleration as Developed by the Brethren of the Common Life in the Netherlands, 1374-1489* (Unpubl. doct. diss., University of Michigan, 1946).
Stern, Virginia F. *Gabriel Harvey: A Study of His Life, Marginalia and Library* (Oxford: Clarendon Press, 1979).
Stock, Brian. *Implications of Literacy* (Princeton: Princeton Univ. Press, 1980).
Stupperich, Robert. 'Zur Biographie des Erasmus von Rotterdam. Zwei Untersuchungen,' *Archiv für Reformationsgeschichte*, 65 (1974), 18-36.
Sylvester, Richard. 'The Problem of Unity in the Praise of Folly,' *English Literary Renaissance* 6 (1976), 125-39.

Telle, Emile V. 'Erasmus's *Ciceronianus*: A Comical Colloquy,' in *Essays on the Work of Erasmus*, ed. R. L. DeMolen (New Haven: Yale Univ. Press, 1978).
Thomas à Kempis [Thomas Hemerken a Kempis]. *Opera Omnia*, ed. M. J. Pohl, 7 vols. (Fribourg, 1902-22).
Thomas von Kempen - Beiträge zum 500. Todesjahr. (Kempen, 1971).
Thompson, Craig R. *The Translations of Lucian by Erasmus and St. Thomas More* (Ithaca, N. Y., privately printed, 1940).

Thomson, D. F. S. 'Erasmus as a Poet in the Context of Northern Humanism,' *De Gulden Passer* 47 (1969), 192 ff.
Thomson, D. F. S. and H. C. Porter. *Erasmus and Cambridge: The Cambridge Letters of Erasmus* (Toronto: Univ. of Toronto Press, 1963).
Torre, Arnaldo Della. *Storia dell'Academia Platonica di Firenze* (Firenze: Carnesecchi e figli, 1902).
Treadgold, Warren, ed. *Renaissances before the Renaissance: Cultural Revivals of Late Antiquity and the Middle Ages* (Stanford: Stanford Univ. Press, 1984).
Trilling, Lionel. *Sincerity and Authenticity* (Cambridge, Mass.: Harvard Univ. Press, 1972).
Trinkaus, Charles. 'Humanism, Religion, Society: Concepts and Motivations of Some Recent Studies,' *RenQ* 29 (1976), 676-713.
Trinkaus, Charles and Heiko Oberman, eds. *The Pursuit of Holiness: Studies in Medieval and Reformation Thought*. X, (Leiden: Brill, 1974).

Underhill, Evelyn. *Mysticism*, rev. ed (New York: Dutton, 1930).

Vahlen, J. 'Lorenzo Valla,' in *Almanach der kaiserlichen Akademie der Wissenschaften*, 14 (Wien 1864), 181-225.
Valla, Lorenzo. *Opera Omnia* (Basel 1540; rptd. Turin, 1962).
Valla, Lorenzo. *De Voluptate*. ed A. K. Hieatt and Maristella Lorch (New York: Abaris Books, 1977).
Verheijen, Luc. *La Règle de Sainte Augustin*, vol. I, (Paris: Etudes Augustiniennes, 1967).
Vervliet, Hendrik D. L., ed. *Post-Incunabula and their Publishers in the Low Countries* (The Hague: Nijhoff, 1978).
Voigt, Georg. *Die Wiederbelebung des klassischen Altertums oder das erste Jahrhundert des Humanismus*, 2nd ed. (Berlin: G. Reimer, 1880-1).

Wansem, C. van der. *Het onstaan en de geschiedenis der Broederschap van het gemene leven tot 1400* (Leuven: Universiteitsbibliotheek, 1958).
Waterbolk, E. H. *Verspreide Opstellen* (Amsterdam: Bert Bakker, 1981).
Weiss, James Michael. '*Ecclesiastes* and Erasmus: The Mirror and the Image,' *ARG* 65 (1974), 83-108.
Weiss, Roberto. *Humanism in England during the Fifteenth Century*, 2nd ed. (Oxford: Blackwell, 1957).
Wentzlaff-Eggebert, F.-W. *Deutsche Mystik zwischen Mittelalter und Neuzeit: Einheit und Wandlung ihrer Erscheinungsformem*, 3 ed. (Berlin: de Gruyter, 1969).
White, Helen C. *The Tudor Books of Private Devotion* (Madison: Univ. of Wisconsin Press, 1951).
Whitehead, A. N. *The Aims of Education*. (New York: Mentor, 1949).
Woodward, William Harrison. *Vittorino de Feltre and Other Humanist Educators* (Cambridge: Cambridge Univ. Press, 1897).
Worstbrock, F. J. 'Die Antikenrezeption in der mittelalterlichen und der humanistischen Ars Dictandi.' in *Die Rezeption der Antike*, ed. A. Buck (Hamburg: Hauswedell, 1981).

Zielinski, Tadeusz. *Cicero im Wandel der Jahrhunderte* 4th ed, (Leipzig: Teubner, 1929).
Zilverberg, S. B. J. *David von Bourgondie, Bisschop van Terwaan en van Utrecht* (Groningen: J. B. Wolters, 1951).
Zunggo, J. A. *Historia generalis et specialis de ordine canonicorum regularium S. Augustini Prodromus*, 2 vols. (Tiguri, 1742).

INDEX NOMINORUM

In the main the principles set forth in *Contemporaries of Erasmus,* ed. P. Bietenholz are followed – that is, to employ the name in the vernacular, except where the Latinized or Graecized form is more familiar today. But complete consistency is not always possible; for the forms of names in quotations will vary in different languages, and some of the studies in this volume predated the publication of *Contemporaries of Erasmus* by a number of years.

Adolph of Burgundy 84
Adrian VI, Pope 106
Aegidius Viterb. = Giles of Viterbo
Aeneas Sylvius (Pope Pius II) 53, 61, 63
Aeschylus 152
Aesop 59
Agricola, Rudolph 31 ff., 36, 40 ff., 62, 73, 95, 99, 112, 114
d'Ailly, Pierre 32, 35, 57, 91
Albertus Magnus 73
Alcuin 112
Alexander the Great 147
Alexander of St. Elpidio 55
Allen, P. S. 41, 50-1, 72, 98
Almain, Jacques 107
Ambrose, St. 59-60, 66, 141, 148
Anna van Borssele 85, 95-6
Anthony, St. 58
Aphthonius, Aelius 131, 135
Aquinas, St. Thomas 58, 73, 104, 148
Aristophanes 132
Aristotle 60, 114, 141
Ascham, Roger 140
Augustijn, C. 11
Augustine, St. 9, 55, 58-61, 66, 68, 70-2, 93, 102, 141, 148
Augustinus Triumphus 55
Aulus Gellius 59, 115, 132
Ausonius 118

Bade/Badius, Josse 36
Bainton, Roland H. 129
Bakhtin, Mikhail 129
Baldwin, T. W. 118, 120
Barbirianus, Jacobus 44
Barker, Ernest 147
Baron, Hans 44
Barzizza: see Gasparino
Basil, St. 58
Bataillon, Marcel 18, 149
Batt, Jacob 68, 93-6

Beatus Rhenanus 50, 52, 81-2, 97
Béda, Noël 107 ff.
Bede, the Venerable 58, 103
Benda, Julien 19-20
Bergen family: see Hendrik, Jan van Bergen
Bernard, St. of Clairvaux 32, 58, 65
Bernard of Cologne 42
Bernays, Jacob 11
Berrong, Richard M. 129
Betti, Emilio 86
Blackmur, R. P. 17, 28, 111
Blount, Anthony, Baron Mountjoy 95, 118
Bloy, Léon 89
Bodin, Jean 138, 153
Boethius 58, 113
Bleicher, Josef 87
Bombace, Paolo 80
Bonaventura, St. 9, 32, 58
Boniface VIII, Pope 55
Bostius, Arnoldus 102
Bouwsma, William J. 150, 152
Bouyer, Louis 18, 20
Bowen, William G. 12
Bracciolini, Poggio 61
Braudel, Fernand 11
Bricot, Thomas 107
Brown, Peter 9
Browne, Sir Thomas 142
Bruni, Leonardo 44
Buchanan, George 107
Budé, Guillaume 108, 148-50, 153
Burckhardt, Jacob 10
Burgundy: see David, Philip, etc.
Burton, Robert 122
Busch, Johannes 35, 59
Buschius, Hermann 36
Busleyden, Jerome de 148-9
Butterfield, Herbert 145, 153

171

Calvin, Jean 150
Cambrai, Bishop of: see Hendrik van
 Bergen
Cantelius, – 60
Canter, Jacob 69, 97
Carbone, Ludovico 41
Cartland, Barbara 137
Casaubon, Isaac 11
Caspari, Fritz 120
Cassianus, St. 148
Castellio, Sebastian 150
Catullus 111, 132
Cave, Terence 44, 140, 153
Celtis, Conrad 42
Chapman, George 122
Charlemagne 112
Charles V, Holy Roman Emperor 91, 97
Charles IX 151
Charles the Rash (of Burgundy) 64
Chaucer, Geoffrey 50
Chomorat, Jacques 127, 131
Chrysoloras, Manuel 119
Chrysostom, St. 58, 141
Cicero 43, 59-60, 66, 80, 82, 113, 115
Classen, C. J. 43
Claudian 60
Clichtove, Josse 107
Colet, John 61, 69-70, 73, 117-8
Columbus, Christopher 99
Conrad, Willem 94
Constable, Giles 50
Cop, Nicolas 108
Copernicus, Nicolas 152
Croke, Richard 118
Curtius, Ernst Robert 26, 111, 113, 128
Cusa/Kues/Cusanus, Nikolaus von 32, 42, 145, 148, 150
Cyprian, St. 66, 141

Dalberg, Johann von 44
Dante 19
Dati, Agostino 61
David van Bourgonië, bishop of
 Utrecht 63-4, 72, 96, 102
Demosthenes 141
Denifle, H. 104
D'Entrèves, A. P. 152
Descartes, René 107
Devereux, E. J. 118, 120
Dolet, Etienne 25, 120

Donne, John 122
Donoghue, Denis 111
Dorne, John 139
Dorp, Martin van 22, 41, 128, 131, 133
Dorsten, Jan van 137 ff.
Dürer, Albrecht 121

Eckhart, Meister 32 ff., 80, 157
Eco, Umberto 130
Edward IV of England 91
Eliot, T. S. 53, 98, 127-8
Elizabeth (a nun) 51
Egerton, Thomas, Lord Ellesmere 138
Emden, A. B. 104
Erasmus:
 – family: brother, Pieter 53, 56, 68, 97
 father, Pieter Helius 114
 – works:
 Adages 20-1, 27, 41, 53, 115 ff., 119-20, 127, 132, 140, 147, 157
 Antibarbari 68, 73, 85, 90, 92-4, 97-8, 115, 121
 Apologiae 115
 Ciceronianus 20, 42, 119-20, 141
 Colloquies 20, 115, 127, 140, 147, 158
 De Contemptu Mundi 42, 53, 64 ff., 73, 85, 94, 97
 De Conscribendis epist. 82, 141
 De Copia 141-42
 Declamationes 141
 Ecclesiastes (De ratione concionandi) 115
 Education of a Christian Prince 20, 117, 131
 Enchiridion (Handbook of a Christian Warrior) 22, 24, 55, 95, 114, 117, 131-32, 147, 158
 Epigrammata 93
 epitaphs 51 ff., 69
 Inquisitio De Fide 26
 Lucian translation 117
 New Testament 20-2, 114, 117
 Paraclesis 20, 114
 poems 52 ff.
 Praise of Folly 20, 115, 117, 127 ff., 147, 157-8
 Ratio verae theologiae 20, 22

172

Philosophia Christi 18, 26, 42, 44-5, 49, 72, 99
Euripides 59, 141
Eyb, Albrecht von 43

Faber, Jacob 36, 45
Farge, James K. 105 ff.
Febvre, Lucien 114
Ferguson, Wallace K. 147
Ficino, Marsilio 43, 59, 83, 145, 148, 151
Filelfo, Mario 53, 61, 81-3
Fisher, Bishop John 17, 118
Flitner 149
Florentius 60
Forster, Leonard 8
François I, king of France 149
Freud, Sigmund 139
Froben, Johann 81

Gaguin, Robert 84, 95, 101-102, 107
Galen 141
Gansfort, Wessel 40, 42
Garin, Eugenio 10, 113
Garland, John of 46
Gasparino Barzizza of Bergamo 61
Gay, Peter 18
Geertz, Clifford 89
Geldenhower, Gerard 36
Gelder, H. A. van 18
Gelida, – 150
George of Saxony 149
Gerard, of Kloster 36
Gerard, Cornelius (of Gouda) 36, 68-9, 92, 94, 97
Gerlo, Aloïs 80
Gerson, Jean 32, 35
Ghellinck, J. de 141
Ghisbrecht de Bréderode 63
Giles of Viterbo 70
Gilles, Pieter 92, 149
Gilles of Rome 71
Gilmore, Myron P. 11
Goclenius, Conrad 36-7
Goldschmidt, E. P. 116
Gordon, D. J. 119
Gilles de Gourmont 127
Gozewijn/Goswin, of Halen 37
Grassi, Ernesto 128, 131
Gregory, St. 58-9

Gregory IX, Pope 101
Gregory of Rimini 71
Grey, Thomas 102
Grote, Gerald 32 ff.
(Groote, Geert)
Grunnius 50, 53, 60
Guarino da Verona 41, 43, 61, 114, 119
Guarino, Battista 41
Gutmann, Elspeth 36

Hadewych, Sister 32
Halkin, L.-E. 11, 37
Hammarskjöld, Dag 157
Harbison, E. H. 129
Harvey, Gabriel 138
Heaney, Seamus 83
Hegius, Alexander 36, 40 ff., 45-6, 73, 95, 99, 114
Helye, Gerardus = Erasmus, father of
Hendrik van Bergen, bishop of Cambrai 68, 72, 83, 85, 89 ff., 102
Henry VII of England 91
Henry VIII of England 91
Hermann, Haio 42
Hermans, Willem 37, 68, 72, 84, 93, 95-6
Hertling, L. SJ 55
Heyen, Berta de 51, 69
Heyen, Margareta Honora 69
Hilary, St. 141
Hirsch, E. D. 86
Holbein, Hans, The Younger 7, 121
Homer 128, 132
Hooker, Richard 152
Horace 60, 132
Hughes, Philip 129
Hugolin d'Orvieto 71
Huizinga, Johan 7, 10, 19, 61, 98, 129
Hunne, Richard 23
Hyma, Albert 42, 59, 67
Hythloday, R. 93

Innocent III, Pope 65
Innocent VIII, Pope 57
IJsewijn, Jozef 7, 11
Irenaeus, St. 141
Ivanov, Vjačeslav 27

Jan van Bergen 85
Jan Christiaanse 57

Jedin, H. 149
Jerome, St. 18, 58-60, 65-6, 68, 141
Jodocus/Joost van Schoonhoven? 94
Jordan, W. K. 144
Julius II, Pope 80
Justinus 59
Juvenal 60

Kaiser, Walter 131
Kelley, Donald R. 149
Kempis = Thomas à Kempis
Kenney, E. J. 113
Kessler, Eckhard 8
Kisch, Guido 149
Knafla, Louis A. 138
Knoringen, Christoph von 43
Knowles, David 37
Knox, John 107
Koch, A. C. F. 41, 45, 53
Koechman, Jan 37
Kristeller, Paul O. 10, 80, 92, 113
Kuiper, Gerdien C. 8

Lactantius Firmianus 66, 147
Ladurie, LeRoy 11
Lambin, Denis 119
Lecler, J. 149
Leclerc, Nicolas 107-8
Lee, Edward 128
Lefèvre d'Etaples, Jacques 112
Leijenhorst, C. G. van 42, 69
Leo X, Pope 53
Lewis, C. S. 23, 133
Lewis, of Bavaria 55
Lindner, R. M. 89
Lipsius, Justus 80
Listrius, Gerardus 37
Livy 141
Lombard, Peter 104
Lorch, Maristella 128
Loyola, Ignatius 32-3
Lubac, H. de 18, 20
Lucian 18, 128, 130, 132-3, 141
Luder, Peter 43
Lupset, Thomas 148-9
Luther, Martin 10, 22-4, 42, 63, 145
Lyndewode, William 139

Maartens/Martens, Dirk/Th. 64, 81
McConica, James K. 118, 120, 149

Macropedius, Georgius 37
Mair/Major, John 107
Mande, Hendrik 33
Mann, Nicholas 9
Manutius, Aldus 116
Margolin, J.-C. 8, 10, 11, 18, 149
Marsiglio of Padua 55
Martens = Maartens
Martial 60, 133
Maurois, André 89
Maximilian I 91
Melanchthon, Philip 41, 140
Merton, Thomas 98
Metsys, Quentin/Quintin 121
Miller, Clarence H. 128 ff.
Milton, John 121
Minchling, Gustav 145
Mirabeau, Honoré-Gabriel de R. de 153
Mombaer, Jan 102
Montaigne, Michel de 11, 19, 52, 122, 140, 144, 153
More, Thomas 18, 21-6, 27, 66, 69, 91-93, 95, 117-8, 122, 128, 130, 145 ff.
Mountjoy: see Anthony Blount
Murdoch, John E. 103
Muret/Muretus, Marcus Antonius 119
Mutianus, Conradus 42

Nardi, E. 149
Nigri/Negro, Francesco 82

Obrecht, Jacob 99
Occo, Pompeius 42
Ockham, William of 32
Olin, John C. 18-9
Ovid 52, 60, 128

Pafraet, Richard 40, 45
Pattison, Mark 11
Paul, St. 65
Perotti, Niccolò 82
Persius 60
Peters, Gerlach 33, 56
Petit, Guillaume 107-8
Petrarca/Petrarch, Francesco 7, 9, 50, 65, 82-3, 95, 97, 112
Pfeiffer, Rudolf 141
Pflug, Caesar & Julius 149
Philip of Burgundy 64, 85, 90, 96, 132
Philip the Handsome 91

Phillips, Margaret Mann 18, 94, 116
Pico della Mirandola, Giovanni 21-2, 43, 99, 113, 148, 151
Piccolomini: see Aeneas Sylvius
Pio, Alberto 128
Plantin, C. 151
Plato 118, 132
Platt, Michael 58
Plautus 84
Pliny the Younger 59, 80, 82, 128, 141
Plutarch 118, 128, 133, 141, 147
Poggio: see Bracciolini
Pole, Reginald 148
Poliziano/Politian, Angelo 43, 59, 82, 99, 120
Pomerius, Henry 32
Popes: see Adrian VI, Gregory IX, Innocent III & VIII, Julius II, Leo X, Sixtus IV
Post, R. R. 34 ff., 37 ff., 70, 72-3
Postel, Guillaume 138, 144 ff.
Powicke, F. M. 104
Prévost, André 149
Priscian 61
Propertius 60
Publicius (Rufus) 43

Quintilian 60, 113, 131, 135

Raabe, Paul 8
Rabelais, François 20, 63, 116, 122, 129, 132-3, 137, 140
Rademaker, C. S. M. 8
Radewijn, Florens 33-4
Rashdall, Hastings 104-5
Reedijk, Cornelius 64, 68
Renaudet, Augustin 18
Reuchlin, Johann 59, 112
Reulos, Michel 148
Rhenanus: see Beatus Rhenanus
Richter, Michael 11
Robert de Sorbon 103
Robinson, Edwin Arlington 15
Rogerus/Rogers, Servatius 64, 67, 82, 97-8
Romains, Jules 89
Roper, William 21, 23
Rummel, Erika 87
Ruysbroeck, Jan van 32
Ryan, Lawrence V. 8

Sabbadini, Remigio 113
St. German, Christopher 24
Sallust 59-60
Salutati, Coluccio 61, 82
Scaliger, J. C. 120
Scaliger, J. J. 11, 112, 118
Scevole, Daniele 80
Schirmer, Walter F. 120
Schlatter, Richard 26
Screech, M. A. 130, 135, 140
Seneca 42, 44, 60, 114, 132
Servatius: see Rogers, Servatius
Servet/Servetus, Michel 150
Servotte, Herman 128
Shakespeare, William 116
Sidney, Sir Philip 121
Simenon, Georges 137
Sixtus IV, Pope 91
Smith, Preserved 10, 17, 92
Snell, Bruno 146
Snoy, Reyner 68, 96
Socrates 144
Solf, Sabine 8
Sophocles 42, 152
Soto, Domingo da 107
Sowards, J. K. 80
Spitz, Lewis W. 8, 43, 45
Standonck, Jan 97, 107
Starkey, Thomas 148
Statius 60
Stern, Virginia F. 138
Stevens, Linton 149
Stock, Brian 57
Strozzi, Titus 41
Stupperich, Robert 149
Sturm, Johannes 140
Suárez, Francesco 107
Suetonius 132, 141
Surtz, E., SJ 148
Sylvester, Richard S. 131, 135
Synesius 128
Synthen, John 36, 40 ff.

Terence 59-60, 141
Tertullian 148
Theodoricus, Franciscus 68
Thomas, St.: see Aquinas
Thomas à Kempis 33, 35, 49, 54, 60, 70, 114, 157
Thompson, Craig R. 7, 26, 115, 141

Thomson, D. F. S. 120
Tibullus 60
Tunstall, Cuthbert 24
Tuynman, Pierre 8
Tyndale, William 24

Valerius Maximus 59
Valla, Lorenzo 43, 61, 82, 85, 95, 98-9, 103
Van Dorsten: see Dorsten, Jan van
Vinet, Elie 118-9
Virgil 60-1
Vitoria, Francisco da 107
Voltaire 10, 18, 20
Volz, Paul 19

Vrije, Antoon 40

Waterbolk, E. H. 122
Werner, Nicolas 102
White, Helen C. 140
Whitehead, A. N. 84, 99
Winckel, Peter 51, 97
Wolfe, John 139, 143

Xenophon 141

Yates, Frances 152

Zeno 147
Zerbolt, Gerard 33